The Changing Role of the Management Accountants

Panida Chotiyanon
Vassili Joannidès de Lautour

The Changing Role of the Management Accountants

Becoming a Business Partner

palgrave
macmillan

Panida Chotiyanon
Bangkok, Thailand

Vassili Joannidès de Lautour
Grenoble École de Management
Grenoble, France
Queensland University of Technology
Brisbane, Australia

ISBN 978-3-030-07986-4 ISBN 978-3-319-90300-2 (eBook)
https://doi.org/10.1007/978-3-319-90300-2

Softcover re-print of the Hardcover 1st edition 2018

Printed on acid-free paper

This Palgrave Macmillan imprint is published by the registered company Springer Nature Switzerland AG
The registered company address is: Gewerbestrasse 11, 6330 Cham, Switzerland

For Khun Suchin

Acknowledgment

This book originates from a practitioner's curiosity associated with the career development of management accountants and the implications of this for the future careers of finance practitioners in general. It evolved into a five-year research collaboration project entailing a long but fruitful journey, and has resulted in rich and profound insight that is beneficial to both the academic and professional communities alike. In the process we would like to thank Valerie Sabatier and the excellent DBA program team of the Grenoble Ecole de Management for project support, Damon Golsorkhi, Lukas Goretzki, and the late Bernard Gumb for invaluable comments and insights, and Anek Jandrakholiga and Maneshka Mahtani for their valuable insights and support contributing to the success of the research project. Last but not least, we would like to thank our families, especially Suchin Chotiyanon and Rachael de Lautour, for nurturing our passion and joy, and providing continuous support in our quest for knowledge.

February 8, 2018

Panida Chotiyanon
Vassili Joannidès de Lautour

Introduction

This book is about the self-orienting process of management accountants, key to their emerging new role as business partners. Contemporary professional and academic literatures have informed of the significant change in the role of management accountants since the early 1990s. From the traditional role of "bookkeepers" (Beard 1994; Bougen 1994; Friedman and Lyne 2001; Dimnik and Felton 2006; Jeacle 2008; Chen et al. 2012), they have grown increasingly "business-oriented" (Granlund and Lukka 1998), becoming "business partners" (Järvenpää 2007). In everyday practice the new business-oriented role takes various shapes, being specific to local sites and associated business contexts (Ahrens 1996, 1997; Ahrens and Chapman 2002, 2007; Jørgensen and Messner, 2010; Fauré and Rouleau 2011; Morales and Lambert 2013; Nama and Lowe 2014; Janin 2016). We see the new breed of management accountants as being active outside their traditional domain in areas that would previously have been unthinkable, such as helping the sales manager decide how to counter-offer a sales promotional campaign or solving the sales discount structure issue with a salesman (Ahrens 1997), working with buyers to decide on the new menu for the restaurant managers (Ahrens and Chapman 2007), acting as a gatekeeper in granting loans to customers (Ahrens 1997), setting financial thresholds for the approval of new product development (Jørgensen and Messner 2010), assisting in the supply chain process of private equity fund management (Nama and Lowe 2014), helping middle managers in the budgeting process (Ahrens 1996, Fauré and Rouleau 2011), or even advising a football club in dealing with the Football Association's rules (Janin 2016). Although the new role is prevalent in various organizations across industries worldwide, establishing such a role in an organization is not a straightforward matter. So far, management accounting research has shed light on how the external elements such as the sociopolitical and economic forces, the change in the organization, and the agency of key organizational players can influence the establishing of the new role in the organization. Nevertheless, it is found that not all management accountants are orienting toward business. Some of them are found to have "irreconcilable" role orientation toward the narrower accounting role, while others are oriented toward a broader "business partnering" role (Järvenpää 2007; Friedman and Lyne 1997; Burns and Baldvinsdottir 2005; Byrne and Pierce 2007). This indicates the importance of understanding the process through which the management accountants "internalize" the new role, an area which we still have little knowledge about (Goretzki et al. 2013; Guo 2017).

This book takes its readers along a journey in time that explores the diverse work life experiences of finance practitioners. For the first time it provides a deep insight into how and why management accountants orient toward business in order to become business partners. Using a unique research method influenced by the oral history tradition coupled with the data analysis of Strauss and Corbin (1998), we mobilize Schatzki's notions of teleoaffective structure and practice memory (Schatzki 2002, 2006) to make sense of the narratives of four finance practitioners from different career tracks and conceptualize the Business Partner Developing Model (BPDM). This model helps to explain how management accountants become business partners through their lifelong self-orienting processes, one of the most important aspects of the changing role of management accountants. For the first time, readers will gain not only a deep insight into the entire work lives of management accountants but also an understanding of how and why each of them has coped with continuously changing work contexts and gradually become the relevant business partner.

Although the book is aimed primarily at future management accountants who are embarking on building a career in management accounting, management contemplating on establishing the new role within their organizations, finance educators designing the program curriculum, and the finance community in general, we hope that our unique longitudinal approach and the BPDM that we have developed will be beneficial in helping research on the practitioners in other practices, that are as equally diverse as management accounting, thereby enriching our knowledge in the broader area of sociology of profession.

The book is organized into three parts. Part I provides the background for the emergence of the new role of management accountants and their self-orienting processes. We begin in Chap. 1 by looking at the phenomenon of the new role from three perspectives: the macro-level, concerning the sociopolitical and economic environment, the meso-level, concerning the organizational change, and the micro-level, focusing on the agency of the key organizational players in order to identify the key drivers of the change. In the process we have identified management accountants' self-orienting process as one of the most important aspects of their changing role. In order to gain a better understanding about the process we review the contemporary theoretical approaches to the self-orienting process in Chap. 2, and highlight the advantages of Schatzki's practice theory and its notion of teleoaffective structure and practice memory (Schatzki 2002, 2006) in making sense of the lifelong self-orienting process of management accountants. Next, in Chap. 3, we mobilize Schatzki's framework to theorize the BPDM, a product of our research project,[1] which explains the phenomenon of becoming business partners through the lifelong self-orienting process of management accountants. The model is built on three micro-processes, consisting of the associated purposeful actions of management accountants aligned toward becoming business partners, together with the underlying key notion of the career turning point, and it is capable of explaining not only the lifelong self-orienting process but most importantly the variation in the degree of business orientation found in everyday practices as well.

In Part II we use the BPDM to look at the real-life experiences of management accountants in their lifelong self-orienting processes. From four diverse career tracks we provide a deep insight and understanding into how and why each of the four selected finance practitioners gradually orients toward business to become who he/she is at present. We begin in Chap. 4 with the narrative of Carol as she navigates the course of her career in corporate financial service, beginning as an audit apprentice and becoming a finance manager, aligning short-term personal objectives to the long-term end with a few significant turning points on the way. Following suit in Chap. 5 is the story of Anne, who is on the financial planning and analysis career track. Her lifelong self-orienting process takes her from a financial apprentice to an expert in financial planning and analysis,

[1] Chotiyanon, P. (2018). Becoming a Business Partner, a lifelong self-orienting process. (Doctoral dissertation) Grenoble Ecole de Management, Grenoble, France.

up to the point where she has to make one of the most important decisions in her work life. In Chap. 6 we look at Madelyn's career in commercial finance. From being a controller in a "mundane" chemical industry to her appointment as the commercial director of an exciting but challenging fast-moving consumer goods industry, she maneuvers through the drastic changes in the business contexts, becoming increasingly business oriented and being accepted as a true business partner by all her peers. In Chap. 7 we follow Alain's management control career. Without any prior relevant background in business, we see how his lifelong self-orienting process is influenced by the changing management philosophy and business contexts; how his role is extended beyond business partner to become the change agent; how corporate culture influences his course of actions; and how his course of actions in turn contributes to a new corporate culture.

In Part III, learning from these real-life experiences, we mobilize the BPDM and propose an internal career development program in Chap. 8. This is aimed at helping to prepare future management accountants for the challenges that come with the continuously changing business environment.

The book closes with the concluding Chap. 9, in which we discuss the key points related to the lifelong self-learning process of management accountants, one of the most important aspects of their changing role, and our contributions to knowledge in empirical, theoretical, managerial, and methodological terms, together with the implications.

References

Ahrens, T. (1996). Styles of accountability. *Accounting, Organizations and Society, 21*(2–3), 139–173.

Ahrens, T. (1997). Talking accounting: An ethnography of management knowledge in British and German brewers. *Accounting, Organizations and Society, 22*(7), 617–637.

Ahrens, T., & Chapman, C. S. (2002). The structuration of legitimate performance measures and management: Day-to-day contests of accountability in a U.K. restaurant chain. *Management Accounting Research, 13*(2), 151–171.

Ahrens, T., & Chapman, C. S. (2007). Management accounting as practice. *Accounting, Organizations and Society, 32*(1–2), 1–27.

Beard, V. (1994). Popular culture and professional identity: Accountants in the movies. *Accounting Organizations and Society, 19*(3), 303–318.

Bougen, P. D. (1994). Joking apart: The serious side to the accounting stereotypes. *Accounting Organization and Society, 19*(3), 319–335.

Byrne, S., & Pierce, B. (2007). Towards a more comprehensive understanding of the roles of management accountants. *European Accounting Review, 16*(3), 469–498.

Burns, J., & Baldvinsdottir, G. (2005). An institutional perspective of accountants' new roles – The interplay of contradictions and praxis. *European Accounting Review, 14*(4), 725–757.

Chen, C. C., Jones, K. T., Scarlata, A. N., & Stone, D. N. (2012). Does the Holland model of occupational choice (HMOC) perpetuate the Beancounter-Bookkeeper (BB) stereotype of accountants? *Critical Perspectives on Accounting, 23*(4–5), 370–389.

Dimnik, T., & Felton, S. (2006). Accountant stereotypes in movies distributed in North America in the twentieth century. *Accounting Organizations and Society, 31*(2), 129–155.

Fauré, B., & Rouleau, L. (2011). The strategic competence of accountants and middle managers in budget making. *Accounting, Organizations and Society, 36*, 167–182.

Friedman, A. L., & Lyne, S. R. (1997). Activity-based techniques and the death of the beancounter. *European Accounting Review, 6*(1), 19–44.

Friedman, A. L., & Lyne, S. R. (2001). The beancounter stereotype: Towards a general model of stereotype generation. *Critical Perspectives on Accounting, 12*(4), 423–451.

Goretzki, L., Strauss, E., & Weber, J. (2013). An institutional perspective on the changes in management accountants' professional role. *Management Accounting Research, 24*, 41–63.

Granlund, M., & Lukka, K. (1998). Towards increasing business orientation: Finnish management accountants in a changing cultural context. *Management Accounting Research, 9*, 185–211.

Guo. (2017). The odyssey of becoming: Professional identity and insecurity in the Canadian accounting field. *Critical Perspectives on Accounting*. https://doi.org/10.1016/j.cpa.2017.10.008.

Janin, F. (2016). When being a partner means more: The external role of football club management accountants. *Management Accounting Research*. https://doi.org/10.1016/j.mar.2016.05.002.

Järvenpää, M. (2007). Making business partners: A case study on how management accounting culture was changed. *The European Accounting Review, 16*(1), 99–142.

Jeacle, I. (2008). Beyond the boring grey: The construction of the colourful accountant. *Critical Perspectives on Accounting, 19*(8), 1296–1320.

Jørgensen, B., & Messner, M. (2010). Accounting and strategising: A case study from new product development. *Accounting, Organizations & Society, 35*(2), 184–204.

Morales, J., & Lambert, C. (2013). Dirty work and the construction of identity. An ethnographic study of management accounting practices. *Accounting, Organizations and Society, 38*, 228–244.

Nama, Y., & Lowe, A. (2014). The 'situated functionality' of accounting in private equity practices: A social 'site' analysis. *Management Accounting Research, 25*, 284–303.

Schatzki, T. R. (2002). *The site of the social: A philosophical account of the constitution of social life and change*. University Park: Pennsylvania State University Press.

Schatzki, T. R. (2006). On organizations as they happen. *Organization Studies, 27*(12), 1863–1187.

Strauss, A. L., & Corbin, J. M. (1998). *Basics of qualitative research: Techniques and procedures for developing grounded theory*. Thousand Oaks: Sage.

Brief Contents

Contents

List of Figures

List of Tables

List of Key Definitions

Keywords	*Descriptions*
Actions	Group of activities
Business partners	The "new" role of management accountants characterized by being business oriented (Granlund and Lukka 1998), having a significant level of engagement in commercial practices and being accepted as a value-adding member by peers
Career	A work life history of a practitioner (Bailyn 1989; Barley 1989), a series of related and definable stages or phases of a given sphere of activity that a group of people goes through in a progressive fashion (that is, one step leads to another) in a given direction or on the way to a more or less definite and recognizable end point or goal or series of goals. (Roth 1963, p. 94)
Career path	The course of the career with milestones marking key events.
Career turning point	The point at which one makes a turn and decides to go on a different path in one's career
Emotions	Manifested feeling associated mostly with short-term goals
End	The long-term goal, the totality of goals in Heidegger's sense (Dreyfus 1991), usually associated with motivations
Expertise	The combination of knowledge and skill
Goals	The short- to intermediate-term objectives
Knowledge	Static knowledge mostly acquired from formal sources inside and outside the workplaces (such as schools)
Know-how	The part of the static knowledge that is acquired from workplaces, such as corporate financial policy and manuals
Orientation	State of orienting
Orienting	Performing actions geared toward a specific goal/end

Keywords	*Descriptions*
Skill/ know-how -to	Knowledge in action: the ability to apply acquired knowledge and know-how to work in various contexts, the equivalent of Schatzki's practical understanding
Work life profile	The profile of work life in chronological order

References

Bailyn, L. (1989). Understanding individual experience at work: Comments on the theory and practice of careers. In M. Arthur, D. Hall, & B. Lawrence (Eds.), *Handbook of career theory* (pp. 477–489). Cambridge: Cambridge University Press.

Barley, S. (1989). Careers, identities, and institutions: The legacy of the Chicago School of Sociology. In M. Arthur, D. Hall, & B. Lawrence (Eds.), *Handbook of career theory* (pp. 41–65). Cambridge: Cambridge University Press.

Dreyfus, H. (1991). *Being-in-the-world. A commentary on Heidegger's being and time, division I.* Cambridge, MA: The MIT Press.

Granlund, M., & Lukka, K. (1998). Towards increasing business orientation: Finnish management accountants in a changing cultural context. *Management Accounting Research, 9*, 185–211.

Roth, J. A. (1963). *Timetables: Structuring the passage of time in hospital treatment and other careers.* Indianapolis: Bobbs-Merrill.

PART I

The Emerging New Role and the Self-Orienting Process

CHAPTER 1

The Emergence of Business-Oriented Role

Contemporary management accounting research informs us of the recent emergence of the new role of management accountants. From the traditional role of "bookkeepers" they have become more "business-oriented" (Granlund and Lukka 1998) more of a "business partner" type (Järvenpää 2007; Beard 1994; Bougen 1994; Friedman and Lyne 2001; Dimnik and Felton 2006; Jeacle 2008; Chen et al. 2012). In everyday practice, the new business-oriented role takes various shapes, being specific to local contexts (Ahrens 1996, 1997; Ahrens and Chapman 2002, 2007; Jørgensen and Messner 2010; Fauré and Rouleau 2011; Morales and Lambert 2013; Nama and Lowe 2014; Janin 2016). Management accounting research has suggested a few key drivers that have contributed to the emergence of this new role over time (Byrne and Pierce 2007). On the macro-level, there are the broad changes in the sociopolitical environment and economic forces (Loft 1986; Miller and O'Leary 1987; Berland and Chiapello 2009). Within the organization the new role has been associated with the changes in corporate culture, broader organization restructuring, and general changes in management philosophy (Simon et al. 1954; Granlund and Lukka 1998; Ahrens and Chapman 2002; Burns and Baldvinsdottir 2005; Järvenpää 2007; Nor-Aziah and Scapens 2007; Ahrens and Mollona 2007; Lambert and Pezet 2011; Lambert and Sponem 2012; Goretzki et al. 2013). At the micro-level, significance has been placed on the agency of key players, such as the

P. Chotiyanon, V. Joannidès de Lautour,
The Changing Role of the Management Accountants,
https://doi.org/10.1007/978-3-319-90300-2_1

leaders of organizations and in particular the leaders of the finance functions (Hopper and Macintosh 1993; Chua 1995; Briers and Chua 2001; Burns and Baldvinsdottir 2005; Baxter and Chua 2008; Goretzki et al. 2013), the operational managers (Hopper 1980; Windeck et al. 2015), as well as the management accountants themselves (Byrne and Pierce 2007; Goretzki et al. 2013; Morales and Lambert 2013; Janin 2016; Guo 2017).

Being business oriented (Granlund and Lukka 1998; Ahrens and Chapman 2000; Burns and Baldvinsdottir 2005; Byrne and Pierce 2007; Goretzki et al. 2013) for today's management accountants means placing an increasing emphasis on a more strategic, forward-looking, and collaborative role orientation (Granlund and Lukka 1998; Burns and Baldvinsdottir 2005; Byrne and Pierce 2007). However, becoming business oriented might not be straightforward. It has been found that not all management accountants are orienting toward business. Some of them are found to have "irreconcilable" role orientation toward the narrower accounting role, while the others are oriented toward a broader "business partnering" (Järvenpää 2007; Friedman and Lyne 1997; Burns and Baldvinsdottir 2005; Byrne and Pierce 2007). This indicates the importance of understanding the process through which management accountants internalize their new role, an area about which we still have little knowledge (Goretzki et al. 2013; Guo 2017).

1.1 The Emergence of the Business-Oriented Role of Management Accountants

The realm of management accountants' activities has been internally oriented toward their internal clients, for example the general managers, production managers, and sales managers; providing support in "scorekeeping," that is, traditional performance record keeping and producing periodic financial reports such as budget and actual numbers; "attention directing," such as performing variance analysis, and "problem-solving" or internal consulting, in terms of preparing special financial analyses to aid in decision-making—such as whether to invest in a particular machine or not (Simon et al. 1954). These activities can also be broadly categorized as "controlling" (scorekeeping and attention directing), which is detached from the business, and "consulting" (problem-solving), which is more oriented toward the business, as management accountants align themselves more with the operating managers (Mouritsen 1996; Ahrens 1996, 1997). In some cases the realm of activities has broadened to include specialized financial areas of banking, international cash management, capital structure, and administration, with direct involvement in customer credit and suppliers' relationships as well. Management accounting research has attributed these developments mainly to broad sociopolitical and economic forces, organizational changes, and the agency of key organizational players.

1.1.1 *Sociopolitical and Economic Influences*

The management accountants' role orientation has been associated with the broader development in the sociopolitical situation. For example, it has been suggested that management accounting practice such as budgeting emerged out of concern for the failure of capitalism during the 1930s to 1950s, which caused major economic problems such as unemployment after the two world wars. Instead of going back to the prior system, which favored the privileged few—the owners, rather than the employees—social reformers decided to "fix" capitalism by implementing budget control systems, responsibility accounting, and management by objectives, which enabled the employees to share wealth with the owners. In this context of the new "spirit of capitalism" (Berland and Chiapello 2009), management accounting practice emerged not just as a calculative practice but also as a disciplinary practice (Loft 1986; Miller and O'Leary 1987), with management accountants tending to orient hierarchically toward top management to help in the process of monitoring and controlling as they worked toward the overall corporate goals (Hopper and Macintosh 1993).

1.1.2 *Organizational Changes*

The wave of economic forces during the 1980s and 1990s affected corporate culture and management philosophy in such a way that it led to broad organization restructuring, which in turn provided an opportunity for the general increase in business orientation of management accountants (Granlund and Lukka 1998; Järvenpää 2007). During this period big companies expanded their operations across national borders and became internationalized or globalized. Faced with fiercer competition at home and abroad, managements shifted their attention toward customers and cost management. In the beginning this development led to decentralization of formerly centralized functions, such as production, sales, and finance, to accommodate the higher need for control and cooperation among dispersed units of operation that spanned national borders. Management accountants' teams were also reorganized into those who were located centrally, performing traditional bookkeeping and preparing reports, and those located within the dispersed operating units to watch over the company's well-being, taking part in management decision-making and becoming advisors and sometimes change agents. This latter group of localized management accountants was characterized as being "business oriented"; that is, placing more emphasis on the future and strategic imperatives, for example by using financial forecast or estimates for strategic decision-making rather than being concerned about the accuracy of the past data as their colleagues at the corporate center were; being good at cross-boundary collaboration and comfortable communicating across functional lines to coordinate activities within the dispersed units as well as at the centralized unit where they functionally belonged (Granlund and Lukka 1998).

Globalization and the rapidly changing markets situation during the 1990s provided a backdrop from which a new business-oriented role of business partner (Järvenpää 2007) emerged. For example, in the telecommunication industry, deregulation coupled with new technologies and the new kind of services available in the industry forced a Finnish global leader in telecommunication business to focus more on the customer dimension of the business, providing an opportunity for the management accountants to take up the new role of business partners. The business orientation in this company evolved over the period of ten years from 1992 to 2001 along with a broad organizational restructuring, which led to a continuous improvement culture that was shared within the company. This new customer-oriented philosophy put pressure on management accountants to be more in line with the new customer focus. The change began with the decentralization of controlling functions into the strategic business units of the company in the early 1990s in order to provide dedicated support to the business. Between 1994 and 1995, after the customer account management teams were established to capture the specific needs of customers, the controllers were given the opportunity to move to a more business-oriented role by taking part in customer account team meetings and preparing customer financial analyses. Besides being part of the customer account management teams they also took part in the appraisal of new product alternatives and in controlling new products development, acting as research and development (R&D) controllers. They acted as a link between the marketing and the research and development activities, providing the much-needed answers to management on questions of timing, risk, and most importantly the economic consequence of alternative actions. Then there was the big change when basic accounting such as bookkeeping and payroll was organized into a shared service center in 1998. This had the effect of clearly separating the promising new role of business partner from the traditional bookkeeping role in the organization. At the same time there was an overhaul of the accounting system brought about by the implementation of the integrated SAP information system (an enterprise resource planning software developed by a German company, SAP SE), which helped to simplify and homogenize the basic accounting information system and provided an opportunity for management accountants to provide value-added services in terms of a rolling forecast, the standardization of the cost system, and accounting innovations such as activity-based costing. In addition, in terms of performance measurement the management accountants began to play an important role in target-setting and measurement, involving non-financial measures which were relevant to the business operation. To facilitate the change processes, human resource management provided management accountants with training on the business, customers, and competitors, including career planning, making sure that each of them was ready for this business-oriented role. As part of the corporate cultural change, the top management provided role models by being hands-on and proactively participating in business. Moreover, there was storytelling about the success of the management accountants who became business partners in the subsidiaries. Both the role modeling and storytelling by top management helped to inspire the management accountants toward being more business oriented and taking up the new role of business partner, being characterized as equal and active members of the management team, having a business mind, being cooperative, and having good business understanding.

The emergence of the new business-oriented role seems to be prevalent in all kinds of industries across national borders: examples are a UK restaurant chain (Ahrens and Chapman 2002), a Malaysian public utility firm (Nor-Aziah and Scapens 2007), and a UK mining company (Ahrens and Mollona 2007) at about the same time. Most of the time in everyday life this new breed of management accountants sit close by their business counterparts dealing with day-to-day operation issues in domains that would previously have been unthinkable. Examples include helping the sales manager deciding on how to counter-offer a sales promotional campaign or solving a sales discount structure issue with the salesman

(Ahrens 1997), working with buyers to decide on the new menu for the restaurant managers (Ahrens and Chapman 2007), acting as a gatekeeper in granting loans to customers (Ahrens 1997), setting financial thresholds for the approval of new product development (Jørgensen and Messner 2010), assisting in the supply chain process for private equity fund management (Nama and Lowe 2014), helping middle managers in the budgeting process (Ahrens 1996; Fauré and Rouleau 2011), or even advising a football club in how to deal with the football association's rule (Janin 2016). In general, they spend less time on the technical side of the practice, such as preparing information and scorekeeping, and more on analyzing and consulting. They are active outside their traditional domain, contributing to various business achievements such as strategic formulation, system development, organizational design, and change management. This broadened role is forward-looking (Byrne and Pierce 2007; Granlund and Lukka 1998), requires a wider business point of view (Vaivio 1999, 2006; Vaivio and Kokko 2006), a good knowledge about the business area in which the firm operates, good communication skills, and a demonstrated appreciation for cross-functional activities (Granlund and Lukka 1998) as their responsibility expands beyond the accounting figures production of the past to the application of these figures in business decisions.

This business-oriented role, generally referred to as a "business partner" role type, can be described as "an equal member of the decision making team" with "the authority and responsibility to tell the operating executive why particular types of information may or may not be relevant to the business decision at hand and is expected to suggest ways to improve the quality of the decision" (Siegel and Sorensen 1999; Burns and Baldvinsdottir 2005; Weber 2011; Goretzki et al. 2013). It is recognizable in management accountants at entry level as well as in the top echelons, such as chief financial officers (CFOs) (Ahrens and Chapman 2000; Baxter and Chua 2008), who are members of management teams that make decisions affecting the whole organization (Granlund and Lukka 1998). They all share a common understanding of their main role as bringing an "economic consciousness" to operating managers within their own organizations (Ahrens 1996, 1997; Ahrens and Chapman 2000).

1.1.3 The Agentive Force

On the micro-level, prominent management accounting research, such as the works of Hopper and Macintosh (1993), Burns and Baldvinsdottir (2005), Goretzki et al. (2013), and Briers and Chua (2001) have shown how the agency of key organizational players, that is, the top managers, the operational managers, and the management accountants, themselves influence the role orientation of management accountants.

By analyzing the autobiography of Harold Geneen, an accomplished accountant and the chief executive of the International Telephone and Telegraph (ITT), Hopper and Macintosh (1993) describe the process by which a powerful actor established management accounting as a disciplinary practice and constituted managers as amenable, docile, obedient subjects within the organization during the 1970s. The case study begins by providing the educational and professional background from which Geneen emerged as a "disciplined disciplinarian" who was well versed in the disciplinary disciplines (ibid., p. 182), before demonstrating how he set up a very tight controlling system not unlike those described by Foucault's "Discipline and Punish: The Birth of the Prison" (Foucault 1979). For example, the discipline of the space or the enclosure principle, which is the first of the three principles of Foucault's model, can be seen in the form of responsibility centers that he established for hierarchical control. Disciplining time, which is the second principle of an efficient body, can be seen in the budget schedule, in which he specified when the budget was to be submitted, reviewed, approved, and finally cascaded down to the members of the organization. To monitor performance, the operational managers were required to submit monthly operating reports against the budget to Geneen and his team for regular review. We also see how Geneen established a surveillance system, with the comptroller and other staff from the headquarters auditing the business managers. Geneen's Panopticon took various forms, both direct and indirect, and his managers had no idea whether he was looking or not looking at them, or whether someone else at headquarters was watching.[1] The comptrollers themselves were also watched over in the same manner; and in addition to having a direct reporting line to Geneen, they were subjected to a specific rating system called "Comptroller Grid." This decided their fate: promotion or demotion. Such a system rendered them obedient, disciplined, and willing, not unlike the rest of the organizational members (ibid., p. 205). In short, management accountants at ITT were completely embedded in the sys-

[1] The Panopticon refers to a type of institutional building designed by the English philosopher and social theorist Jeremy Bentham in the late eighteenth century. The concept of the design is to allow a single watchman to observe the inmates of an institution without them being able to tell whether they are being watched (Bentham's preface in Bozovic 1995).

tem, being passive and oriented toward top management—in other words Harold Geneen.

Studying the implementation process for a new business-oriented role for management accountants in the manufacturing division of a pharmaceuticals organization during the 1990s, Burns and Baldvinsdottir (2005) adopt the model of Seo and Creed (2002) to identify a few "contradictions" that motivate the embedded "institutional entrepreneurs" to take certain actions aimed toward organizational change.[2] Such contradictions are found in the contradicting institutional logics,[3] that is, research versus marketing and customer oriented versus cost orientation, and other interinstitutional incompatibilities which become apparent after a slowdown in economic performance. In this context the study highlights how a senior finance manager with broad business acumen and links with business schools enacts the role of the institutional entrepreneur in instituting the change in the role of management accountants toward a more business-oriented role. Such a role change is part of the overall organizational restructuring process that the company has undertaken over five years from the mid- to late 1990s, which is necessitated by a business downturn. This in turn is caused by economic pressure from government price control and the expiry of the company's major drug patents. With the aim of increasing efficiency in its business process and being more responsive to the market and its customers, the company streamlines its operation by implementing the so-called "process way of working," reorienting all functions toward the products and introducing a business plan that realigns all functions in the same direction. Under this strategy, an entire business process chain from customer order through to after-delivery service for each individual product is realigned to a single site. Seizing this opportunity to capitalize on the contradicting logics, and sensing the support from top management, a senior finance manager skillfully mobilizes internal and external support in order to introduce the new role of "hybrid accountants," who gets more involved in the day-to-day operation of the "product stream" as opposed to previous transaction-oriented activities. He reorganizes the finance function by centralizing the

[2] Embedded entrepreneurs are organized actors who envision new institutions as a mean of advancing interests they value highly yet that are suppressed by extant logics (DiMaggio 1988).

[3] Taken-for-granted, resilient social prescriptions, sometimes encoded in laws, specifying the boundaries of the field, its rules of membership, and the role identities and appropriate organizational forms of its constituent communities (Friedland and Alford 1991).

transaction-related service and statutory reporting on one site and integrating the rest of the finance team into the "product stream." The latter team consists of finance managers, who provide advice supporting the product stream leaders in strategic decision-making, and financial analysts, dealing with day-to-day operational issues and working side by side with other product stream team members. Supporting this change are the human resource department's efforts in "skill transfer," involving recruiting managers from outside and offering internal financial training programs for non-finance managers, covering, among other subjects, budget setting and management, product costing, and capital expenditure, in order to create financial awareness among the business managers and the culture of "money does matter" in the organization. In analyzing the role of an embedded agency in the process of change, this case also highlights the importance of the senior finance manager's micro-level activities in changing others' and management accountants' perception of this new role, through self-reorienting and in building trust and relationship within and among the process stream teams. This overcomes cultural obstacles and contributes to the successful implementation of the new role over the years.

From the institutional perspective Goretzki et al. (2013) add a valuable insight into how a new CFO, an external agent, institutes the new business oriented role of management accountants, over the period of seven years from 1993 to 2010 through legitimizing the "business partner" role, *re*-constructing the management accountants' role identities and linking the intra-organizational level with an institutional environment sharing the desire for the role change. Their study also highlights the importance of re-orienting of the management accountants' role identity in instituting the new role. The process begins when the new CFO introduces a new integrated enterprise resource planning (ERP) system, which helps to free management accountants from data inconsistency issues created by the legacy system so they can spend more time creating and analyzing the value-added reports that the operating managers want. This new information and the statistics compiled are shared and appreciated by operational managers as well as by customers, thereby solidifying the management accountants' role as business oriented. The CFO then decentralizes the management accounting function in order to draw local managers into closer proximity and offer opportunities for the management accountants to gain business knowledge. Besides working "on site" to gain knowledge of local business management, accountants are encouraged to proactively and constantly prove the value of their work, and to be "visible"—presenting their craft whenever opportunity arises. While the new role is gaining ground, and being accepted by the operational manager, the CFO also promotes it among management accountants as the springboard for a management career; thus they accept the new role as well. In other words, he reconstructs the new role model as business/management oriented and convinces the management accountants to accept it. In addition, he sends management accountants on outside training with the relevant professional training organization in order to instill an externally legitimized "controller philosophy" among them, inspiring them to internalize their new role.

From the Actor Network Theory perspective, Briers and Chua (2001) provide an insight into the process of change in a management accounting system. They examine the manufacturing strategic business unit of a major Australian mining company from late 1988 to 1991, and reveal how an active lead management accountant seizes the opportunity presented by an overall change in the business model, from manufacturing centered to product centered, to make the case for a new accounting system based on activity-based costing (ABC). Playing the role of the innovator, he skillfully mobilizes the network of external consultants, other actors in the academic circle, and key internal executives such as the engineers and the managing director, as well as tools such as ABC and management accounting textbooks, to support the change. As part of a broader organizational change, the role of management accountants gradually changes into a more "value-added" role, through "know-your-business" and other off-site accounting training (ibid., p. 251).

Besides the actions of top managers, the reaction to and acceptance of operational managers play a significant role in the outcome of the implementation process regarding the changing role of management accountants (Hopper 1980; Mouritsen 1996; Burns and Baldvinsdottir 2005; Nor-Aziah and Scapens 2007; Goretzki et al. 2013; Morales and Lambert 2013). It is suggested that operational managers can be "enrolled" to accept the new role of management accountants and to help in dispersing the concept of "business partnering" throughout the organization. This enrollment process involves the implementation of corporate strategy, the business plan, and the new SAP system. There is also a reorganization of sales function, with the management accountants, being part of the sales organization, sharing the destiny of the sales function, and participating in the sales review. This gives them an opportunity to learn about the business, prove their value, and win acceptance from their peers (Windeck et al. 2015).

Management accountants' current roles result not only from the actions of top management and reactions from the line functions but also from the interplay between management accountants' own aspirations, self-orientation, and expertise which they mobilize (Mouritsen 1996; Burns and Baldvinsdottir 2005; Goretzki et al. 2013). Being business oriented (Granlund and Lukka 1998; Ahrens and Chapman 2000; Burns and Baldvinsdottir 2005; Byrne and Pierce 2007; Goretzki et al. 2013) for today's management accountants means placing increasing emphasis on a more strategic, forward-looking, and collaborative role orientation (Granlund and Lukka 1998; Burns and Baldvinsdottir 2005; Byrne and Pierce 2007). This requires certain individual characteristics and competencies, such as business knowledge, interpersonal and communication skills, IT skills, flexibility, personal qualities, technical skills, monitoring skills, and organizational influence (Byrne and Pierce 2007). In addition, contemporary management accounting researches have informed that how management accountants orient themselves affects their current roles (Ahrens 1996, 1997; Burns and Baldvinsdottir 2005; Ahrens and Chapman 2007; Jørgensen and Messner 2010; Morales and Lambert 2013; Janin 2016). Nevertheless, this self-orienting process might not be straightforward. It has been found that individual management accountants seem to have an "irreconcilable" role orientation toward the narrower accounting or broader "business partnering" role (Järvenpää 2007; Friedman and Lyne 1997; Burns and Baldvinsdottir 2005; Byrne and Pierce 2007). This prompts us to look more closely at the process through which each individual management accountant orients toward business, an area about which so far we have limited knowledge.

1.2 Business Orientation of Management Accountants

While broader sociopolitical and economical forces provide the backdrop or the context, and the actions and reactions/responses of top managers and operational managers open up the opportunity to become business oriented, it is how management accountants orient themselves toward business that influences the individual degree of business orientation (Mouritsen 1996; Granlund and Lukka 1998).

1.2.1 General Self-Orienting Strategies

In the context of change, social studies have informed us of three general self-orienting strategies, all involving intentional acts (Ahrens 2009) and manifested identities that are the outcomes of the self-orienting process. These are full compliance or full alignment, partial compliance or adapting, and rejection or resistance to change. For the full alignment strategy Thornborrow and Brown (2009) demonstrate how the British Parachute Regiment acts upon the new members' orienting process by mobilizing the aspiring identity which each member draws upon for the meaning of what it is to be a member of the elite organization and the disciplinary process that must be gone through in order to meet the expectations of the role. Becoming fully compliant might also involve sacrificing one's own identity, as indicated in the case of an Italian company, NouvoPignone (NP). After being taken over by General Electric, the management philosophy changed drastically from noble bureaucratic management to money-making machine. Under the new culture of "making the numbers," NP managers and employees were forced to sacrifice their identities, becoming "*Homo economicus*" in order to survive in the highly competitive work environment (Macintosh et al. 2009). On the other hand, the adapting strategy allows one to maintain one's own identity while reorienting toward the new role. For example, in a case study of a large public teaching hospital in Australia, Abernethy and Stoelwinder (1995) find that when the highly profession-oriented doctors who prefer autonomy are hired into the bureaucratic organization with tight control, conflicts usually arise. In order to minimize such conflict, it is suggested either that the doctors reorient themselves less to their profession by giving up part of their professional identities or put in place the control mechanism that allows a certain degree of self-regulation that accommodates their professional orientation. In another case, Allsop and Calveley's (2009) study of the impact of mining industry privatization on miners' identity finds that miners draw upon their identity as autonomous workers in order to mediate the impact of technology on their working practices. When new technological working practices are introduced, they reorient themselves by learning how to combine the new technology and their unique expertise at the coalface, to help management in the control process while maintaining their own identities as autonomous workers. Nevertheless, in most cases, despite the picture of smooth transition there are those who resist the role change, shunning the reorienting process completely (Burns and Baldvinsdottir 2005; Morales and Lambert 2013).

1.2.2 *Self-Orientation in Everyday Life*

Contemporary management accounting researches influenced by the "practice turn" suggest that the degree of self-orientation together with its meaning or the essence of being today's management accountants is manifested in day-to-day actions (Schatzki 2001).[4] Complementing the earlier work of Hopper and Macintosh (1993) on disciplinary practice, Lambert and Pezet (2011) adopt Foucault's practice theory and illustrate that being management accountants of a French automobile equipment manufacturer means being "knowing subjects" and "producers of truthful knowledge." This involves being accountable for the bidding price in the auction that the company participates and subjecting oneself to the subsequent management review or the "trial of truth" system.

From an ethnographic study of management accounting practice at a French industrial aeronautics firm, Morales and Lambert (2013) inform us that, for the management accountants under the study, being recognized as "business partners" involves not participating in activities related to "bean counters," such as reviewing and correcting accounting errors; these are part of what the study refers to as the "dirty work" (Hughes 1951). Some others, however, do not mind doing such work, and also enjoy taking control of how the accounting data are constructed—thereby revealing their orientation toward being traditional accountants. Most importantly, the study suggests that by performing business-partner-typed actions, such as participating in board meetings or decision-making, one does not become a business partner. Rather, it is in the way those actions are performed: for example, whether one sits silently in a board meeting while decisions are being made or just validates the preapproved investment informs the direction of the self-orientation.

Studying the budgeting conversation in a French construction company, Fauré and Rouleau (2011) provide an insight into the strategic orientation of management accountants. This involves drawing upon practical

[4] The "practice turn" (Schatzki 2001), which represents a move away from problematic dualisms (Giddens 1984) such as structure versus action and subject versus object, and offers a field of practices as the "site of social," includes the works of prominent social philosophers and theorists such as Michel Foucault, Pierre Bourdieu, Bruno Latour, Anthony Giddens, and Theodore Schatzki. Although practice theorists agree that social practices are arrays of activities, they differ on how the practices are organized and the way in which they govern an individual's activities and in turn sustain the practices (Taylor 1995; Schatzki 1997). Most importantly, the practice theory suggests that the role identity of each member of the practice is constituted within the practice (Schatzki 2001, 2002, 2005; Whittington 2011).

understanding (Schatzki 2002) of accounting and reporting in close collaboration with the site engineers in the context of strategic execution. Such orientation is manifested in their actions of invoking the usefulness of numbers to activate local projects; constructing the acceptability of numbers to report them to external partners; and authorizing the plausibility of numbers to reconcile local contingencies and global coherence.

1.2.3 Self-Orienting in Cultural Context

Management accounting research tells us that the self-orienting process is influenced by the broad occupational and corporate culture (Ahrens and Chapman 2000), as manifested in the styles of accountability (Ahrens 1996). For example, under the same business context German management accountants would prefer to act as "scorekeepers" respecting the functional accountability of their business counterparts, while British management accountants, being more of the "business partners" type, would be getting involved in business decisions, bringing in economic logic together with an understanding of the business to support their business counterparts. In everyday life the self-orienting is a situated phenomenon, and can be attributed to management accountants' capability to switch their roles vis-à-vis operations that marks out the identity of management accountants from other accountants (Ahrens 1997). An example of this is a formal budget meeting in which a British business partner is asked to fill in the budget shortfall. He switches role from business partner to corporate controller and begins to challenge the business units' budget.

> Amongst management accountants, who had experienced the divided loyalties to which their simultaneous roles as 'partners' of operational management and 'financially objective informers of the board' could give rise, the professional identity which distinguished management accountants was expressed by pointing towards the contradictory demands of their work. (Ibid., p. 633)

1.2.4 Self-Orienting, Culture, and Past Practices

In a rare study on the self-orienting process, Baxter and Chua (2008) explore the influence of past habits on the process. Experimenting with Bourdieu's practice theory, they explain how a new CFO orients himself in a new company where there is a different corporate culture and different financial practices. With the notion of "habitus," which is defined as the "habitual way that we (as the agents) have of entering into relationships with the social world" (Baxter and Chua 2008, pp. 214, 224), this insightful study points to the significant role of past habit in constituting the position of the CFO in the new organization. We see how the new CFO mobilizes his previously acquired social capital, which is described as "high-profile accomplished accounting professional" (ibid., p. 217), and symbolic capital, such as first-class air travel and company car, to establish and distinguish his position as a high-ranking officer in the new organization. He exercises the balance sheet management, arranging for a weekly corporate finance meeting and other informal meetings in an effort to form a financial community. These and other related activities are to convey the new meaning of the finance management, and thereby change the culture, the practice and the role of management accountants in the company.

1.2.5 Self-Orienting as a Life Journey

In the context of the consolidation of three Canadian accounting associations, Chartered Accountant, Certified Management Accountants, and Certified General Accountant, into one, Chartered Professional Accountant, during 2011–2012, Guo (2017) has found that besides the current professional standing or how the accountants perceive themselves in relation to others in the profession, their lifelong professional experiences of "becoming" accountants play an important role in defining their work identity. The lifelong professional journey, consisting of activities *oriented* towards becoming the member of the accounting profession, contributes to their identity work, in the sense that it feeds into the perception of standing in the profession, and at the same time the perception guides their everyday activities during their journey to become who they are today.

References

Abernethy, M., & Stoelwinder, J. (1995). The role of professional control in the management of complex organizations. *Accounting, Organizations and Society, 20*, 1–17.

Ahrens, T. (1996). Styles of accountability. *Accounting, Organizations and Society, 21*(2–3), 139–173.

Ahrens, T. (1997). Talking accounting: An ethnography of management knowledge in British and German brewers. *Accounting, Organizations and Society, 22*(7), 617–637.

Ahrens, T. (2009). Everyday accounting practices and intentionality. In C. S. Chapman, D. J. Cooper, & P. Miller (Eds.), *Accounting, organizations, and institutions* (pp. 30–47). Oxford: Oxford University Press.
Ahrens, T., & Chapman, C. S. (2000). Occupational identity of management accountants in Britain and Germany. *The European Accounting Review, 9*(4), 477–498.
Ahrens, T., & Chapman, C. S. (2002). The structuration of legitimate performance measures and management: Day-to-day contests of accountability in a U.K. restaurant chain. *Management Accounting Research, 13*(2), 151–171.
Ahrens, T., & Chapman, C. S. (2007). Management accounting as practice. *Accounting, Organizations and Society, 32*(1–2), 1–27.
Ahrens, T., & Mollona, M. (2007). Organisational control as cultural practice – A shop floor ethnography of a Sheffield steel mill. *Accounting, Organizations and Society, 32*(4–5), 305–331.
Allsop, D., & Calveley, M. (2009). Miners' identity and the changing face of the labour process within the UK coal mining industry. *Qualitative Research in Accounting & Management, 6*(1/2), 57–69. https://doi.org/10.1108/11766090910940665.
Baxter, J., & Chua, W. F. (2008). Be(com)ing the chief financial officer of an organisation: Experimenting with Bourdieu's practice theory. *Management Accounting Research, 19*, 212–230.
Beard, V. (1994). Popular culture and professional identity: Accountants in the movies. *Accounting Organizations and Society, 19*(3), 303–318.
Bentham, J. (1995). In M. Bozovic (Ed.), *The Panopticon writings*. London: Verso.
Berland, N., & Chiapello, E. (2009). Criticisms of capitalism, budgeting and the double enrolment: Budgetary control rhetoric and social reform in France in the 1930s and 1950s. *Accounting, Organizations and Society, 34*, 28–57.
Bougen, P. D. (1994). Joking apart: The serious side to the accounting stereotypes. *Accounting Organization and Society, 19*(3), 319–335.
Briers, M., & Chua, W. F. (2001). The roles of actors-networks and boundary objects in management accounting change: A field study of an implementing of activity-based costing. *Accounting Organizations and Society, 26*, 237–269.
Burns, J., & Baldvinsdottir, G. (2005). An institutional perspective of accountants' new roles – The interplay of contradictions and praxis. *European Accounting Review, 14*(4), 725–757.
Byrne, S., & Pierce, B. (2007). Towards a more comprehensive understanding of the roles of management accountants. *European Accounting Review, 16*(3), 469–498.
Chen, C. C., Jones, K. T., Scarlata, A. N., & Stone, D. N. (2012). Does the Holland model of occupational choice (HMOC) perpetuate the Beancounter-Bookkeeper (BB) stereotype of accountants? *Critical Perspectives on Accounting, 23*(4–5), 370–389.

Chua, W. F. (1995). Experts, networks and inscriptions in the fabrication of accounting images: A story of representation of three public hospitals. *Accounting, Organizations and Society, 20*(2/3), 111–145.

DiMaggio, P. J. (1988). Interest and agency in institutional theory. In L. G. Zucker (Ed.), *Institutional patterns and organizations: Culture and environment* (pp. 3–21). Cambridge, MA: Ballinger.

Dimnik, T., & Felton, S. (2006). Accountant stereotypes in movies distributed in North America in the twentieth century. *Accounting Organizations and Society, 31*(2), 129–155.

Fauré, B., & Rouleau, L. (2011). The strategic competence of accountants and middle managers in budget making. *Accounting, Organizations and Society, 36*, 167–182.

Foucault, M. (1979). *Discipline and punish: The birth of the prison*. New York: Vintage Books.

Friedland, R., & Alford, R. R. (1991). Bringing society back in: Symbols, practices, and institutional contradictions. In P. J. DiMaggio & W. W. Powell (Eds.), *The new institutionalism in organizational analysis*. Chicago: University of Chicago Press.

Friedman, A. L., & Lyne, S. R. (1997). Activity-based techniques and the death of the beancounter. *European Accounting Review, 6*(1), 19–44.

Friedman, A. L., & Lyne, S. R. (2001). The beancounter stereotype: Towards a general model of stereotype generation. *Critical Perspectives on Accounting, 12*(4), 423–451.

Giddens, A. (1984). *The constitution of society outline of the theory of structuration*. Cambridge: Polity Press.

Goretzki, L., Strauss, E., & Weber, J. (2013). An institutional perspective on the changes in management accountants' professional role. *Management Accounting Research, 24*, 41–63.

Granlund, M., & Lukka, K. (1998). Towards increasing business orientation: Finnish management accountants in a changing cultural context. *Management Accounting Research, 9*, 185–211.

Guo. (2017). The odyssey of becoming: Professional identity and insecurity in the Canadian accounting field. *Critical Perspectives on Accounting*. https://doi.org/10.1016/j.cpa.2017.10.008.

Hopper, T. M. (1980). Role conflicts of management accountants and their position within organisation structures. *Accounting, Organizations and Society, 5*(4), 401–411.

Hopper, T. M., & Macintosh, N. (1993). Management accounting as disciplinary practice: The case of ITT under Harold Geneen. *Management Accounting Research, 4*, 181–216.

Hughes, E. C. (1951). Mistakes at work. *Canadian Journal of Economics and Political Science, 17*(3), 320–327. (Reprinted in *The sociological eye*. Selected papers, New Brunswick: Transaction Publishers, pp. 316–325).

Janin, F. (2016). When being a partner means more: The external role of football club management accountants. *Management Accounting Research*. https://doi.org/10.1016/j.mar.2016.05.002.

Järvenpää, M. (2007). Making business partners: A case study on how management accounting culture was changed. *The European Accounting Review, 16*(1), 99–142.

Jeacle, I. (2008). Beyond the boring grey: The construction of the colourful accountant. *Critical Perspectives on Accounting, 19*(8), 1296–1320.

Jørgensen, B., & Messner, M. (2010). Accounting and strategising: A case study from new product development. *Accounting, Organizations & Society, 35*(2), 184–204.

Lambert, C., & Pezet, E. (2011). The making of the management accountant – Becoming the producer of truthful knowledge. *Accounting, Organizations and Society, 36*(1), 10–30.

Lambert, C., & Sponem, S. (2012). Roles, authority and involvement of the management accounting function: A multiple case-study perspective. *The European Accounting Review, 21*(3), 565–589.

Loft, A. (1986). Towards a critical understanding of accounting: The case of cost accounting in U.K., 1914–1925. *Accounting, Organizations and Society, 11*(2), 137–170.

Macintosh, N. B., Shearer, T., & Riccaboni, A. (2009). A Levinasian ethics critique of the role of management and control systems by large global corporations: The General Electric/NuovoPignone example. *Critical Perspectives on Accounting, 20*, 751–761.

Miller, P., & O'Leary, T. (1987). Accounting and the construction of the governable person. *Accounting, Organizations and Society, 12*(3), 235–265.

Morales, J., & Lambert, C. (2013). Dirty work and the construction of identity. An ethnographic study of management accounting practices. *Accounting, Organizations and Society, 38*, 228–244.

Mouritsen, J. (1996). Five aspects of accounting departments' work. *Management Accounting Research, 7*, 283–303.

Nama, Y., & Lowe, A. (2014). The 'situated functionality' of accounting in private equity practices: A social 'site' analysis. *Management Accounting Research, 25*, 284–303.

Nor-Aziah, A. K., & Scapens, R. W. (2007). Corporatisation and accounting change: The role of accounting and accountants in a Malaysian public utility. *Management Accounting Research, 18*(2), 209–247.

Schatzki, T. R. (1997). Practices and actions: A Wittgensteinian critique of Bourdieu and Giddens. *Philosophy of the Social Sciences, 27*(3), 283–308.

Schatzki, T. R. (2001). Practice theory: An introduction. In T. R. Schatzki, K. Knorr Cetina, & E. von Savigny (Eds.), *The practice turn in contemporary theory* (pp. 1–14). London: Routledge.

Schatzki, T. R. (2002). *The site of the social: A philosophical account of the constitution of social life and change*. University Park: Pennsylvania State University Press.

Schatzki, T. R. (2005). The sites of organizations. *Organization Studies, 26*(3), 465–484.

Seo, M. G., & Creed, W. E. D. (2002). Institutional contradictions, praxis, and institutional change: A dialectical perspective. *Academy of Management Review, 27*(2), 222–247.

Siegel, G., & Sorensen, J. E. (1999). *Counting more, counting less, the 1999 practice analysis of management accounting*. Montvale, NJ: Institute of Management Accountants.

Simon, H. A., Guetzkow, H., Kozmetsky, G., & Tyndall, G. (1954). *Centralization vs. decentralization in organizing the controller's department*. New York: The Controllership Foundation.

Taylor, C. (1995). *Philosophical arguments*. Cambridge: Harvard University Press.

Thornborrow, T., & Brown, A. (2009). 'Being regimented': Aspiration, discipline and identity work in the British parachute regiment. *Organization Studies, 30*(4), 355–376.

Vaivio, J. (1999). Examining "the quantified customer". *Accounting, Organizations and Society, 24*, 689–715.

Vaivio, J. (2006). The business controller, non-financial measurement and tacit knowledge. *The Finnish Journal of Business Economics, 2*, 194–212.

Vaivio, J., & Kokko, T. (2006). Counting big: Re-examining the concept of the bean counter controller. *The Finnish Journal of Business Economics, 1*, 49–74.

Weber, J. (2011). The development of controller tasks: Explaining the nature of controllership and its changes. *Journal of Management Control, 22*, 25–46.

Whittington, R. (2011). The practice turn in organization research: Towards a disciplined transdisciplinary. *Accounting, Organizations and Society, 36*, 183–186.

Windeck, D., Weber, J., & Strauss, E. (2015). Enrolling managers to accept the business partner: The role of boundary objects. *Journal of Management & Governance, 19*(3), 617–653. https://doi.org/10.1007/s10997-013-9277-2.

CHAPTER 2

Self-Orienting Process and Schatzki's Lens

Management accounting research informs us that the emergence of business-oriented management accountants is influenced by sociopolitical and economic forces, organizational changes, and agency. It also hinges on management accountants' lifelong self-orienting process. Contemporary research has found that the degree of business orientation is associated with management accountants' understanding of what it is to be business-oriented: this is drawn from everyday practice, the broader cultural context, past habits, and certain personal characteristics. Despite these valuable insights, there is still a need for further investigation into the entire process of self-orienting: how and why management accountants orient towards business over the span of their professional lives, and how the above-mentioned external and internal elements play out in influencing the degree of business orientation in such a process.

To study and gain an understanding of the lifelong self-orienting process as an individual level phenomenon that is embedded in the broader social environment, one requires a model that not only appreciates the influence of the social and respects individual intentionality but is also capable of relating various activities across time and accounting for variations. Such a model can be found in the research under the practice theory.

P. Chotiyanon, V. Joannidès de Lautour,
The Changing Role of the Management Accountants,
https://doi.org/10.1007/978-3-319-90300-2_2

2.1 The Turn to Practices

During the 1970s, most management accounting research concentrated on finding the economic models that render the "best" accounting techniques, such as economic profit and residual income, which could help in optimizing management decisions. In the early 1980s, confounded by the vast diversity in management accounting practices, a relatively high number of researchers began to look at management accounting changes in order to find the reasons behind the different "best" techniques that were used in various organizations. Their research approach was influenced predominantly by positivism with theoretical frameworks, such as the contingency theory, being adopted. Expanding earlier economic models to explicate the phenomena, additional data were gathered from surveys or questionnaires and processed using statistical models such as the regression model to find a relationship between the different practices and some "independent variables." This helped with gaining an understanding of, for example, why some organizations used residual income in their capital budget decisions whereas others used return on investment or the budget, for example, to control their investment.

Later, in the 1980s into the 1990s, when most of the economic models failed to explain the diversity in the practice, other disciplines such as organizational and social theories were mobilized in studies of management accounting changes and related processes of change in order to gain a deeper insight into management accounting practice. The research during this period expanded to include interpretative and critical approaches. In addition to the quantitative research, with mathematic models built on data from surveys or questionnaires, we began to see more qualitative research with an increasing number of case studies. Out of this development arose an alternative school of thought, which represented a broad non-rational approach to management accounting research (Baxter and Chua 2003). This stream of research was influenced by institutional theory and a new approach called practice theory. The latter school of thought, sometimes broadly referred to as the "practice turn," included the works of prominent social philosophers and theorists such as Michel Foucault, Pierre Bourdieu, Bruno Latour, Anthony Giddens, and Theodore Schatzski.

In general, the practice turn represents a move away from problematic dualisms (Giddens 1984), such as structure versus action and subject versus object. It argues that in order to study practices there are not only activities but also practice organizing structures to be considered. In other words, we cannot consider one without the other. This new approach posits a field of practices as the "site of social" and most importantly suggests that the role of each member is made only in the practice (Schatzki 2001, 2002, 2005a; Whittington 2011). Although practice theorists agree that social practices are arrays of activities, they differ on how the practices are organized and the way in which they govern an individual's activities and in turn sustain the practices (Taylor 1985; Schatzki 1997). Foucault, for example, views social practices in terms of power relations. To him the only appropriate relation for power is that of government: "To govern ... is to structure the possible field of actions of others."[1] Accordingly, disciplinary practice comprises the actions of one or more persons that enable or constrain the action of others for the purpose of government; whereas Callon, Law, and Latour of the Actor Network Theory (ANT) school conceptualize social as the constellations of networks: any element of the network is itself a network of further elements.[2] This means that if we take a slice of social it is nothing but networks. In fact, "networks are immersed in nothing."[3] Both Foucault and the ANT theorists conceive social as consisting of the same kind of "textures," be they power relations or simply the networks. On the other hand, Bourdieu, Giddens, and Schatzki conceive social as immersed in the "*con*textures" of social formations, having the power of determination vis-à-vis people.[4] Bourdieu talks about the structuring structure that lies in the actors, the "habitus," which is more or less the embodiment of the social structure; for example, the culture and belief system. It is the habitus that selects the action for the actors in various situations. In contrast, Giddens (1984) explains the social constitution and change with his structuration theory, which is based on the mutual constitutive power of structure and actions; that is, structure guides the activities and the activities

[1] Foucault, M. The Subject and Power. Critical Inquiry, 8(4), Chicago: University of Chicago Press, 777–795.

[2] Callon, B. & Law, J. (1989). On the Construction of Sociotechnical Networks: Content and Context Revisited, Knowledge and Society: Study in the Sociology of Science Past and present, ed. Lowell Hargens, Robert Alun Jones, and Andrew Pickering. Greenwich, Conn.: JAI Press, 57–83, 62, 78.

[3] Latour, B. (1993). We Have Never Been Modern, trans. Catherine Porter, Cambridge, MA: Harvard University Press.

[4] According to Schatzki (2002) "contexturalists" such as Bourdieu and Giddens maintain a position that is close to that of "socialism." That is, the determination power vis-à-vis people is attributed to social formations, as opposed to "individualism," which gives the power of determination to individuals.

shape the structure. Giddens shares the concept of practice intelligibility governing the activities in Bourdieu's habitus with his "practice conscious," whereas Schatzki contends that activities are organized or governed by four practice modalities: shared practical understanding, rules, teleoaffective structure, and general understanding (Schatzki 2002).

The following discusses some of the previous research that relates to the change in the role of management accountants, mobilizing five prominent theoretical lenses: the institutional theory, the Foucauldian approach, the ANT approach, and the practice theories of Bourdieu and Giddens. Three aspects of these are explored: the time span of the study (present versus past), the elements used in associating activities (internal inherent micro-level element versus external macro-level element), and the change agency (management accountant's own action/will versus other players'), as summarized in Table 2.1. These help us to assess in what way the frameworks being used help to explain the lifelong self-orienting process: how and why management accountants orient themselves towards business, and when the business orientation emerges in each individual, which is discussed in Sect. 2.2.

2.1.1 *Institutional Theory Study*

Institutional theory can be broadly categorized into two branches: "Neo-Institutionalism" which focuses on external factors and their influences on the organizational structure, and "Old Institutionalism," which looks at the internal factors and its implications for organizational change. The Neo-Institutionalism school comprises the New Institution Economic, attributing the organizational change to economic factors such as transaction costs which decide what activities are to be performed within the organization or by the market outside the organization, and New Institutional Sociology, looking at other contingencies as determinant factors of the organization structure (Scapens 2006). Most of the research that adopts Neo-Institutionalism looks at convergence or normalization and stability in the organization and explains how external factors force the organization to align itself with other organizations and create a new role for management accountants in the process. For example, in the context of fierce competition in the market that led to the commercialization of a Malaysian public utility, Nor-Aziah and Scapens (2007) indicate that there has been an attempt to change the role of state accountants into that of financial advisors as part of the overall organizational change.

Table 2.1 Comparative theoretical lens

Theoretical lens	*Levels of analysis*	*Focused time span of study*	*Change agency*	*Elements associating activities across time*	
				External macro-level elements	*Internal inherent micro-level elements*
Institutional theory (Burns and Baldvinsdottir 2005; Nor-Aziah and Scapens 2007; Goretzki et al. 2013)	Organizations and organizational actors	Present and past	Actions of the leaders of the organizations	External forces, institutional goals	
Foucauldian approach (Hopper and Macintosh 1993; Lambert and Pezet 2010)	Practices, practitioners	Present	Actions of the CEO, management accountants	Power relations	Power relations
ANT (Briers and Chua 2001)	Practices, practitioners	Present	Actions of the finance leader	Network relations	
Bourdieu's practice theory (Baxter and Chua 2008)	Practitioners, practices	Present	Actions of CFO/ management accountant	Habitus	Past habits
Giddens' structuration theory (Guo 2017)	Practices, practitioners	Present	Action of the accountants	Past and present practices	Practice intelligibility

On the other hand, Old Institutionalism, such as Old Institution Economics, looks inside the organization to explain divergence and change. This approach leads some researchers to focus on the "embedded agency paradox," in which embedded organizational members strive for change (Seo and Creed 2002). By implicating the activities of actors in the process of change, this stream of research has led to some insightful management accounting studies on the change in the role of management accountants. An example is the work of Burns and Baldvinsdottir (2005).

Studying the emergence of a new role for "hybrid accountants" in the manufacturing division of a multinational pharmaceuticals organization,

Burns and Baldvinsdottir (2005) attribute the change in role to broader changes in the competitive arena that result in broad organizational change; examples are the stricter government control of drug prices, the increase in competition, and the expiry of "backbone" drug patents. In the same manner as Nor-Aziah and Scapens (2007), the study attributes the change in the role of management accountants to the efforts of a senior finance manager, who takes the role of an institutional entrepreneur,[5] an embedded agent who seizes an opportunity for change in the institutional contradictions (Seo and Creed 2002). Seeing the contrasting business logics, research and development versus the market, he seizes the opportunity to institute the new role of management accountants as hybrid accountants who have a higher degree of engagement in the business. The study provides an insight into a series of initiatives made by the key organizational players within the change event. This begins with the key actions taken by lead managers between 1994 and 1996: the establishment of a strategic business plan by the management committee in 1994, emphasizing a new strategic direction focusing on customer value and cost reduction; and broad organizational restructuring in 1995, putting all business processes related to a product, from customer ordering to customer delivery, on one site under the leadership of a business stream leader. These two key actions helped to cultivate a cross-functional work culture, the "process way of working," providing a backdrop and opening up an opportunity for the senior finance manager to establish new business-oriented management accountants by decentralizing the finance function in order to assist the process stream leaders with their strategic imperatives and day-to-day operations. For this study all of the purposeful concerted efforts intended to help counter the stronger competitive forces that the company was facing are related to one change event: the current role of management accountants as hybrid accountants.

On the other hand, in a comprehensive case study Goretzki et al. (2013) look at a series of change events related to the changing role of management accountants in a German manufacturing firm from 1993 to 2010, as led by the company's new chief financial officer (CFO). Each individual event is distinctively associated with the specific time-bound business and organizational contexts. For example, the former bean counter role during

[5] Institution entrepreneur is defined as organized actors who envision new institutions as a mean of advancing interests they value highly yet that are suppressed by extant logics (DiMaggio 1988).

1993–1997 is associated with the company's focus on the German market and the emphasis on the marketing function; the subsequent role of reporters during 1998–2002 comes with the shrinking German market and the restructuring of the sales function; the navigator role during 2003–2005 is associated with the internationalization of the organization; and finally the business partner role during 2006–2010 is associated with the opening up of the emerging market and the introduction of channel management (ibid., Figure 2, page 49). In turn, the activities within each particular change event are geared towards specific institutional goals; for example, developing a group controlling department as well as local controlling departments is aimed at building a navigator role to support the internationalization of the firm so it can compete in the global market. It appears that all event-related activities are geared towards the ultimate goal of countering external forces.

Mobilizing the institutional theory, all three case studies attribute the change in the role of management accountants to external forces, such as broader government policy (Nor-Aziah and Scapens 2007), or to market forces (Burns and Baldvinsdottir 2005; Goretzki et al. 2013) and the agency of the leaders of the organization. In addition, by virtue of tracing series of change events across timelines, Goretzki et al. (2013) has not only demonstrated how to expand the framework to systematically trace the process of change and link activities across the time span but also highlighted the importance of management accountants' internalizing of the new role or their long-term self-orienting processes.

2.1.2 *Foucauldian Study*

Management accounting researches benefit from the work of Michel Foucault in two areas. First, in the history of management accounting practice it is argued that management accounting does not arise from a linear relationship and is not path-dependent, as described by Chandler (1962). The advent of cost accounting and management accounting innovation, such as standard costing and budgeting, is a result of specific conditions.[6] Together they form a calculative practice, which is a part of a broader apparatus of power emerging out of the development in scientific management and industrial psychology during the last three decades of the twentieth century. This had the aim of constructing the individual

[6] Or "particulars" (Schatzki 2005a).

person as a more manageable and efficient entity (Loft 1986; Miller and O'Leary 1987). As such, management accounting is viewed as a "power tool" that can be used to discipline the members of the organization (Hoskin and Macve 1986; Hopwood 1987; Preston 1992).

Foucault's second contribution to management accounting research is in the area of disciplinary practice. Shedding some light onto the role of management accountants in disciplinary practice Hopper and Macintosh (1993) demonstrate how the chief executive office (CEO) establishes a controlling structure and system that governs the activities in the everyday lives of the members of the organization. In effect the system renders all members of the organization, including the management accountants, docile and amenable subjects (Foucault's "Discipline and Punishment", 1979).

While Hopper and Macintosh (1993) focus on the agency of the leader of the organization, Lambert and Pezet (2010) provide an insight into how management accountants in an automobile equipment manufacturer portray themselves as the producers of truthful knowledge at the moment when they participate in a reverse online auction, thereby committing themselves together with the company to a long-term project.

Compared with the earlier longitudinal case studies under the institutional theory, Foucauldian studies focus on the present stage of the change; in other words the activities surrounding the present role. And while they have attributed the change in role to the agency of the powerful player in the case of Hopper and Macintosh (1993), and management accountants themselves in the case of Lambert and Pezet (2010), they suggest one universal inherent motivation for those agencies; that is, the power relation. In their view, the present self-orienting activities of management accountants are acted upon by the agency of influential organizational players or involve the act of subjecting themselves to other organizational players.

2.1.3 The Actor Network Theory Study

ANT (Latour 1996) shares with Foucault's theoretical framework the way in which they conceptualize practice as existing in the same textures.[7] While Foucault talks about the "textures" of power relations, ANT talks

[7] By "textures" Schatzki (2002) means the same elements forming a backdrop to the activities in which they are immersed, as opposed to different ones that are called "contextures."

about the networks. In other words the ANT school conceptualizes social as constellations of networks: any element of the network is itself a network of further elements. This means that if we take a slice of social it is nothing but networks. In fact, "networks are immersed in nothing" (Schatzki 2002).

Most ANT-based management accounting research looks at the networking process and its implications. An example is the work of Chua (1995), which has demonstrated how knowledgeable experts come together to form a network of humans and non-humans, such as software, in the process of implementing a new management accounting practice, Diagnostic Result Group, in public hospitals. In another study Briers and Chua (2001) have attributed the change in management accounting and the corresponding change in the role of management accountants to a single element; that is, the broad network of global and local actors and actants through the agency of the lead accountant.

In the same manner as the Foucauldian studies, ANT research is interested in current activities surrounding a present role. However, they differ in the sense that ANT studies are more concerned about the process of networking rather than the internal inherent elements such as the personal motivation.

2.1.4 *Bourdieu's Practice Theory Study*

While Foucault's and ANT's theoretical frameworks talk about social as existing in the same textures of power relations and networks respectively, Bourdieu places the emphasis of the power of determination vis-à-vis people on "contextures" (Schatzki 2002).[8] He calls the structuring structure that lies in the actors "habitus", which is more or less the embodiment of the society's structure, its culture and belief system. According to Bourdieu it is the habitus that selects the action for the actors in various situations.

Adopting Bourdieu's practice theory"; Baxter and Chua (2008) conduct a study on an event of change related to a personal experience of becoming a new CFO of a large Australian retail organization. The study relates the activities within the event to one internal and inherent micro-level element; that is, past habits of the new CFO residing in Bourdieu's "habitus". Capitalizing on his prior experiences he manages to change the way corporate finance is practiced while firmly establishes his position in the company that he has newly joined.

[8] "Contexturalists" such as Bourdieu and Giddens place the determination power on social formation such as states, social facts, totalities of structures, and modes of production.

Even though this case study focuses on the present stage of the change, the new CFO position in the organization, as in most of the earlier cases under practice theory's lens, it differs in the sense that it attributes the role change to one's own will and actions as opposed to being acted upon by the influential organizational players. It also demonstrates the importance of past habit and experiences in influencing the way in which one orients in the present environment.

2.1.5 *Giddens' Structuration Theory Study*

With his structuration theory, Giddens (1984) explains his concept of social constitution and change through the mutual constitutive power of structure and actions; that is, structure guides the activities and the activities shape the structure. Accordingly, practice is built by the activities of the actors, who draw upon the structure that exists virtually outside the realm of practice but leaves some residual in "practical conscious," which perpetuates routines that sustain the practice through time and space (Giddens 1984). This concept suggests associating actions with the practical conscious.

In a recent study of accountants' professional identity in the context of the unification of three Canadian accounting associations, Guo (2017) finds that such identity consists of two aspects;[9] that is, identity ranking, which is a self-privileged standing in perceived social pecking orders or how one is positioned compared with others, and identity experiencing, which is a result of one's past and expected future professional life journey, which is laden with cognition, meanings, and emotions. These two aspects of identity are coconstitutive in the sense that professional identity governs the activities of the accountants in their everyday lives and that their activities both at present and in the past feed into professional identity. And while it focuses on the present stage of the new role as in other studies under the lens of practice theory, this study brings a crucial aspect to the study of the change in role enacted by management accountants; that is, the past dimension in terms of the experiences of management accountants as they move along their "professional life journey" (ibid.) to become who they are today.

[9] The process in which the identity is formed or reconstructed: Guo (2017).

2.2 Taking Stock

At this point we look at how far the five theoretical frameworks have taken us, and in what way Schatzki's framework (Sect. 2.3) can help to explain the lifelong self-orienting process: how and why management accountants orient themselves towards business and when the business orientation emerges in each individual, by assessing the frameworks mobilized in previous studies in three aspects: the time span of the study (present versus past), the key elements used in associating activities (inherent internal micro-level element versus external macro-level element), and the change agency (a management accountant's own action/will versus other players') (Table 2.2). While the first aspect concerns the time span relevant to the lifelong self-orienting process (Guo 2017) the last two aspects are indicatives of whether the frameworks are relevant to the volition and motivation of management accountants in their self-orienting processes (Goretzki et al. 2013).

The self-orienting of management accountants is a lifelong process (Guo 2017). Investigating such a process would require a longitudinal study of the activities of management accountants during their entire work life journey towards becoming today's business partners, including the related volition or motivation. From this view, evaluating the previously mobilized theoretical frameworks by looking at the "Change agency" element (column 4, in Table 2.2), "Internal inherent micro-level elements associating activities" (column 6, in Table 2.2) and "Focused time span of study" (column 3, in Table 2.2), it seems that the frameworks of Foucault, Giddens, and Bourdieu[10] might partially meet the study's requirement, by virtue of their focus on the activities and motivation of the management accountants. However, they have been mobilized to explore only the *present* stage of change rather than the required entire work life span. On the other hand, the institutional theory, which demonstrates how to explore the activities surrounding *past* as well as *present* change events in the long history of the organization (Goretzki et al. 2013), seems to fulfill the requirement regarding the time span of the study but has yet to delve into the internal element inherent to the management accountants. In view of these limitations we turn to Schatzki's theoretical framework

[10] ANT's framework is not included as it focuses only on the present role and attributes the role change to the networking process rather than the internal inherent elements, as in other frameworks under Practice Theory.

Table 2.2 Comparative theoretical lenses-extended

Theoretical lens	*Levels of analysis*	*Focused time span of study*	*Change agency*	*Elements associating activities across time*	
				External macro-level elements	*Internal inherent micro-level elements*
Institutional theory (Burns and Baldvinsdottir 2005; Nor-Aziah and Scapens 2007; Goretzki et al. 2013)	Organizations and organizational actors	Present and past	Actions of the leaders of the organizations	External forces institutional goals	
Foucauldian approach (Hopper and Macintosh 1993; Lambert and Pezet 2010)	Practices, practitioners	Present	Actions of the CEO, management accountants	Power relations	Power relations
ANT (Briers and Chua 2001)	Practices, practitioners	Present	Actions of the finance leader	Network relations	
Bourdieu's practice theory (Baxter and Chua 2008)	Practitioners, practices	Present	Actions of CFO/ management accountant	Habitus	Past habits
Giddens' structuration theory (Guo 2017)	Practices, practitioners	Present	Action of the accountants	Past and present practices	Practice intelligibility
Schatzki's site of social (Fauré and Rouleau 2011; Ahrens and Ferry 2016)	Practices, practitioners	Present	Actions of the leader of local government authority, management accountants	Culture, past practices	Goals, ends, emotions, motivation, practical understanding

which can fulfill all of the requirement of the study with its notion of "teleoaffective structure".

In terms of the time span, with the notion of "teleoaffective structure" (Sect. 2.3.1.3), Schatzki (2002) contends that an activity is not just an occurrence in time but it is associated with a specific personal goal and imbued with "affectivity" or "emotion-in-action." In the process of aligning short-term and long-term goals, the purposeful actions are driven by motivations (what matters) towards an ultimate end (Schatzki 2010). In this respect the time span of the study can be expanded from the present event of a role change, which is the focus of earlier studies mobilizing Foucault's, Giddens', and Bourdieu's frameworks, so that it covers past events by linking purposeful activities associated with present role change events to those of the past through the goal alignment mechanism (Sect. 2.3.4). Furthermore, as the teleoaffective structure is open ended, in the sense that activities can be alternately aligned to various goals, it can help bring another dimension to the analysis: the variation in role orientation, compared with generalization under Bourdieu's, Giddens' and Foucault's frameworks (Baxter and Chua 2008; Hopper and Macintosh 1993; Schatzki 1997), to explain the various degree of business orientation.[11] In terms of the personal elements that Schatzki's teleoaffective structure offers, not only the personal goals/ends but also the affectivity or "emotion-in-action" which is associated with the motivations or "what matters" to the person, is added—a new dimension of analysis that is relevant to personal decision-making and how management accountants internalize their new role.

In summary, longitudinal studies under institutional theory have explained the process of changing role for management accountants via a series of related activities of the organizational players over a long period of time, and have suggested the importance of how management accountants internalize their new role (Goretzki et al. 2013). And while they have shown how the actions of lead organizational players can open up opportunities for management accountants to orient themselves towards new roles in this context, they have yet to delve into how and

[11] Bourdieu's model suggests that habitus directs the present actions, implying duplication of the old role template (Baxter and Chua 2008). In the same manner, under Foucault's model, the role is stipulated by those who have power allowing for no variation (Hopper and Macintosh 1993), whereas Giddens' suggests the notion of routines (Schatzki 1997).

why (motivation) management accountants have internalized their new role. On the other hand, the practice theories of Foucault, Bourdieu, and Giddens have shed light on the why by attributing self-orienting activities to power relations, habitus, and practice intelligibility, respectively. Nevertheless they have so far focused on present everyday self-orienting rather than the entire lifelong self-orienting process. This leaves room for Schatzki's theoretical framework and the notions of "teleoaffective structure" and "practice memory" (Sect. 2.3.3), to combine strengths in breadth (in terms of study timeline with the Institution framework) and in depth (in terms of personal experiences offered by the frameworks of Foucault, Giddens and Bourdieu), making it an appropriate framework to be mobilized in the study and in making sense of the lifelong self-orienting process of management accountants. Next we present an overview of Schatzki's practice theory, before demonstrating in Sects. 2.3.4 and 2.3.5 how the two key notions of "teleoaffective structure" and "practice memory" have been mobilized in previous management accounting research.

2.3 Schatzki's Practice Theory

2.3.1 Practices as the "Site of Social"

Compared with other theoretical frameworks that have been mobilized to study activities and actions of agents in the social setting related to the change in the role of management accountants, Schatzki's is perhaps the only one that offers an inherent tool that can be directly and systematically used to study volition of the agent across time. Schatzki's "teleoaffective structure" (Schatzki 2002) associates various activities in time with personal goals. It argues that each activity is not just an occurrence in time; it is associated with a specific personal goal and imbued with "affectivity" (ibid.) or "emotion-in-action." In the process of short-term and long-term goals alignment, the purposeful actions are also aligned and driven by motivations (what matters) towards an ultimate end. This theoretical framework is robust in the sense that it can be systematically mobilized not only in analyzing activities across time but also in explaining the variation in those activities.

In his "Sites of Social," Schatzki (2005a) conceptualizes social as bundles of practices and material arrangements. He contends that social orders exist and evolve in the context of practices, and that human coexistence transpires through practice.[12]

> Social orders are not self-standing or self-propagating configurations but they instead exist and evolve only in some *context* encompassing them ... This context is a nexus of social practices. To say that the social orders through and amid which human coexistence transpires are established in this nexus is to say that the relations, meanings, identities, and positions, of their components (*as well as change in these*) are beholden to certain organized bundles of human activities. This state of affairs entails, in turn, that human lives hang together, not just through social order, but also through social practices... the overall site specific to human coexistence is a mesh of orders and practices. (Schatzki 2002, p. 59, emphasis added)

He further defines practices as arrays of organized activities:

> By practices, I mean organized human activities. Examples are political practices, cooking practices, educational practices, management practices, shop floor practices, and design practices. Any practice is an organized, open-ended spatial-temporal manifold of actions. (Schatzki 2005a, p. 471)

Practice is spatial-temporal in the sense that the activities composing the practice are spatially and temporally dispersed; that is, each of them takes place somewhere in objective space at some point in or over some duration of objective time.[13] In forming a nexus, these activities are organized and connect through such relations as causality and intentional directedness (Schatzki 2012, p. 15).

Although Schatzki agrees with other practice theorists such as Foucault, Bourdieu, and Giddens that practice is an array of human activities, he differs in how the practice is organized and in the way that

[12] Schatzki (2002) conceives social orders as the ensembles or arrangements of entities through and amid which social life transpires. These elements consist of people, artifacts, organisms, and things which the ANT school of thought broadly categorizes into human and non-human elements.

[13] Schatzki (2005b, 2010) differentiates between "objective time," which is the traditional time that we have when one event (past one) precedes the next (present one) and this in turn precedes the next (future one), and "activity time," in which past (what matters), present (the action), and the future (for the sake of which) occur instantaneously in the action.

practice governs the activities of the members. While Bourdieu and Giddens place special emphasis on the role of practice intelligibility in terms of habitus and practice consciousness or certain rules/routines and resources in governing the activities of the members and the key binding factors of the practices, Schatzki contends that besides the practice intelligibility and routines there are also four other practice modalities: the practical understanding, the rule, the teleoaffective structure, and general understanding, that organize the practice (Schatzki 2001, 2002, 2005a, 2012).

2.3.1.1 *The Practical Understanding*

> By 'knowing how to x' I mean knowing which of the doings and sayings of which one is capable would constitute x-ing *in current circumstances.* (Schatzki 2001, emphasis added)

Schatzki's practical understanding is a know-how-to-do, a skill gained in practice more or less in the same manner as Bourdieu's and Giddens' practice intelligibility. However, it differs in the sense that it never decides on what action to take (Schatzki 1997). In fact, it executes the action that the practice intelligibility has pointed to. Examples are in the understanding of how to prepare an analysis for a specific customer, how to draw a financial budget, or to prepare a capital budget for a particular manufacturing site.

2.3.1.2 *The Rule*

> By 'rules' I mean explicit formulations that enjoin or school in particular actions such as statute law, 'rules of thumb,' and explicit normative enjoining. (Schatzki 2001)

According to Schatzki, the rule is the explicit rule that binds the member to the practice. It is the rule that all members observe and regard as such. For example, in the management accounting practice it could be the accounting rule, such as how to treat an expense item as either variable or fixed cost, or the format or the depth of a financial analysis.

2.3.1.3 *The Teleoaffective Structure*

> *Teleology*, as noted, is *orientations* toward ends, while *affectivity* is how things matter. (ibid., emphasis added)

Influenced by Heidegger (1962), Schatzki (2006) describes "telos" as what one is going forward to; for example, one has an inclination towards being a business leader.[14] As for the "affectivity," it is what one is coming from or what matters; for example, one has the inclination to become a leader as one loves to have people looking up to one. In Schatzki's words the teleoaffective structure is about end-project-activities imbued with emotion or a combination of end-project-activities. This teleoaffective structure is manifested in the projecting agency.

2.3.1.4 *The General Understanding*

> ...general understandings are abstract senses, for instance, of the beauty of an artisanal product or of the nobility of educating students. They are not ends for which people strive but senses of the worth, value, nature, or place of things, which infuse and are expressed in people's doings and sayings. (Schatzki 2012, p. 16)

The general understanding concerns the understanding related to a particular "site" as shared by many practices within the site (Jørgensen and Messner 2010), such as the accountability of operational managers and management accountants in the organizational control practice (Ahrens 1996). It could also be a common fate, such as the case of the Shakers, which forms the basis of study in Schatzki (2002)'s "The Site of the Social," or the shared concern for profitability in the management control practice (Ahrens and Chapman 2007; Jørgensen and Messner 2010).

2.3.2 *Practices Perpetuating Through Variations*

Schatzki avers that perpetuity is the default mode of practice. Although he argues that human nature is to follow the norm he does not equate the perpetuity with being forever in status quo without any change. Indeed, the perpetuation of a practice as well as the emergence of new ones occur because practices allow for "variations," in which the new practice

[14] "Being" a business leader here means a way of life as opposed to being appointed a CFO or CEO, which is an accomplishment (Dreyfus 1991).

structures are taken in while the traces of the old one are maintained. Thus drastic change can only be exogenous (Schatzki 2005a).

> An organization, construed as a practice-arrangement bundle, (1) is a product of actions performed in extant practices, (2) is a mesh that embraces existing, to varying degrees altered, practices (possibly supplemented with new ones) and a mix of new and old material arrangements, and (3) continues in existence via a perpetuation of its practices and a maintenance of its arrangements that accommodates evolution and focused changes in the mesh. (Ibid., p. 476)

And it is indeed in the persistence of the practice organizing structure from the past into the present that perpetuates the practice (Schatzki 2006, p. 1868).

> Carrying on the variant practices requires drawing on acquired know-how, acquiring additional know-how, and becoming familiar with whatever different rules, ends, projects, and equipment are germane to the new practice-arrangement bundle. (Schatzki 2005a, p. 476)

This structure from the past is embraced in the notion of "practice memory."

2.3.3 Practice Memory Linking Activities Across Time

On the four modalities of practice structure mentioned earlier, Schatzki (2006) contends that there are some that are present when the action unfolds while some are not. The parts of the practice structure that do not govern the performances of the present action but continue to exist during and between these performances are called "practice memory"

This term does not signify the collection or the sum of the members' memory. It consists of how to do things, the rule that enjoined the members, what matters for the members that is intelligible for all of them and binds them together over the life of the practice. In order for the practice to persist, Schatzki argues that it is enough that some members carry the practice memory, even if not all of them do. Most important is that it is available to and intelligible within the practice. Such a memory is distributed among members according to status, experience, and position.

> This memory is also a feature of the practice involved, not an aggregation of features of participants in it, for instance an aggregation of individual memories. What in individual people corresponds to the structure of a practice are different combinations of versions, or incarnations, of structural understandings, rules, and teleologies. Practice memory is not equivalent to the continuing existence of these incarnations. Nor is it secured by their continuing existence. It is secured, instead, by a status-, experience- and position-based distribution among participants of actions, thoughts, experiences, and readinesses that express these incarnations or focus on and react to their expressions. Practice memory is an interactionally maintained feature of practices. (ibid, p. 1869)

Management accounting researches under Schatzki's lens tend to focus on the practice rather than the practitioners (Hui et al. 2017). Nevertheless they provide a useful insight into how the framework can be mobilized to explain the purposeful actions of the practitioners. The following sections elaborate on some of the management accounting researches that have mobilized Schatzki's framework, highlighting how his notions of "teleoaffective structure" and "practice memory" have been used, and how they can be extended to analyze and make sense of the self-orienting process of management accountants. They enable us to understand how and why management accountants orient towards business and when business orientation emerges in them.

2.3.4 *Self-Orienting, Teleoaffective Structures Orchestrating*

With Schatzki's model, various past as well as present activities relating to the self- orienting process can be conceptually aligned across time through the orchestrating of teleoaffective structures. To this effect, Ahrens and Chapman (2007) demonstrate how various purposeful actions of the organizational actors are aligned through an overarching organizational goal in a study of management control practice at a UK restaurant chain. Under Schatzki's theoretical lens (Schatzki 2005a) they conceptualize the management control practice as "a bundle of practices and material arrangements" situated in offices and workshops, using configurations of machines and computers. Actions concerning management control practice performed by various organizational members, such as negotiating strategies, budgets, and performance targets, discussing ways of realizing them, alerting others to contingencies, giving orders, following, disputing, or circumventing instructions, generating reports and making comparisons, giving and receiving advice, finding excuses, and taking corrective action are all associated with specific goals of the organizational players. These goals are aligned to the overall strategic goal of the company through the business review process.

Aligning the various goals in the weekly business review meeting, the restaurant managers and the area managers negotiate the course of action as governed by each organizational member's teleoaffective structure and the normative general understanding of how to run a successful restaurant chain. In order to achieve the overall food margin the restaurant managers may choose the compliance strategy by closely watching food cost, reducing wastage, for example in burnt steak, the proportion of food thrown away, or may choose to be a little more rebellious, orienting more towards their own objectives, such as having the reputation of running an excellent restaurant with the best chef with the associated pride (affectivity) of being recognized as a legendary manager—despite the associated higher or "overspent" operating expenses and perhaps a lower profit margin, with a higher sales volume and profit contribution. These goal-oriented activities imbued with emotions are discussed and agreed upon in the meeting, and constitute the new general understanding. For example, it is fine to overspend as long as the profit contribution is high, creating a "new" variation in the practice. In all, this case demonstrates how to align activities through goal alignment mechanisms, and the different ways in which restaurant managers orient towards the same corporate goal; that is, becoming a "good boy" or a "renegade," as explained through the notion of teleoaffective structure.

Orchestrating the teleoaffective structure can be either vertically or horizontally, top down or bottom up. While Ahrens and Chapman (2007) demonstrate the case in which the hierarchy of teleoaffective structures is orchestrated towards a unified orientation for the single overall goal of the restaurant chain, Jørgensen and Messner (2010) bring to light the bottom-up collaborating activities in clarifying the overall project goals through the orchestrating of teleoaffective structures among peers in a new product development process.

2.3.5 Self-Orienting, Teleoaffective Structure, Practice Memory, Cultural Memory

So far practice researches under Schatzki's lens have suggested that among the four practice modalities it is the teleoaffective structure that could be mobilized to link and align present activities of the management accountants and make sense of the present process of self-orienting as well as the variation in the role. Adopting the notion of "practice memory," Ahrens and Ferry (2016) add in the past dimension of the activities and show how present activities can be influenced by past ones through the teleoaffective structure as well. Besides past activities, the study has demonstrated how the broader culture can affect the present practice in the same manner.

In a response to the decision in 2012 by central government to cut the budget of local government by 30% between 2013 and 2016, Newcastle City Council (NCC) prepared and published a so-called "heat map," which was a graphic presentation highlighting the areas where cuts would hurt most and giving a new three-year local budget depicting where money could be saved to finance the statutory community services so that they could survive.[15] The case showed how this action to change the local budget practice was imbued with the emotions or feelings that were associated with being treated unfairly by central government. On a broader scale, the NCC was rallying the mood of the local people in its attempt to change the field of central–local budget practice by drawing upon the broad cultural template (Assmann 2011) that related to the strained relationship between the poor North to which Newcastle belongs and the rich South where Westminster is situated, together with the past practice of how central–local budgeting is prepared.

Complementing the previous research, this case highlights the significant role of "affectivity" in the teleoaffective structure and in both affecting the change and explaining the variations (Ahrens and Chapman 2007; Jørgensen and Messner 2010). It also demonstrates how broader external forces such as history and culture influence change through affectivity.

In all, compared with other theoretical models that have been mobilized to study the activities of agents in the social setting related to the changing role of management accountants, Schatzki's is perhaps the only one that offers a framework consisting of the internal inherent elements that can be directly and systematically used to study the volition of agents across a time span. Schatzki's "teleoaffective structure" (Schatzki 2002) associates various activities in time with personal goals. It argues that each activity is

[15] Ahrens and Ferry (2016) treat NCC as an institutional entrepreneur, that is, an agent rather than an organization with various members.

not just an occurrence in time, but it is associated with specific personal goals and imbued with the "affectivity" (ibid.) or "emotion-in-action." Through the alignment of short-term and long-term goals, the purposeful actions are aligned and driven by motivations (what matters) towards an ultimate end. This analytic framework is robust in the sense that it can be systematically mobilized to study not only activities across time but also variations within those activities as well.

References

Ahrens, T. (1996). Styles of accountability. *Accounting, Organizations and Society, 21*(2–3), 139–173.

Ahrens, T., & Chapman, C. S. (2007). Management accounting as practice. *Accounting, Organizations and Society, 32*(1–2), 1–27.

Ahrens, T., & Ferry, L. (2016). Institutional entrepreneurship, practice memory, and cultural memory: Choice and creativity in the pursuit of endogenous change of local authority budgeting. *Management Accounting Research*. https://doi.org/10.1016/j.mar.2016.11.001.

Assmann, J. (2011). *Cultural memory and early civilization: Writing, remembrance, and political imagination*. New York: Cambridge University Press.

Baxter, J., & Chua, W. F. (2003). Alternative management accounting research-whence and whither. *Accounting, Organizations and Society, 28*, 97–126.

Baxter, J., & Chua, W. F. (2008). Be(com)ing the chief financial officer of an organisation: Experimenting with Bourdieu's practice theory. *Management Accounting Research, 19*, 212–230.

Briers, M., & Chua, W. F. (2001). The roles of actors-networks and boundary objects in management accounting change: A field study of an implementing of activity-based costing. *Accounting Organizations and Society, 26*, 237–269.

Burns, J., & Baldvinsdottir, G. (2005). An institutional perspective of accountants' new roles – The interplay of contradictions and praxis. *European Accounting Review, 14*(4), 725–757.

Chandler, A. (1962). *Strategy and structure*. Cambridge, MA: MIT Press.

Chua, W. F. (1995). Experts, networks and inscriptions in the fabrication of accounting images: A story of representation of three public hospitals. *Accounting, Organizations and Society, 20*(2/3), 111–145.

DiMaggio, P. J. (1988). Interest and agency in institutional theory. In L. G. Zucker (Ed.), *Institutional patterns and organizations: Culture and environment* (pp. 3–21). Cambridge, MA: Ballinger.

Dreyfus, H. (1991). *Being-in-the-world. A commentary on Heidegger's being and time, division I*. Cambridge, MA: The MIT Press.

Fauré, B., & Rouleau, L. (2011). The strategic competence of accountants and middle managers in budget making. *Accounting, Organizations and Society, 36*, 167–182.

Foucault, M. (1979). *Discipline and punish: The birth of the prison*. New York: Vintage Books.

Giddens, A. (1984). *The constitution of society outline of the theory of structuration*. Cambridge: Polity Press.

Goretzki, L., Strauss, E., & Weber, J. (2013). An institutional perspective on the changes in management accountants' professional role. *Management Accounting Research, 24*, 41–63.

Guo. (2017). The odyssey of becoming: Professional identity and insecurity in the Canadian accounting field. *Critical Perspectives on Accounting*. https://doi.org/10.1016/j.cpa.2017.10.008.

Heidegger, M. (1962). *Being and time* (trans: Macquarrie, J. & Robinson, E.). Oxford: Blackwell Publishers Ltd. (Original work published 1953).

Hopper, T. M., & Macintosh, N. (1993). Management accounting as disciplinary practice: The case of ITT under Harold Geneen. *Management Accounting Research, 4*, 181–216.

Hopwood, A. G. (1987). The archaeology of accounting systems. *Accounting, Organizations and Society, 12*(3), 207–234.

Hoskin, K. W., & Macve, R. H. (1986). Accounting and the examination: A genealogy of disciplinary power. *Accounting, Organizations and Society, 13*(1), 37–74.

Hui, A., Schatzki, T. R., & Shove, E. (2017). Introduction. In A. Hui, T. R. Schatzki, & E. Shove (Eds.), *The nexus of practices, connections, constellations, practitioners* (pp. 1–7). Oxon: Routledge.

Jørgensen, B., & Messner, M. (2010). Accounting and strategising: A case study from new product development. *Accounting, Organizations & Society, 35*(2), 184–204.

Lambert, C., & Pezet, E. (2010). The making of the management accountant, becoming the producer of truthful knowledge. *Accounting, Organizations and Society, 36*(1), 10–30.

Latour, B. (1996). On actor-network theory. A few clarifications plus more than a few complications. *Soziale Welt, 47*, 369–381.

Loft, A. (1986). Towards a critical understanding of accounting: The case of cost accounting in U.K., 1914–1925. *Accounting, Organizations and Society, 11*(2), 137–170.

Miller, P., & O'Leary, T. (1987). Accounting and the construction of the governable person. *Accounting, Organizations and Society, 12*(3), 235–265.

Nor-Aziah, A. K., & Scapens, R. W. (2007). Corporatisation and accounting change: The role of accounting and accountants in a Malaysian public utility. *Management Accounting Research, 18*(2), 209–247.

Preston, A. M. (1992). The birth of clinical accounting: A study of the emergence and transformation of discourses on costs and practices of accounting in U.S. hospitals. *Accounting, Organizations and Society, 17*(1), 63–101.

Scapens, R. W. (2006). Understanding management accounting practices: A personal journey. *The British Accounting Review, 38*(1), 1–30.

Schatzki, T. R. (1997). Practices and actions: A Wittgensteinian critique of Bourdieu and Giddens. *Philosophy of the Social Sciences, 27*(3), 283–308.

Schatzki, T. R. (2001). Practice theory: An introduction. In T. R. Schatzki, K. Knorr Cetina, & E. von Savigny (Eds.), *The practice turn in contemporary theory* (pp. 1–14). London: Routledge.

Schatzki, T. R. (2002). *The site of the social: A philosophical account of the constitution of social life and change.* University Park: Pennsylvania State University Press.

Schatzki, T. R. (2005a). The sites of organizations. *Organization Studies, 26*(3), 465–484.

Schatzki, T. R. (2005b). Where times meet. *Cosmos and History: The Journal of Natural and Social Philosophy, 1*(2), 1–14.

Schatzki, T. R. (2006). On organizations as they happen. *Organization Studies, 27*(12), 1863–1873.

Schatzki, T. R. (2010). *The timespace of human activity: On performance, society, and history as indeterminate teleological events.* Lanham, MD: Lexington Books.

Schatzki, T. R. (2012). A primer on practices. Theory and research. In J. Higgs, C. Sturt, R. Barnett, S. Billett, M. Hutchings, & F. Trede (Eds.), *Practice-based education perspectives and strategies* (pp. 13–26). Rotterdam: Sense Publishers.

Seo, M. G., & Creed, W. E. D. (2002). Institutional contradictions, praxis, and institutional change: A dialectical perspective. *Academy of Management Review, 27*(2), 222–247.

Taylor, C. (1985). *Philosophy and the human sciences. Collected papers* (Vol. 2). Cambridge: Cambridge University Press.

Whittington, R. (2011). The practice turn in organization research: Towards a disciplined transdisciplinary. *Accounting, Organizations and Society, 36*, 183–186.

CHAPTER 3

Business Partner Developing Model (BPDM)

Schatzki's theoretical approach has been demonstrated to have an advantage in making sense of the lifelong self-orienting process. By virtue of its teleoaffective structure it is capable of relating various activities across a time span and accounting for variations. Mobilizing Schatzki's framework (Schatzki 2002, 2005a, b) in relation to the entire work lives of four selected financial practitioners, we have theorized the Business Partner Developing Model (BPDM), the product of our research project on the lifelong self-orienting process of management accountants (Chotiyanon 2018). This model explains the changing role of management accountants through their lifelong self-orienting processes.

3.1 Conceptualize the Self-Orienting Process

BPDM contends that the lifelong self-orienting process of management accountants towards business in order to become business partners is the key feature of their changing role. The process consists of three micro-processes: becoming a financial apprentice, becoming a financial expert, and becoming a business partner; these are aligned through the teleoaffective structure (Schatzki 2002). With its notion of a turning point, the model explains how internal inherent personal goals and ends, personal characteristics and motivations, as well as external broader organizational and corporate cultures can simultaneously affect how one decides to orient towards becoming a business

P. Chotiyanon, V. Joannidès de Lautour,
The Changing Role of the Management Accountants,
https://doi.org/10.1007/978-3-319-90300-2_3

partner in the course of one's career.[1] The model is robust in the sense that it is able to not only explain the phenomenon concerning the changing role of management accountants through the self-orienting process but also predict the different degree of business orientation of those management accountants who are to be found in earlier management accounting research (Ahrens 1996, 1997; Morales and Lambert 2013).

Drawing upon Schatzki's practice theory, BPDM establishes relations between activities across a time span through a teleoaffective structure. It contends that each activity is associated with a specific personal goal imbued with affectivity (Schatzki 2002) or "emotion-in-action." Through short-term and long-term goals aligning, the purposeful actions are aligned and driven by motivations (what matters) towards an ultimate goal/end; for example, becoming a business partner, or forming a lifelong self-orienting process (Fig. 3.1). Among the five key actions in the process, acquiring practical know-how, acquiring (or gaining additional) practical

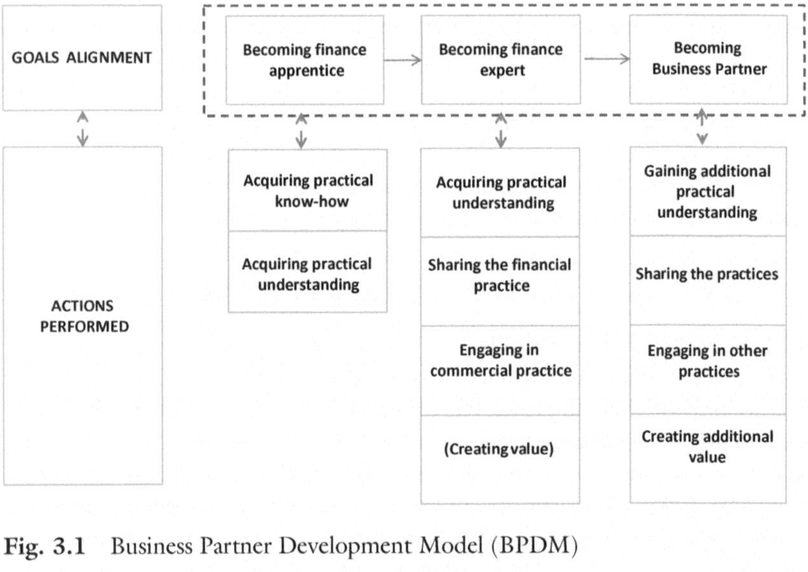

Fig. 3.1 Business Partner Development Model (BPDM)

[1] "Business partner" in this book refers to a management accountant who is business- or commercial- oriented (Granlund and Lukka 1998; Järvenpää 2007) having significant level of engagement in commercial or business practices and is accepted as a value-adding member by commercial peers.

understanding, sharing the practice, engaging in the commercial practice, and creating (additional) value, BPDM suggests that the action of creating (additional) value represents the hallmark of business orientation while acquiring (additional) practical understanding is the crucial action sustaining the self-orienting process.

3.1.1 *Becoming a Finance Apprentice*

The first micro-process in the model is characterized by activities centered around on-the-job learning, primarily to gain basic knowledge and practical know-how about the analytical tools of the trade. It involves acquiring knowledge about the business language, such as accounting; becoming acquainted with the accounting terminology and the structure of accounting reports, such as the profit and loss statement and the balance sheet, and the underlying relationship in general; and "site-specific" analytical tools, such as the product or customer profit and loss statements, Z-score modeling for customers' credit assessment, and brand analytics. After this basic knowledge is well established, the process is more about building practical understanding of how the acquired technical know-how can be applied in specific business contexts; for example, how to model the customer margin analysis by deciding which cost is relevant to a particular customer or group of customers in a particular market. By practicing the analytical craft in everyday life, one gains attention to detail and opportunities not only to sharpen analytical skills but also to build up an analytical framework that can be used to make sense of commercial activities at a later stage. This process starts on the first day on the job and can last between six months and two years. It usually starts again when there is a major change in work contexts, such as a change in sites across industries which can take place as a result of job changes—for example, moving from the accounting industry to the banking industry or from the oil or gas industry to a fast-moving consumer products industry; or on a smaller scale moving from marketing support to sales support within the same industry or the same organization. As the main purpose of this initial phase is to build up technical knowledge and site-specific analytical skill, there is little or no direct business engagement in the process. The entire process of learning on the job is usually guided by a "master" of the financial analysis craft, that is, someone who has gone through the same kind of practical training and has demonstrated a high level of knowledge and practical understanding (Schatzki 2002) related to the site.

3.1.2 Becoming a Finance Expert

The second micro-process focuses on building on acquired know-how and gaining practical understanding by the sharing of financial practice through the teaching or training of commercial colleagues. It usually involves directly engaging in commercial practice through providing relevant financial advice or regularly participating in commercial meetings and creating value from specific areas of financial expertise, such as financial analysis or budgeting by introducing new analytical tools (e.g., customer-dimension profit and loss statement, raw material price impact stimulation), or in some cases an entire new process such as a simplified or standardized budget process. The emphasis of this process is on building solid "on-the-ground" experiences that draw upon the previously acquired attention to detail, integrated with an understanding about business contexts, while engaging in the commercial practice in order to gain a broader "big picture" perspective. It is during this process that management accountants have the opportunity to become immersed in business and decide to embark upon the path to become business partners, with a gradual increase in the degree of business orientation (Sect. 3.2). This process takes two to three years in general and usually includes the critical career turning point (Fig. 3.2), the point at which one decides whether to become a business partner or not. During this phase, business orientation begins to be manifested in some cases through the creating of value actions, the hallmark of becoming a business partner.

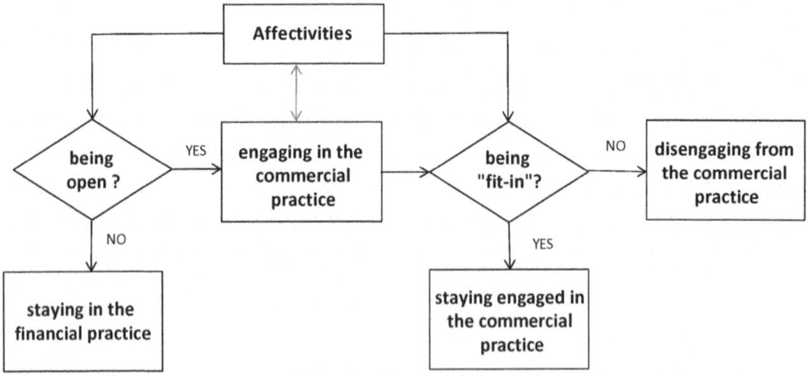

Fig. 3.2 Turning points in career

3.1.3 Becoming a Business Partner

The last micro-process focuses on the depth and breadth of business engagement. It is about dispersing an economic consciousness to the rest of the organization, be it the sales, the production, human resources, or general administration functions, through coordinating internal activities or sharing best practices with external partners, such as tax, banking, audit, or other business communities. It can also be about finding ways of doing "commercial finance" better, continuously adding value to the local, regional and global commercial partners within the global environment.[2] This process draws upon the significant wealth of experience built up over lifelong professional journeys, of over 20 years in general. Besides the significantly higher level of business engagement, this process is also marked with a high number of value-creating activities.

3.2 Self-Orienting Process, Teleoaffective Structure

BPDM contends that all the activities related to the self-orienting process are aligned through the teleoaffective structure both in the short term and the long term (Table 3.1). And while management accountants may decide to become a business partner or not at the turning point,[3] being influenced by elements inherent to the practitioners such as personal goals, personal characteristics (i.e., being open, being proactive, being logical) through "affectivities" or emotions-in-action that occur as they engage in commercial practices, in the long run it is motivation (what matters) that drives them consistently towards an ultimate goal. For example, in the case of Carol (Chap. 4), a former certified public accountant, what matters to her is to acquire financial knowledge and skill (motivation) in order to become a knowledgeable financial practitioner (end). Along the way, she has logically made a few turns in career, aligning and realigning her career goals towards this ultimate end. Each action that she performs, each decision that she has made at various turning points in her career, is associated with certain emotions. For example, performing auditing she feels that she likes the analysis part more and that she dislikes work-related traveling.

[2] Commercial finance is a branch of financial practices with dedicated commercial service and support.

[3] This is the point at which one makes a turn and decides to go on a different career path.

Table 3.1 Teleoaffective structures underlying the self-orienting process

Motivations (things that matter)	*Affectivities (emotions-in-actions)*	*Self-orienting activities*	*Goals*	*Ends*
Gaining additional knowledge and skill	Being excited about learning new things	Self-learning, quitting when not learning anything new	Being corporate financial practitioner	Being knowledgeable financial practitioner
Family life	Dislike for work-related traveling	Leaving audit job for corporate finance job	Being corporate financial practitioner	Being knowledgeable financial practitioner
Continuous improvement	Being passionate about commercial initiatives	Getting involved in commercial activities, innovating in terms of process, tools and people	Being commercial finance practitioner	Being "business partner"

This makes her decide to move away from auditing towards a corporate finance career. While pursuing an MBA degree in order to gain the financial knowledge in order to embark upon this, she discovers that she feels good about numbers. This makes her decide to search for a job in financial analysis. Later on, when the financial institute that she joins is in financial distress, she experiences some fear and anxiety about the future of her career. Yet being logical, and at the same time motivated by her quest for knowledge and skill in finance analysis, she balances these negative emotions with the excitement related to the chance of working closely with the CFO, thereby learning about financial practice in the finance industry; and she decides to stay on despite the fact that most of her colleagues have already left. Making all these turns, she stays on course to become a knowledgeable corporate financial practitioner, her end goal. Or in the case of Madelyn (Chap. 6), a commercial finance practitioner who is passionate about commercial activities, it is the drive for continuous self-improvement that motivates her to pursue a career in commercial finance practice, actively engage in commercial practices, implement significant changes in terms of value-added tools and systems, and organizational culture and practices, while aiming to become a business partner, her ultimate career goal (Table 3.1).

Although BPDM explains how management accountants could become business partners through the three micro-processes and the alignment of the teleoaffective structure, it does not imply that each and every management accountant who has gone through such processes will become a business partner. On the contrary, whether one becomes a business partner depends pretty much on one's own experiences at the career turning points that can occur on several occasions during one's professional life journey (Guo 2017), in particular when one has the opportunity to be deeply engaged in commercial practices.

3.3 The "Turning Point" and Affectivity

Underlying the BPDM is the critical concept of a career's turning point, which is the point at which one decides whether to make a turn towards becoming a business partner or not. At this turning point, when management accountants engage in business, BPDM postulates that the external macro-level elements such as the culture as well as the internal inherent micro-level elements such as personal goals/ends, motivation, and personal characteristics can simultaneously influence the degree of business orientation through affectivity. As shown in Fig. 3.2, being opened to new opportunities (Burns and Baldvinsdottir 2005; Goretzki et al. 2013), while engaging in commercial activities, might make management accountants feel that they "love," "enjoy," "are excited" about the experience, or "fit in" in general and decide to take the path to become a business partner. On the other hand they might feel that they do not "fit in" and choose not to become a business partner (Järvenpää 2007; Friedman and Lyne 1997; Burns and Baldvinsdottir 2005; Byrne and Pierce 2007). BPDM and its notion of a turning point can help explain not only the internal decision-making of management accountants in general but also the varying degree of business orientation, as manifested in the way that they engage in commercial activities; for example, being proactive and actively participating in a commercial meeting or sitting quietly throughout the whole ordeal. It suggests that a high degree of business orientation is manifested in being proactive in engaging in commercial activities with all the associated positive emotions-in-action, such as being happy, joyful, and excited.

3.4 Self-Orienting, Organizational and Cultural Context, Past Practice, and Affectivity

Besides the internal micro-level elements inherent to management accountants, BPDM argues that external macro-level elements such as organizational or corporate culture, including management philosophy, can affect the self-orienting process through affectivities or emotions-in-action. All the cases explored in Chaps. 4, 5, 6, and 7 demonstrate how an open and supportive organizational culture, in terms of the opportunities for management accountants to engage in commercial practices and the support from their direct bosses, can help make management accountants feel confident enough to actively engage in business and embark on the path to becoming business partners. Furthermore, in some cases, for example that of Madelyn (Chap. 6), under the lens of BPDM it is demonstrated how past practices can influence present decisions and actions in the self-orienting process. In Madelyn's case this includes revamping the current budget process drawing upon her previous experiences in the chemical and pharmaceutical industries, which she feels is "right" and makes sense for the new company that she has joined (Baxter and Chua 2008; Guo 2017).

In summary BPDM explains the changing role of management accountants through their lifelong self-orienting process. This process, which is organized by teleoaffective structure, consists of three main micro-processes: becoming finance apprentice, becoming finance expert, and becoming business partner. With its notion of the career's "turning point," BPDM also explains how external macro-level elements, such as corporate/organizational cultures (e.g., supportive, caring culture), past practices, and internal inherent micro-level elements (e.g., personal goals and ends, motivations, and certain personal characteristics, such as being passionate about commercial activities), *simultaneously* affect a career decision at the point when management accountants engage in commercial activities. Being positively affected by these elements and feeling as if one fits in, one continues to be engaged in commercial practices, creating additional value and eventually becoming a business partner. On the other hand, when one feels that one does not fit in, one attempts to disengage from commercial engagement (Fig. 3.2). This varied degree of business orientation is manifested in the manner in which management accountants engage in commercial activities and their "emotions-in-action", both of which BPDM highlights as the hallmarks of self-orienting towards business.

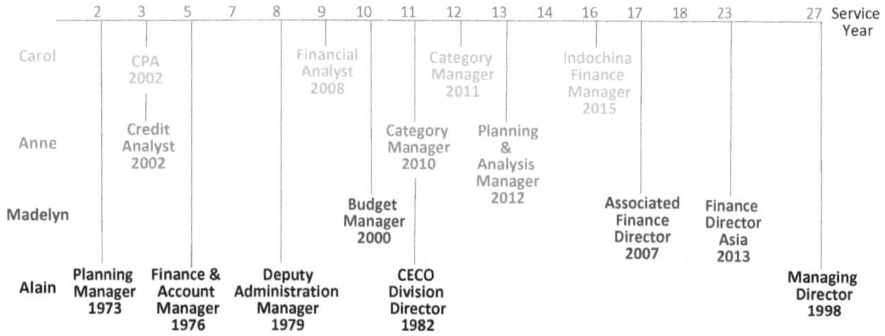

Fig. 3.3 Work life profile

3.5 Self-Orienting Study, the Longitudinal Approach

Who we are today depends pretty much on our life journey (Guo 2017). Each and every action that we have performed at any point in our lives is not a mere occurrence in time.[4] In fact, our actions are guided by specific goals and ends, and imbued with certain emotions as described by the teleoaffective structure (Schatzki 2002). Underlying this structure is the notion that, in tandem with "objective time" that is running in succession along the timeline that we are familiar with, there is "activity time" (Schatzki 2005b, 2010), in which the "past" that we come from, the motivations or "what-matters" to us,[5] and the "future" towards which the action is projecting, instantaneously occur when we perform the action, in the "present." This implies that the place we would find these two types of time is in human activity.[6] Hence, in order to gain an understanding of how and why management accountants orient towards business in order to become business partners, we trace the activities in their work lives across the traditional timeline (Fig. 3.3) and analyze the underlying teleoaffective structure at the same time.

[4] Objective time (Schatzki 2005b, 2010).

[5] Dreyfus (1991).

[6] Influenced by Heidegger's (1962) existential temporality, Schatzki (2005b, 2010) distinctively makes a difference between the traditional "objective time" and "activity time", underlying the notion of teleoaffective structure, and argues that both types of time meet in human activities.

Table 3.2 Profiles of the selected financial practitioners

Practitioners	*Career tracks*	*Work experience spanning*	*Number of years of experience in financial practice*	*Prior relevant educational background*
Carol	Corporate financial service	Early 2000s–2016	13	Yes
Anne	Financial planning and analysis	Early 2000s–2016	13	Yes
Madelyn	Commercial finance	Early 1990s–2016	24	Yes
Alain	Management control	Early1970s–late 1990s	25	No

Our study of the lifelong self-orienting process of management accountants within the work context is influenced by the oral history tradition and its interview technique.[7] In the process of data collection we have invited four financial practitioners drawn from two traditional educational backgrounds that are generally associated with the management accounting career path (Ahrens and Chapman 2000). We have three practitioners with prior relevant business educational backgrounds, close to the tradition of the German controller, having attended the business economics program (Betriebswirtschaftslehre, or BWL), and one without any prior relevant business educational background in the tradition of members of the British Chartered Institute of Management Accountants. The selected practitioners come from different career tracks in two starkly different industries, having working experience of over ten years spanning the period from the early 1970s to 2016 (Table 3.2). Each of them has provided a rich narrative of his/her work life shedding light on the personal journey towards becoming who he/she is.

In order to have a coherent story with a sufficient level of detail for a later in-depth analysis (Chaps. 4, 5, 6, and 7), we have created four work life profiles, lining up the key events in the work life as marked by career milestones in chronological order along the career timeline (Fig. 3.3). With this timeline in mind and each career milestone as a reference point, we manage to systematically follow each story and delve deeper into the

[7] Chotiyanon, P. (2018). Becoming a Business Partner, a lifelong self-orienting process. (Doctoral dissertation) Grenoble Ecole de Management, Grenoble, France.

narratives surrounding each key milestone in each individual work profile. This becomes useful in later analysis,[8] and was also important in theorizing the BPDM in Sect. 3.1.

References

Ahrens, T. (1996). Styles of accountability. *Accounting, Organizations and Society, 21*(2–3), 139–173.

Ahrens, T. (1997). Talking accounting: An ethnography of management knowledge in British and German brewers. *Accounting, Organizations and Society, 22*(7), 617–637.

Ahrens, T., & Chapman, C. S. (2000). Occupational identity of management accountants in Britain and Germany. *The European Accounting Review, 9*(4), 477–498.

Baxter, J., & Chua, W. F. (2008). Be(com)ing the chief financial officer of an organisation: Experimenting with Bourdieu's practice theory. *Management Accounting Research, 19*, 212–230.

Burns, J., & Baldvinsdottir, G. (2005). An institutional perspective of accountants' new roles – The interplay of contradictions and praxis. *European Accounting Review, 14*(4), 725–757.

Byrne, S., & Pierce, B. (2007). Towards a more comprehensive understanding of the roles of management accountants. *European Accounting Review, 16*(3), 469–498.

Chotiyanon, P. (2018). *Becoming a business partner, a lifelong self-orienting process.* Doctoral dissertation. Grenoble Ecole de Management, Grenoble.

Dreyfus, H. (1991). *Being-in-the-world. A commentary on Heidegger's being and time, division I.* Cambridge, MA: The MIT Press.

Friedman, A. L., & Lyne, S. R. (1997). Activity-based techniques and the death of the beancounter. *European Accounting Review, 6*(1), 19–44.

Goretzki, L., Strauss, E., & Weber, J. (2013). An institutional perspective on the changes in management accountants' professional role. *Management Accounting Research, 24*, 41–63.

Granlund, M., & Lukka, K. (1998). Towards increasing business orientation: Finnish management accountants in a changing cultural context. *Management Accounting Research, 9*, 185–211.

Guo. (2017). The odyssey of becoming: Professional identity and insecurity in the Canadian accounting field. *Critical Perspectives on Accounting*. https://doi.org/10.1016/j.cpa.2017.10.008.

[8] Using Strauss and Corbin's (1998) technique.

Heidegger, M. (1962). *Being and time* (trans: Macquarrie, J. & Robinson, E.). Oxford: Blackwell Publishers Ltd. (Original work published 1953).

Järvenpää, M. (2007). Making business partners: A case study on how management accounting culture was changed. *The European Accounting Review, 16*(1), 99–142.

Morales, J., & Lambert, C. (2013). Dirty work and the construction of identity. An ethnographic study of management accounting practices. *Accounting, Organizations and Society, 38*, 228–244.

Schatzki, T. R. (2002). *The site of the social: A philosophical account of the constitution of social life and change*. University Park: Pennsylvania State University Press.

Schatzki, T. R. (2005a). The sites of organizations. *Organization Studies, 26*(3), 465–484.

Schatzki, T. R. (2005b). Where times meet. *Cosmos and History: The Journal of Natural and Social Philosophy, 1*(2), 1–14.

Schatzki, T. R. (2010). *The timespace of human activity: On performance, society, and history as indeterminate teleological events*. Lanham, MD: Lexington Books.

Strauss, A. L., & Corbin, J. M. (1998). *Basics of qualitative research: Techniques and procedures for developing grounded theory*. Thousand Oaks, CA: Sage.

PART II

Self-Orienting Process: The Lifelong Experiences

CHAPTER 4

Corporate Financial Services Career

I have put in my development plan that I want to learn more. And this is what I want. (Carol's comment on what matters to her in her work life)

Our journey begins with Carol, a young manager in her early 30s and a mother-to-be. She held the position of Indochina finance manager, being in charge of the consolidation of financial reports for all Indochinese subsidiaries and associated companies of CONSUMCO, an American leader in fast-moving consumer goods (FMCG). She began her career as a junior auditor. After three years of rigorous audit apprenticeship and finally becoming a certified public accountant (CPA), she decided to embark on a new career path in financial analysis. She began again as a financial planning analyst in a subsidiary of a big European financial institution, remaining there for about two years before leaving for her dream job as a brand analyst at CONSUMCO-T, a subsidiary of CONSUMCO. After about five years with CONSUMCO, and shortly after being promoted to Indochina finance manager, she decided to leave, citing a desire to devote more time to her young family.

Carol is a person who knows what she wants. She is purposeful, always plans ahead, makes her choices rationally, and follows through with her decisions. She saw her career life as a self-development program in which

P. Chotiyanon, V. Joannidès de Lautour,
The Changing Role of the Management Accountants,
https://doi.org/10.1007/978-3-319-90300-2_4

she step by step accumulated work know-how and practical understanding in preparation for the next phase in her career.[1]

> I sort of had what I want to do laid down to 1, 2, 3, 4, and I would follow those steps. And I would not be distracted.

In this chapter we trace her activities, observing key career milestones in her career life: being a CPA, being a financial analyst, being a category analysis manager, and being Indochina finance manager (Sects. 4.1, 4.2, 4.3, and 4.4). Adopting BPDM we identify five key actions: acquiring (additional) technical know-how and acquiring practical understanding, sharing the practices, engaging in commercial practice, and creating (additional) value, which together form a lifelong self-orienting process in which the teleoaffective structure plays a significant role in organizing those activities towards the goals of becoming financial analyst and then financial expert (Sect. 4.5). We also demonstrate how at each turning point in her career the internal inherent elements, such as personal characteristics, goals/ends, and motivations, as well as external elements such as organizational culture, simultaneously affected her career decision to embark on the path to become who she is today.

4.1 Becoming a CPA (2002–2005)

4.1.1 Acquiring Technical Knowledge

Carol had an inclination for business administration. However, when it came to career choice, she followed her mother's advice to turn to professional accounting.

> My mother said anyone could do [business] administration. But accounting was an expertise. She wanted me to study accounting first. So I selected the accounting [department] when I sat for the entrance examination and have been studying accounting from then on.

[1] "Know-how" refers to the work-related knowledge acquired at work, for example an accounting reporting structure or other work-related knowledge specific to an industry or company. Whereas Schatzki's notion of practical understanding or "know-how-to," which is sometimes referred to as "skill" in this book, is about knowing how to use acquired knowledge in the relevant work context.

From accounting college, Carol obtained technical knowledge about accounting principles, accounting mechanisms, such as transaction recording and accounting presentation, and general accounting systems, for example the standard accounting structure and terminology, and the relationship between details of summaries of accounts, including how to build financial statements for trading and manufacturing companies.

4.1.2 Acquiring Practical Know-How and Understanding

After completing a Bachelor degree in Accounting Information Systems (Honors) from one of the best accounting colleges in the country, Carol had no problem getting a job with one of the big three international audit firms. Here she underwent a three-year formal professional apprenticeship, a rigorous well-established formal audit training program that each young aspiring auditor was required to go through. With this program she learned how to perform accounting reconciliation which helped build a practical understanding about how the accounting principle that she learned in school was applied in practice. She began to see the accounting relationship between the detailed sub-ledgers and the summary ledgers/accounts, use the appropriate accounting terminology, and apply the correct order in which accounts were to be summarized and reported in the financial statements. Working under the close supervision of the senior auditors in charge she was guided on how to make a comparison between financial statements of the current and previous years. The practical know-how gained through working on various audit assignments enabled her to understand how the standard accounting principle was applied in the various manufacturing companies that were being audited. She also began to develop her analytical skill through analyzing her client's financial statements.

> When I did audit I gained a lot of things, various kinds of experiences, I was there about three years, three years and a bit more. I gained the experiences. [At the beginning] I did not know what I was supposed to do. But I had got the accounting concept. I knew I had to review the financial statement. [Fortunately] there was a senior auditor guiding me. What I've gained was that I understood the flow or links in the P&L [profit and loss statement]. I understood almost all of the [accounting] items that I did [review] and on how the balance sheet and the P&L were linked. Also I had a chance to deal with all kinds of people as most of my clients were [spread] in the manufacturing

> sectors upcountry. I think I got that. Some were cooperating and some tried to stay away from the auditors. They did not want to have anything to do with the auditors. It's like, "I got my own stuff which I urgently needed to complete." I got experience on how to manage what I needed to do.

The audit experience not only familiarized her with accounting details but also instilled in her a broad overall picture based on the accounting structure; that is, how all the accounts were related and flowed into the financial statements. Carol considered this to give her an advantage over other accountants who were specialists on certain areas of accounting, such as accounts receivable, accounts payable, inventory, and assets. This detailed approach and overall view provided her with an integrated and systematic analysis framework which proved to be beneficial in her later analysis assignments.

> But looking back from the present I think it was very useful doing the audit. We knew [learned about] lots of "pictures." If we started at the corporate from the very beginning and we did 'A' we would be only doing 'A'. But when you were an auditor the first year you did this, then the second year you changed to other areas, third year you would be doing something else. So if we would compare [ourselves] with someone who completed the [same] bachelor degree and started working I think being an auditor we got significantly more knowledge, it might not be in depth but it was broader. We knew the relationship between accounts. I would say we had a little bit of feel for the analytic as well. Like [when] we saw this [number] we would know that the other [related] one would go up or [be] in what kind of trend. This was the thing that audit gave me.

She found she liked the analysis part of the job and credited the experience for establishing the kind of feel for the numbers which became useful in her later career.

> What I liked from the audit background was the analysis part. There was the control weakness part as well, but that was what we gave to the client; but the part that stayed with me in everyday life was the analytical skill.

After a little over three years of rigorous apprenticeship Carol sat for the CPA examination and finally got her certificate. At this point in time she was feeling that auditing was perhaps not the kind of work she would like to do as a career. While she found it useful working on various assignments in various locations in terms of building her knowledge base, she also felt that her work life was "not stable" and yearned for something more "steady."

> Maybe it's during my audit years [when] I got the opportunity to visit various customers in various locations. I felt that the corporate world might be better [for me]. At least they were settled and stable [no moving around]. Being in audit it's continuously moving, new stuff all the time, which might be good but it's not for me. I wanted a steady job like in corporate.

So she decided to leave the audit world and look for a job in a corporate world of business administration, which was an area she aspired to from the very beginning.

4.2 Becoming the Financial Analyst (2008–2010)

4.2.1 Acquiring Practical Know How and Understanding

Determined to embark on a new career in business administration area, Carol took two years off to do a Master in Business Administration (MBA), majoring in Finance and Marketing. During the study she found herself inclined towards finance disciplines. She saw herself as a person who was "good with numbers" rather than being "creative," like those majoring in marketing. After she obtained her MBA she started looking for a job in the corporate finance area, that is in budget and planning. Among the first companies that accepted her application was CREDITCO, a subsidiary of a major European finance company.

> So I started looking for a job in corporate. Also I did not want to do accounting work like bookkeeping. So I decided on a job in budgeting, reporting, and analysis. During the audit work there was also some analysis job. That part I felt I liked. So I planned that after I completed my Masters I would do some financial analyses. There I got a job at the company I told you—CREDITCO.

CREDITCO was, according to Carol, almost like a financial institute. It dealt with installment loans and a credit card business. Getting into the new work environment, the financial business, she got a chance to learn about a management reporting system for the first time.

> Reporting was Excel-based. Sales forecast was Excel-based. But if we wanted to submit anything to overseas it was the Hyperion [reporting system].
>
> I got to know the Hyperion system. I knew what it looked like. And it was my first experience of a management report. It was the first time in my life I did it. I got to see how the analysis of the corporate was done, how to prepare the forecast, and the kind of reporting that they wanted to see.

She learned how to prepare reports in the same manner in which they had been done before by the incumbent budget managers.

> I learned the management reports from the team. At that time there were two people: me and another senior one. The senior one did more. She had been staying for a long time and she was good. So she got allocated with more work. I also learned from the other one who was about to leave after the budget manager [had left]. She told me how to do the estimate, "this is how I do it." In other words [she showed me] how she prepared the management report. So it was a teaching not from a manual, like having a book from the very beginning, but more like an one-on-one teaching, self-learning.

There were not many transactions as business was on a downturn. Carol found most of her assignment easy. She approached her work life at CREDITCO systematically, using the income statement framework and relations she had acquired in her audit days as a standard template. She could recall the interest and loans and how to calculate them. But she failed to make sense of the complete financial statements. She found her template irrelevant at CREDITCO. There were no physical goods to be sold, or sales revenue, just interest income. With her previous experience mostly being in a manufacturing context, she was able neither to adapt nor to make any adjustments to her P&L template, her prime sense-making tool, to fit the new financial institution context. Therefore she carried out her assignments by following instructions from her supervisor without much understanding. Without this practical understanding, the scope of Carol's work and the opportunity to learn new things were rather limited.

> I did not get what it was that I was doing. Why I had to calculate this way, something like this. Like the models that they had [used to calculate the balances of principal and interest] I had no idea what they were about: this formula, [calculating how much out of] each installment had to be deducted

[from the principal amount], one sum at a time, to give the balance of the principal. It could be that I wasn't good at the concept of finance and banking. ...when we closed [the book to see] the interest [balance], how much the [principal] amount should be. [I had no idea about it].

She attempted to draw on her knowledge of accounting relationships from her previous audit experience to make sense of her work. She managed to map the interest income to the sales revenue, but when it came down to the loan amortization she could make head or tail of it.

The interest was the revenue or anything that had to do with the customers. Amortization, the expenses incurred, I had only a rough framework of what they were. But when it came to the [installment] payment for each period, like reduction in principal and interest, I could not compute. I was like now what...

Carol mentioned that this might came about when she was "groomed" for manufacturing of trading goods business transactions rather than financial ones.

I'm not sure whether it's related, but I was auditing manufacturing firms throughout the time when I was the auditor. From there I was familiar with that kind of business. I was familiar with the production process and the trading goods process. When I moved to finance or banking I could not go on.

Yes, yes. In manufacturing you see the picture right in front of you. With finance you have to imagine. You have to think about it yourself.

Less than a year after she joined, the company was under financial duress and began to let people go. Carol decided to stay on for a while. After all the budget managers had left she got the chance to work for the CFO, who would be providing instructions on how to prepare the sales estimates.

When the manager was not there I talked directly to the CFO who guided me a lot, saying this was what was needed. At that time I did not do much. Most of the time the CFO would advise me of the monthly sales and the expenses. I would take the same ratio [of sales-to-date] and if there was something special [that would come on top] she would tell me. That's more or less it. If it were for the week, [and] say we would [like to know that we would] close [the month] at how much sales. It was very easy. I would do the [sales] prorating, like we had made [how much sales for] how many days so far, how much per day, and how many days we had left.

About a year later the company went through a major financial restructuring. Having no means to develop a full understanding of either the business practice or the analytical tools, working at CREDITCO did not serve Carol's purpose anymore. Moreover, she felt that a finance company was not for her.

> If I really put an effort into understanding it I think I would be able to understand. But would I like it? I think I did not like this kind of business for sure.

She finally left to pursue other job opportunities.

4.3 Becoming a Category Analysis Manager (2011–2014)

The third stage in Carol's career was with CONSUMCO-T, which was actually the first company that she had been working with. During her junior year in college, she was given the opportunity to do an internship with COSUMCO-T's treasury department. From that experience she formed a positive impression of the company, and expressed her intention to rejoin after she graduated should there be an opportunity. That opportunity finally arrived, with an opening in the budget and planning section.

> first I was happy about this place and the opening was something I wanted to do from the very beginning. So it was perfect, there was no reason to say no.

4.3.1 Acquiring Additional Practical Know-How

Carol started as a brand analyst. Her work involved analysis of the variance of 11 brands' P&L under two key product categories which represented almost 25% of the company's total sales. Here she was required to focus on detailed analysis of the trade spending, a key commercial action required of a dynamic FMCG company in a fierce competitive environment, which was something new for her. However, she saw no problem in this. In fact she found the job more to her liking as she was able to relate back to her accounting relationship under the manufacturing environment, whereas in her prior experiences with CREDITCO she was not able to make sense of her reporting work at all. Here at COSUMCO-T Carol was back with her familiar P&L statement of the goods manufacturing company: the usual accounts categories, with the top line being the gross sales, then the net sales, the profit margin after the variable cost, the operating expenses, and the operating profit; together with all the other accounts categories that she was well acquainted with. In addition, through various assignments she was able to learn about specific accounting classifications for the different marketing and sales activities, together with their impact on the brand's profit margin.

4.3.2 *Acquiring Practical Understanding Through Sharing the Practice*

Carol's daily work involved detailed analysis of profit margin down to the level of sales keeping units and summarizing this analysis into standard reports at three levels in the product's hierarchical order: brand level, subcategories, then categories levels. She learned from her predecessor how to obtain information from the centralized SAP system (an enterprise resource planning software developed by German company, SAP SE) and put this in her "workbook," which was a set of linked Excel spreadsheets. Most of her analytical work was centered around these Excel spreadsheets, which linked the profitability of the brand through items such as the net sales (selling price, sales volume, and product mix), promotion expenses or trade spending, variable product costs, and operating expenses. The analysis was usually done in two dimensions or in a "matrix" of brand and customers. This workbook and the set of summary reports in the form of Excel spreadsheets were Carol's major "tools of the trade," those that she regularly updated and referred to in her everyday work life. With these tools she made sense of all the marketing and sales activities in terms of the brand's profitability.

Carol's various analyses were prepared mostly for the finance director and for her marketing and sales counterparts, informing them of the detailed development in the standard brand's margin. In a report called "brand snapshot," she summarized the analysis of margin variances from the previous year and from the budget or the latest estimates. Such variances were categorized into "buckets": the change in net sales following the development in average selling price, sales volume, and product mix; the change in trade spending following commercial activities, including new product launches; and the change in variable product costs following changes in material prices and the exchange rate fluctuation. The analysis was performed in two dimensions: by brands and by customers. From this detailed analysis she was able to answer such questions as "why we budget a low percentage of margin for Brand 'A' compared with last year?" Initially Carol needed guidance from the budget manager, who would advise her to "take a look at the margin, compare the budget to last year's actual" or "take a look at the quantification and assumptions built into the budget." After a while, through these daily analyzing exercises she gained an understanding of how the workbook worked and in turn how to work it. Now when she got an inquiry, she knew precisely which table or worksheet she needed to go to and what information she would need in order to perform her analysis. Mastering her workbook, Carol began to learn about how to pick significant items: which product, what variance, what kind of impact to bring to the attention of the management. In the standard "brand snapshot" report she began to add brief comments, bringing the management's attention to significant variation in brand profitability.

Besides this regular brand profitability monitoring for the management, Carol assisted the marketing team in evaluating marketing and sales initiatives or "deals" for the consumers or customers, in terms of their impact on brand profitability. She regularly took part in the commercial meeting at which the marketing and selling activities were shared. This provided her with the necessary insight into commercial activities. In the meeting she was required to provide relevant information about the development of the brands' profitability or the anticipated impact on this from the proposed commercial activities. In the budget and planning process she helped with sales volume planning, by training the brand manager how to work through a planning workbook that Carol designed and maintained, together with her budget colleagues. She also assisted the marketing team in drawing up the planned P&L for the brands. In the budget review session, she assisted in providing the opportunity and risk related to the brands that she was assigned to.

4.3.3 Engaging in Commercial Practices

Carol became accepted as an expert in her field, and demonstrated her understanding through assisting in the implementation of the budget system involving information technology (IT) practice.

> About two years ago we were implementing the budget process. We had tools to be tested with the IT department whether the concept, the logic,

> and calculation were okay. I took the lead in solving the issues [related to the implementation]. We got about 20 of them [issues]. I managed to sign them off talking with IT and making them understand the user's perspective, i.e., why we needed things to be like this (or) that (way). It took several rounds of discussions before they understood the needs. Sometimes we had to be persistent and stood our ground; [they would argue that], "We used to do this, we don't understand why we have to change".

Carol mentioned two important things that helped her to accomplish this task: the support of her boss and her knowledge and understanding of how the system worked from her own experience.

> I think it's the experiences, the understanding of the process, the logic in pricing.

Besides having a good information system, the support from her boss was one of the key elements in Carol's career life. From the earlier years we have seen the important roles of the senior auditor, the CREDITCO's CFO, and now her budget manager at COSUMCO-T. The importance of this support was evinced again during her short-term assignment in Australia, to be discussed later on.

Carol was accepted as an expert in her field of financial analysis. At COSUMCO-T she worked closely with marketing and sales and the management, and identified herself an important member of the commercial team, setting herself apart from the operational finance department (treasury, financial/statutory accounting).

> As we worked closely with the commercial side in FMCG I felt that they recognized that we were important. We were financial support. Every time they had any initiatives they would run to us and ask us to have a look or help them calculate what the financial implication would be. I was rather proud of my role, that we were important for the launch of the product or carrying out the promotion or anything we did to get our products to the consumers. We got involved with the management a lot compared with the (financial) operation (people). In general the commercial [team] got to involve more with the management because we [the company] had to focus on the commercials. We were the finance [people] that got the chance to get involved with the management the most when compared with the accounting or treasury or other department, not counting sales and marketing (people) who were even closer than us.

As a member of the "commercial finance" team, Carol saw herself as a key business partner providing not only support to the commercial team but also monitoring their activities for the management.

> Like I've mentioned a little to you before (that) when they were about to launch the product, (for) whatever product they would launch or whatever promotion they would do, we were the people that gave them the information, the analysis about their financials: [that] their P&L would become like this (and) because of what. That made us feel like we controlled the marketing (on) how their performance was...
>
> They might not know that much. They might know only roughly. But we had in-depth information. We knew what happened to this brand, their products. We looked (to see) if they launched a new product what the income statement would look like in —three to five years. This they could not do. They could not do it themselves. They needed support from us. I felt I was a key (partner) to them as well.

Carol had a certain advantage over other management accountants in the sense that she had a strong accounting knowledge from both her educational background in accounting and her professional background in auditing. From this knowledge base she built on her practical know-how and developed her analytical skill by regularly preparing financial analyses at the audit firm and later at COSUMCO-T. She was able to share her practical knowledge with her colleagues through teaching, thereby demonstrating her practical understanding. Trained to be detail oriented but having an integrated view from her early audit days, Carol was able to make sense of her analysis by working with her commercial partners and learning about their imperatives. Going through detailed analysis assignments catering to her counterparts in the commercial practice, she gained a practical understanding and was able to make sense of the situation at hand. To her commercial counterparts she became first a technical expert and second the business partner whom they relied on for advice while they engaged in the financial analysis practice.

Being able to make sense of the numbers went hand in hand with Carol's experience of being analytical and logical.[2] Therefore, in recruiting new members, she would look for those people with logic who had experienced analytical work.

[2] Logic here is close to Schatzki's notion of practical understanding: the ability to make sense of financial analysis in the commercial context.

> He has to have a prior background in analysis. See I want to have someone with prior experience [with] minimum one or two years in the same kind of work. At least I know he has a little bit of analysis background with him. Then [there's] the personal characteristics, like when we talk we know he has the logic. The way I see it an analyst's work needs logic and sense. It's not like you just glance at it [the number] and find the answer. You need to use sense. When I discuss or choose a subordinate I need to see if the person can use the logic and if he talks in the same language as us.

Being logical and analytical herself, Carol learned to manage challenging assignments in the financial analysis practice with minimum support from her boss. Doing so helped her gained additional practical understanding in the business context and enabled her to cope on her own. Again she relied on the support of good information systems to successfully carry out these assignments.

Carol became an expert in financial analysis. She was able to teach her colleagues how to manage the tools in order to find the answers to questions raised by the management. From her experience, being a competent member of the financial analysis practice would require technical expertise, as well as being reliable, accountable, helpful, resourceful, and collaborative.

After four years with the company doing product margin analysis, Carol gained a full understanding of the reporting system. Her workbook became a part of her work life, the one she always used to make sense of commercial activities. Using the workbook, Carol assisted her partners, the marketing and sales colleagues, in evaluating commercial proposals and pointing to the impact of each choice for further decisions. In no time her analytical skill grew to the point where she was able to anticipate the impact of each commercial action on the brand's P&L and to bring the significant and relevant actions to the attention of the management. She understood that something was wrong when the reports "talked back" to her (Schön 1983).

> I stayed relatively long so I knew the system: how it flowed, what the budget process was like. Regarding seeing the picture, it was the business that I wanted to do: trading goods … The job itself no problem anymore. That one is clear. I knew the system how it worked. [With the] P&L I might not know the detail of every line [item]. For the details of cost [item] I did not know. But I knew about all the KPIs [key performance indicators] that management watched. If this one [KPI] went up what would happen to the

> trend of others, for example. They were all related, and if there was something out of line I would be able to explain why. I would know [that] it should not be and that there was something wrong. Maybe it's because I stayed here a long time and it helped. Also it's the field of analysis which was ingrained in me since starting to work. And it's helping.

After a while it all became like a routine to her. Each request was a repeat of an earlier one. Carol felt that she had reached saturation point in her line of work. When she discussed her career plan with her boss she mentioned that she wanted to expand her horizon but not too far away from budgeting, planning, and reporting, her current "comfort zone."

> Like I have done it all and I felt I did not get anything out of the old work anymore. This is what I meant by saturation. Every kind of work, I have done them all. I know it all, what is to be done and how to do it all.
>
> When I faced the questions or when someone asked me the questions it would be the same old questions. For the same old stories they came back to us. Or the work itself kept on repeating like we had been doing it for the past three years. And now I am bored. Now I want to know more than what I have already known here.
>
> Maybe it's like working until saturation. I feel like I would like to have something new. I might need to look for a new job. Is there any place that provides a job about the same nature but doing other things in addition? Like for example now I am an analyst doing the brand. I have been working for Madelyn [her boss] and I have written in my [career] development plan that I would like to know more about this than before. The same old job still remains but I want to expand my scope to be more than before. But this would [have to be] still be in my department, still something in budget and planning. Once I have worked till saturation for my own job I would like to have additional knowledge.

4.4 Becoming Indochina Finance Manager (2015)

4.4.1 Sharing the Practices, Acquiring Additional Practical Know-How

Carol indicated to her boss a career development plan in which she would like to explore the customer side of the commercial activities when the opportunity came, by getting involved in sales support while maintaining her current role in the budget planning and reporting department.

> Maybe it's that I don't want to leave my comfort zone. As here I am comfortable, I have comfort. My comfort zone is high up to a given level that I probably will not go.
>
> Although there might be other work I still love the work I am doing, budget and reporting. At the same time I'd like to add other scope to myself as well. [But] if everything has to be switched all together it could be difficult to decide. Another thing, staying in the same company for a long time it's like having some kind of comfort zone, so when the time comes to move we have to think hard whether it's a good idea to move.

Staying her course rather than venturing into unknown territory somewhat limited Carol's chance of getting more practical understanding and thus limited her career potential.

> I might have a comfort zone but the comfort zone is this kind of work that I know I like and I am willing to do it.

In the meantime, her boss was appointed to take a larger divisional role so now she reported to a new colleague. Not long afterwards, Carol had the opportunity to join a team of global international internal auditors from the headquarters: she was to be a guest auditor in a short-term audit assignment with an Australian subsidiary for about six weeks. She was quite happy about the prospect of this experience.

> I was happy as I knew it's a rare chance [and] not everyone got [it]. At the same time I was worried. I was afraid whether I could do it.

> It's also a good exposure. First it's the culture. I had never been abroad. Now I was going abroad. It was good … they were nice people always ready to help … I was doing audits but they knew I was not a real auditor. I was one of them so they were more willing to help out.

In addition the audit assignment laid out Carol's responsibilities clearly and summarized the work she had to carry out for the team during the audit period. She also got good support and guidance from the head of the audit team.

> I was looking over the expense and revenue cycle and spending-in-trade. The latter was quite complex. I didn't know much about it.

> At first I was worried about the work. So I called the people at COSUMCO-T who are in charge of the [same] processes and got some information. But no I thought I had no problem. [Anyway I] also told the auditor-in-charge that I did not know much about the stuff.
>
> He joined in the meeting with the (audited) company (people) and helped in listening to the points when he did not have to. He participated and talked for me. He delved into things. He never left me.

This short-term audit assignment experience left Carol with a good impression about working with a new team in a new environment. It encouraged her to be open to new job opportunities.

> It has opened a whole new world for me.

Not long after she went back home, Carol was promoted to the position of finance manager, being in charge of the balance sheet and cash flow reporting for the Indochina sub-region. Compared with her previous stable and systematic world, this was a big change. She found out that there was no reporting system in place and the competency was not there to implement this. She asked her colleagues at COSUMCO-T for some information, but the situation was much more complex than this approach could solve. There was no one she could turn to for the required information and support.

> It's the transition (process). They did not do it very well. The role and responsibility were not very clear. I did not know what they expected of me.
>
> I was working in Brands (level), now it's the company level for management report and I did not have the knowledge. I needed guidance but there was none. What I did was I asked my counterparts who were doing the same thing (at the country level). But things were much more complex. I could not grasp the picture or the process. I needed some guidance.

Looking back, Carol mentioned the lack of knowledge, understanding, and guidance about how to deal with the new situation, and thus her lack of confidence, as being the main issues.

> The way I see it, knowledge would make me confident. One day when I become confident I would want to move.

> I am this kind of person who would say, "No, I would not be able to do it. So it's better not to take it."

Despite this last episode, overall Carol accredited COSUMCO-T as a good place to work owing to its "caring" and supportive corporate culture, which included the company of good and able people, an advanced information system, and the opportunity to work closely with people from other areas of expertise. These three "enablers" made her happy at COSUMCO-T, and she stayed for a relatively long time.

> The culture here was good, not too aggressive. An aggressive person would not fit here. Here it was not too aggressive and caring, caring in the sense that it was very good here. Overall culture for me was good. In addition I think here the system was quite good. There were many tools that helped with the analysis. Actually I was in the analysis field [and] there were many times when they tried to develop more tools than [what] had been in existence up to now. Thirdly, due to the kind of work that I did, I think we got close to our partners. As we worked closely with the commercial side in FMCG I felt they recognized that we were important.

4.5 The Lifelong Self-Orienting Process

Through the lens of BPDM, we can see that Carol's lifelong self-orienting process towards business consists of two main micro-processes: becoming the finance apprentice and becoming the finance expert. These are aligned by the teleoaffective structure and geared towards becoming a knowledgeable finance practitioner (end-goal). In the process we can see how the external elements such as organizational culture, together with internal inherent elements such as personal characteristics, personal goals/end, and motivation, affect Carol's career decision at each crucial turning point, so that she stays on course towards her ultimate goal and becomes who she is today.

4.5.1 Self-Orienting Process, Teleoaffective Structure

Over her career Carol alternately performs four key actions: acquiring the relevant knowledge and practical know-how,[3] acquiring (additional) practical understanding, sharing financial practice and engaging in commercial

[3] In this study (practical) know-how refers to part of the static knowledge acquired in work, such as the specific accounting structure related to the industry or company. On the other hand, the "know-how-to" (Schatzki 2001) is about knowing how to apply the acquired knowledge in practice; that is, the practical understanding.

Table 4.1 List of actions and key milestones of the corporate financial service career

Being CPA	*Being financial analyst*	*Being category analysis manager*	*Being Indochina finance manager*
Acquiring technical knowledge			
Acquiring practical know-how	Acquiring practical know-how	Acquiring practical know-how	Acquiring practical know-how
Acquiring practical understanding	Acquiring practical understanding	Acquiring practical understanding	
		Sharing the practice	Sharing the practice
		Engaging in commercial practices	

practices. These take place at different points, as marked by her career milestones (Table 4.1). In the early stage of her career she spent most of her time and effort acquiring accounting know-how and practical understanding. For example, when she was the junior auditor she was learning how to apply the accounting principle and related rules to audit her clients' financial statements and to make sense of them through financial analysis. After gaining audit experience, she moved on to acquire knowledge about financial management through the MBA program. Thereafter it was all about acquiring practical understanding about financial analysis of a financial institution and an FMCG business in order to become the financial analyst. The act of gaining (additional) practical understanding, typical of management accountants who are facing continuous change, prevailed throughout her career life. This can be in the form of formal training, such as during the audit apprenticeship, or informal training or self-learning through engaging in practices while she was at the financial institution or at CONSUMCO-T. By sharing the practice, teaching finance to non-finance colleagues, or engaging in commercial practice at the later stage of the career, Carol gained additional practical understanding and won acceptance as an expert in her domain of brands' financial analysis.

These actions are not just occurrences in time, but they are performed for specific goals (Schatzki 2002), such as acquiring accounting knowledge or analytical skill in order to become a financial analyst and acquiring additional knowledge and skill through using them in various business contexts in order to become a financial analysis expert. These goal-oriented actions

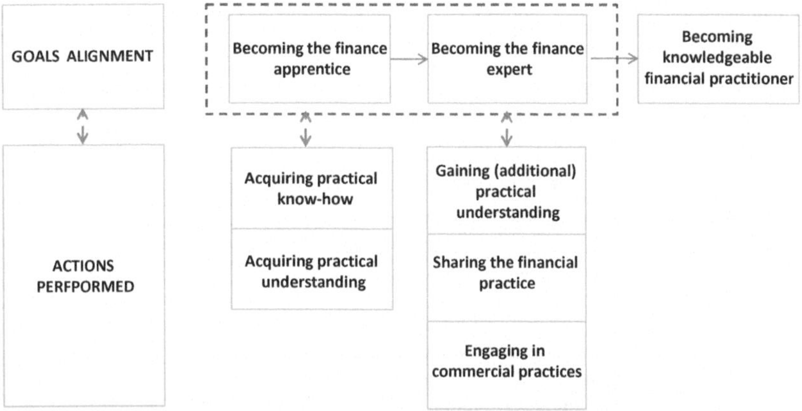

Fig. 4.1 Self-orienting process and goal aligning – corporate financial service manager

can be organized into two main micro-processes that are aimed at two distinct career goals: becoming a financial apprentice and becoming a finance area expert. In turn these are aligned towards the ultimate long-term end goal, which in this case is becoming a knowledgeable finance practitioner, and forming the lifelong self-orienting process that pertains to a corporate financial service career (Fig. 4.1).

While various activities at each point in time are directed towards certain short-term goals, for example, learning accounting in order to join the accounting profession, entering the audit apprentice program in order to get an audit license to be a CPA, getting an MBA in order to explore a financial career, and joining a financial institute in order to gain an experience in financial forecast and reporting, they are also imbued with "emotions-in-action." For example, while engaging in these various practices Carol gets to understand her own work inclination towards finance, as manifested in her feelings of "liking" the financial analysis element, which in turn encourages her to seek additional knowledge in the area in order to become a financial analyst. On the other hand, the dislike of work-related traveling is manifested in her leaving the audit job for a corporate finance job on the way to becoming a financial area expert. While performing reporting and budgeting, which gives her an opportunity to work closely with the management and commercial partners, Carol also feels a sense of pride (Table 4.2).

Table 4.2 Self-orienting and teleoaffective structure – corporate financial service manager

Motivations (things that matter)[a]	*Affectivities (emotions-in-action)*	*Self-orienting activities*	*Goals*	*End-goal*
Gaining additional knowledge and skill related to financial practices	"happy" learning new things	Self-learning, quitting when not learning any new things	Being financial analyst	Becoming knowledgeable financial practitioner
	Dislike for work-related travelling	Leaving audit job for corporate finance job	Being financial areas expert	
	Feeling proud	Joining the commercial practice	Being "a part" of commercial practice	

[a]Dreyfus (1991)

In her self-orienting process these "emotions-in-action" play an important role in affecting the decisions about her career choice at the turning points (Fig. 4.2). For example, while practicing auditing in the audit firm Carol feels that "this is not for me" and that instead she likes the analysis part much more. This positive feeling towards financials drives her away from the auditing practice and towards the financial analysis practice, which is in alignment with the totality of becoming a knowledgeable financial practitioner, her end-goal. Other emotions, such as pride associated with the feeling of being recognized as "an important member," makes her want to stay engaged in commercial practice while being rooted in her area of financial expertise and her comfort zone, financial analysis. Meanwhile, a dislike for moving around from site to site associated with audit work turns her towards a stable corporate life. Over the long run, all these emotion-imbued actions are performed in order to obtain the financial knowledge and skill ("what matters" or motivation) for the sake of becoming a knowledgeable financial practitioner (an end goal).

4.5.2 *Self-Orienting, Personal Characteristics, and Affectivity*

From her own account, Carol seems to be a person who knows herself very well. She is self-driven, logical, and systematic. She thinks through and plans her course carefully. She is also open to opportunities to learn new things.

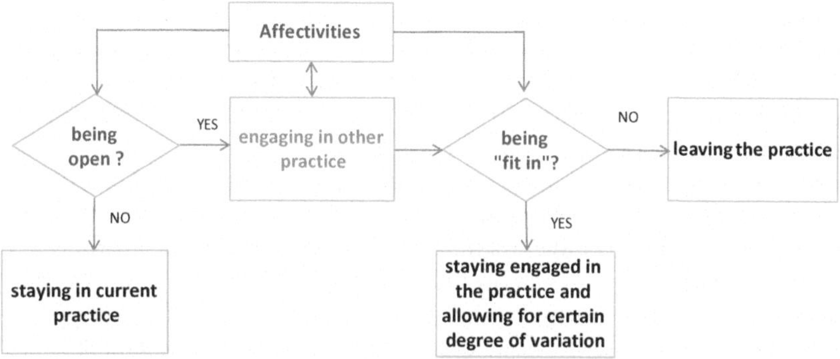

Fig. 4.2 Turning point – corporate financial service manager

These personal characteristics are distinct in the manner in which she maneuvers her career turns. They also play out in the emotions-in-action affecting the course of her career orientation through the "affectivities" part of the teleoaffective structure (Fig. 4.2). For example, while working with the financial institute she experiences some fear about business discontinuity. Nevertheless she draws upon her logic, weighing down the fear with the excitement about the chance to be working closely with the CFO, learning about financial practice in the finance industry; and she decides to stay on despite the fact that most of her finance team has already left.

4.5.3 *Self-Orienting, the Cultural Context, and Affectivity*

When engaging in a new practice, Carol usually draws upon her tools of the trade, for example the "brand snapshot," other Excel workbooks, and her analytical skill. In every stage of her career she has demonstrated how each milestone is achieved by using her tools of the trade skillfully. Learning from others, she knows what is required and how to use the tools to meet the requirements. This learning on the job is facilitated by someone who has the experience of performing the work activities before. Her career life story indicates the important role of the direct boss in mentoring and coaching, helping in the process of self-orientating towards the new work environment. Whether support exists or not, together with the manner in which it is provided, can make or break Carol's work orientation, such as when she leaves CREDITCO and CONSUMCO's Indochina division when there is a lack of support and guidance. This broad supportive organizational culture influences her decisions at turning points through her affectivities, such as feeling that she is able to fit in or being confident that she will have support. Nevertheless, this broad supportive organizational culture can have both positive and negative effects on her career. For example, while the support from her direct boss can make her feel happy in her work and confident about growing vertically in the organization, it can make her feel anxious, even frustrated, about leaving her comfort zone, to an area where the support is perceived to dwindle, thereby limiting her career growth path.

In summary this case of Carol illuminates a self-orienting process that comprises two goal-oriented micro-processes, becoming a finance apprentice and becoming a financial expert, geared towards the end goal of becoming a knowledgeable financial practitioner (Fig. 4.1). It highlights the action of acquiring (additional) practical experience, in terms of practical knowledge and understanding, as the hallmark of the self-orienting process of a management accountant who faces continuous changes and wants to survive them. It also demonstrates how such a process is influenced by internal inherent elements such as personal goals, ends, motivations, and personal characteristics, together with external elements such as the broader organizational culture. Through the "affectivities" (Fig. 4.2), these internal and external elements *can simultaneously* affect the career decisions that lead to the realigning of goals and activities, so that one can stay on course towards one's ultimate goal with a varying degree of business orientation.

References

Dreyfus, H. (1991). *Being-in-the-world. A commentary on Heidegger's being and time, division I.* Cambridge, MA: The MIT Press.

Schatzki, T. R. (2001). Practice theory: An introduction. In T. R. Schatzki, K. Knorr Cetina, & E. von Savigny (Eds.), *The practice turn in contemporary theory* (pp. 1–14). London: Routledge.

Schatzki, T. R. (2002). *The site of the social: A philosophical account of the constitution of social life and change.* University Park: Pennsylvania State University Press.

Schön, D. A. (1983). *The reflective practitioner: How professionals think in action.* New York: Basic Books, Inc.

CHAPTER 5

Financial Planning and Analysis Career

> *...it's about building credibility continuously, building credit trying to make people accept me, that is, continuous learning and building credit for ourselves.* (Anne's comment on how she saw her work life)

Our second story is about the work life of Anne, a young manager in her early 30s who was the financial planning and analysis manager of CONSUMCO-T in charge of overall corporate planning and reporting, a position that most people of her age would be envious of. She began her career at OILCO, one of the biggest international oil and gas companies, as a credit analyst. After gaining about four years of work experience she studied for a Master of Business Administration (MBA) in the USA. Upon returning home she rejoined OILCO, before joining CONSUMCO-T as a category analyst about a year later.

Unlike Carol (Chap. 4) who was self-driven, Anne relied on the advices, actions, and reactions of those who were close to her and whom she trusted.

> [On my recent promotion,] when my mom and my boss praised me, "It [the job promotion]'s very fast, others could not make it to this stage [so soon], not everyone would be able to make it," I was so proud and able to go on.

She did not like taking chances, preferring to stay in her own comfort zone. Compared with Carol, it was less likely that Anne would venture out of her comfort zone without significant encouragement from her

P. Chotiyanon, V. Joannidès de Lautour,
The Changing Role of the Management Accountants,
https://doi.org/10.1007/978-3-319-90300-2_5

supervisor-cum-mentor and other people whom she trusted. But once she decided to take something on she would not give in easily. Her perseverance was one of the virtues that contributed to her career advancement.

According to Anne, her work life was about building credibility. This was achieved through continuous learning on the job, practicing what she learned, and finally winning acceptance as competent, which was very important for her. In this chapter we follow her purposeful actions concerning her key career milestones: at the points in time when she was a credit assistant, credit assessment and control assistant, category analysis manager, and financial planning and analysis manager. By doing so, we will gain an understanding of the process through which she orients herself towards business. We also demonstrate that besides personal goals, ends, motivation, and supportive organizational culture, mentioned in the previous case, certain personal characteristics, such as not being assertive and avoiding confrontation, can influence career choice and the degree of business orientation through "affectivities" or "emotions-in-action" at the "turning point," which is where one is engaging in commercial activities.

5.1 Becoming a Credit Assistant (2002–2006)

5.1.1 Acquiring Practical Know-How and Understanding

Anne graduated magna cum laude in Finance and Banking from one of the top three business schools. She began her career at OILCO, a subsidiary of a Dutch oil and gas company, as a credit assistant. Her work involved evaluating the creditworthiness of the company's customers for the commercial department. She was responsible for both wholesale and retail customers in the three key business units: fuel, oil and lubricants, and bitumen/asphalt. She discovered that the technical finance knowledge she had acquired in school was of little help when it came to the credit management practice of an oil and gas company.

> What I learned from school: financial statement, debit/credit was of… little use. Here at OILCO I learned about the "real" finance such as the credit management of a real business. I learned about the company's policy and the rating model.

Through her assignments, Anne had acquired knowledge about how to assess the credit risk of the customers and how to prepare a credit report for the management. For each customer she obtained the relevant information and evaluated the credit risk using the standard z-score model, thereby ranking the customer according to the company's credit policy. Once the credit line was granted she monitored the performance of the customer in terms of payment record, and suggested credit line adjustment or legal actions for any problem account in the credit report that she regularly prepared and submitted for the management's review.

> I got the information from "Business Online" [a subscribed credit information service] to evaluate the customers' financial position and rated them A, B, C, and D. I looked at their liquidity, debt level, and aligned them with the company global policy. We got [credit] requests from sales. We did the assessment and sent it for credit approval. Then for the reporting we tracked their payment for management and sales team to see if the payment was late, and how late. Say [for] a "big customer" rated A why the payment was so late. Sometimes the credit of USD 10,000 was not enough as the order size was USD 20,000 ... Sales orders got blocked automatically. The credit manager and/or the sales manager were able to unlock the credit.

She was closely guided by her direct boss.

> I reported to my credit assessment manager who in turn reported into the commercial manager.
>
> My boss then was a strong and self-assured person. She was knowledgeable and knew the system very well. ... She taught me and told me to improve suggesting that, for example, when I prepared the report and saw something was wrong I should raise a question.

Her credit assessing was mostly rule-following, avoiding potential conflicts with the sales team.

> I did the credit maintenance and the assessment. I did everything according to authorization.
>
> The sales people they wanted to have a high credit amount and high credit rating for their customers so they could earn high points [to win the salesman award at the end of the year and the year-end bonus]. Overdue amount was one of the salesman's KPIs [key performance indicators]. I heard about one case in which a salesman had achieved the highest sales number but he did not get to win the top salesman rank as one of his customers had a very high overdue amount.

> I did not react emotionally. I always tried to explain the company policy. I explained how the customer's credit request did not match the evaluated creditworthiness and advised them to ask for the bank guarantee or personal guarantee.

She stood firm by the company's credit assessment policy and escalated the issue when needed.

> I said no [to unjustified credit request] and said that if you insisted it would not get the approval anyway.

5.1.2 *Acquiring Additional Practical Understanding*

Preparing the credit assessment regularly, Anne gained not only skill in using the credit assessment model but also insights into the nature of customers.

> The lubricants customers are financially well established like the service centers of Honda while the customers of the last category were mostly construction companies. We had problems with the financial statements of smaller companies. We also got customers who purchased for resale and some used it for their own production.

This knowledge about customer behavior informed her that the standard assessment model might not be applicable to all customers across the board. Anne had the opportunity to give this useful insight to the global team when they came over to evaluate alternative models for credit risk evaluation. According to her, this was one of the proudest moments in her career, as they not only listened to her input but also incorporated it into the new model they later implemented.

> After [working for] one to two years a global corporate finance project team leader who was working on developing a new credit assessment/ rating tool came to ask me for an input for a new tool. I was proud as he took my input into the model which was put to use. In former times the global model which we took from head office was predominantly [financial] measurements like liquidity, debt ratio. Afterwards it had incorporated the [non-financial] data like how many years the customers had been in operation, whether they were the key players, say top five customers. The ratio was 30% for the latter [measure] and 70% for the former whereas in the past we did not have the non-financials at all. Even though I was not leading the project I was proud that the team leader took in my input.

Having the global corporate project team leader taking her input into account was important to her. It meant that she had established enough credibility regarding her practical know-how and understanding of the practice that they had accepted her as a knowledgeable member.

5.2 Becoming a Credit Assessment and Control Assistant (2009)

5.2.1 Acquiring Additional Technical Knowledge, Sharing the Practice, and Gaining Additional Practical Understanding

Anne had always planned to pursue an MBA after acquiring a few years of work experience. So after about four years with OILCO she decided that she had reached her "saturation point" as far as work experience was concerned, and tendered her resignation in order to pursue her MBA.

> I felt comfortable about my work after four years. Then I went to further my study. I was always thinking about continuing my study. It was my aim to do the MBA to progress further. After four years I tendered my resignation to further study in the US.

At this point she began to have an interest in brand management, and took this opportunity to change her field of study to marketing and strategy.

> I knew that investment banking or banking were not for me. I wanted to change the field or learn something else. The way they conducted cases [at the business school] like Pepsi/Coca-Cola was interesting. I was learning about business and strategy. I was getting interested in brand management.

After two years studying for her MBA in Marketing and Strategy Anne came back home. While looking for a job she was offered a short-term contract to do credit management and control at OILCO, her former employer. This time she was helping with the implementation of standard credit management and control process within the SAP system (an enterprise software developed by SAP SE), using her prior knowledge of the company's credit management process. She was also involved with credit management practice of the retail business operation related to the fleet card business.[1] Unfortunately, she felt that most of the time she was doing

[1] Fleet card business involved the company giving a credit line to a corporate client. The client's employees would be given "fleet cards," which allowed each of them to fill up with

the same kind of work she has done before. Disappointed at not having the chance to grow a career at her old workplace, she felt it was pointless to stay on and began to look for a new job.

> My former boss at OILCO called me [and asked] if I was interested to work with them again. I did not have anything at the time so I agreed to be hired in as a contractor working in the [same old] credit assessment department but this time under a new boss looking over fleet card business. They were implementing SAP so I was validating whether the system should go live or whether there would be any hiccup in the process. Basically I did 60% for my old job and 30% for the project. After a while I found the work not interesting and had asked the boss if there was any opportunity to move on. The answer was no. So I decided to leave.

5.3 Becoming a Category Analysis Manager (2010–2012)

Anne learned about the job opportunity at CONCUMCO-T from one of her friends.

> A friend of mine who used to work at OILCO called and informed me about the job opportunity at CONCUMCO-T. She said the job involved business analysis dealing with marketing and preparing reports for management. The prospect sounded exciting to me when compared it with the paperwork at OILCO.

5.3.1 Acquiring Practical Know-How, Sharing the Practice, and Acquiring Practical Understanding

In the beginning Anne was assigned to do a margin analysis of one of the company's key product categories. Despite her prior exposure to credit analysis work at OILCO and her familiarity with the SAP information system, she initially found the work at CONSUMCO-T overwhelmingly challenging, owing mainly to the highly complex analytical tools she had to master.

> CONSUMCO-T also had a standard financial policy. But I found most of the things must be "handed on." I was shocked at first at the so-called "workbook" used in analysis. There were so many columns, so many work-

gas at any of the company's gas stations on credit, the payment being settled every month against the record of gas consumption.

> sheets, plus numerous links. It took me almost two months to learn to maneuver the worksheets, not counting the analysis and reporting to be done, which took me up to six months. It was about the time I completed my probation period before I could manage the thing.

With some help from her predecessor, she tried to cope with the worksheets and the required analysis work at the same time.

> I was looking over the analysis of T&S [product] category. I was lucky that my predecessor was still in the team so I could ask some questions. But the opportunity was limited as she was busy looking after her own [current] category. So I was to learn and manage the worksheets and the analysis and the reporting all by myself.

This self-learning process proved not to be easy for her. Anne felt frustrated every time she was not able to answer a question that she thought she should have known the answer to.

> It's usually someone asking a question. When they asked and I could not answer I felt I had failed.
>
> I didn't feel much about losing face but self-failure. Very often people said, "It's all right not knowing." But I would feel for myself that, "Wait I don't know? They asked but I cannot answer? Hey, I cannot answer!" It's like it's my job but I could not answer. I don't know how to describe it: completely blank or being not able to recall. I felt the self-failure, failure and feeling down on myself.

But instead of giving up, she was determined to make managing of the tool her first priority. Luckily she had someone she could turn to for advice.

> I was heavy-hearted and stressed out in the first two months but I was not giving up. I wanted to prove to myself that I could do it. I looked at my colleagues: if they could do it so could I. The first—seven to eight months was about catching up with my peers. I had the feeling that I was slow and way behind and there was a lot to catch up on. I worked late, so late, as I was trying to catch up on my overwhelming amount of work. After the first seven months, after probation, I began to feel a bit at ease. I was also lucky to have my predecessor around to answer some of the questions.

This self-studying was further facilitated by her boss asking repeated questions, providing guidance relating to standard answers, and pointing to related templates for analysis work.

> I used my boss as the check point [or] like a sounding board. Like if I would say it in this way would she agree with me? This was the first step. I got the feel from my boss first whether she's "in" with me or having confidence in me. Say we said [something] to the boss and she's not saying something like, "What are you talking about? It does not make sense." After that we would gain the courage to talk to others, someone outside the department or other members of the management, other heads of the commercial team.
>
> Most of the time it was my boss coming to ask us and it turned out that she really understood the thing we said and agreed to our explanation and did not interrupt us.
>
> When she asked the question and I answered [correctly], she would say, "Right, right, correct. Very good, right, right, I agree." or "Add something." But as long as she's not going like, "How could you say this? It was incorrect. You should [rather] think [in] this way." If it's not like this then I would gain confidence and be able to see other people afterwards.

Doing detailed analysis on the profit margin of the product category that she was responsible for on a regular basis, under guidance from her boss, Anne gradually developed her analytical skill.

> After three years I felt I had developed an analytical skill which could be considered my strength. I was able to answer the questions raised. I knew how to formulate a set of answers based on a "template" of standard questions developed/guided by my direct boss.

Her analytical skill informed her how to pick up significant variance and explain it with supporting details.

> I just looked to see if it's not normal. For example, I knew that it was always in positive but this year it [the profit number] was so low or in negative I would take a little look to see which [expense] item had been bloated, any significantly big amount [of expenses] that made this P&L [profit and loss] turned negative. So I had to look to review to see if there was anything not normal or worse than the previous year. I would [also] try to find the supporting analysis.
>
> If it were [about] promotion, if we looked at it [promotion expense] and it [also] concerned KPIs say high promotion [expenses], my team would already have this information [readily available and be able to explain], like yes we had this particular campaign with high promotion [expenses]. But if it were

something which we had no [readily available] analysis like factory expenses or advertising cost we would have to go back to the sources, like the commercial team or the supply chain team, to see why these expenses increased.

5.3.2 *Sharing the Practice, Acquiring Additional Practical Understanding*

Regularly practicing her analytical skill Anne began to be able to make sense of the numbers that she reviewed and provide relevant and reliable information for management decisions.

> Yes, it was a [required] step of the [budget] process that they came to consult with us and we did this part [financial analysis] and presented it for the management review. The management would look at the numbers that finance has prepared.

> Well we would not say, "do not pull this deal as it was not good" for we did not know [that much about it]. Sometimes the management could take it. Sometimes their issue was not the margin but that of the [market] share. I felt that my team or I would not say that this promotion would not work. But my team would object them and say, "You put in too high a volume in there so that the P&L would get through or that the statement would look nice for the management. Don't play with the numbers, it does not make sense. If you want to do this you have to include the impact from cannibalization of other products as well." We were trying to make the P&L as realistic as possible. We told them if they did not follow our advice when the management saw it they would kill it themselves. [We might also say,] "Do you think it would be that great by just doing this deal, that sales would increase this much?"

However, Anne limited her role just to providing useful reliable information on the financial impact of the marketing decision and pointing to potential issues, and never imposed her view on her counterparts.

> For example they reviewed in the [meeting] room why the margin was worse, why the price, or why the KPI for this year was so bad compared to last year. We had prepared the analysis to explain how it happened and because of what.
>
> We had increased the selling price for USD 8, why was the margin still not good? We had already the analysis showing them that even though we had increased the price but you had increased proportionately the promotion for this amount of USD XX. Last year you reduced the price by USD 5

but this year you increased it by USD 8. These items canceled out. For I could quantify that the price increase would have an impact of about USD 25 million but the promotion had gobbled up already USD 20 million leaving the [net] new gain to only USD 1 million. When we informed them about this they would not say like, "Really? Was it that we did too much promotion?" They would say, "Oh yes, that's correct." They had this check point, they had it [already] in their mind, but either they did not remember or they did not realize that the promotion went [actually] higher. But when we said it they would [recall] and believe it.

Having management and her counterparts believe in her numbers was important to her. It meant that she had established enough credibility that they had not only listened to her but also accepted her as being a competent category analysis manager.

While Anne had established herself in the organization, CONSUMCO-T was beginning to lose some of its well-trained analysts to competitors.

5.4 Becoming Financial Planning and Analysis Manager (2013–Present)

5.4.1 Engaging in Other Practices, Acquiring Additional Practical Understanding

After about three years on the job, Anne had been promoted to financial planning and analysis manager to replace one of her senior colleagues who had left to join a competitor. She viewed her new work as not very different from her previous job. Instead of the former category view, she was now responsible for the overall picture. With her prior experience of preparing the planned P&L for the category under her responsibility, and having assisted her boss in consolidation work for the total company's P&L from time to time, she was able to manage the planning process; that is, to teach her counterparts on how to use the tool for sales planning purpose, control the process, and provide information and reports, leaving the operation and the decision-making to those responsible for it. She viewed her main output in terms of a realistic P&L plan for the overall company.

My role and responsibility was to control the process and educate the commercial and marketing team on how to use the tools. You see they keyed in the volume only twice a year so sometimes they forgot how to. When they asked that Finance did the input we said we did not have the knowledge of the sales volume driver. Say [when] you have volume launch, in some case you played with volume through promotion. We did not know which promotion worked best for the customers, which promotion worked best? We checked and controlled the process making sure we could provide the answer to our boss/management. We told them if you did this promotion the impact to your margin was this much. Your 2+1 promotion resulted in this margin. So they could see the impact and think for themselves.

Anne continued to work closely with the marketing team in drawing up the P&L. This process began with the marketing team keying in the planned quantity sold, advertising, and promotion, while she would be coordinating and providing for other income and expenses numbers.

For budget and planning we prepared the budget timeline. We coordinated with the marketing and others: who was doing what and when. In two months we had to deliver the company P&L. We issued the timeline, we were the process owner. We educated marketing on the volume [planning] so we could deliver the P&L in time. Marketing could not do the whole P&L themselves even though they had the skill set as they needed us to coordinate with costing on the cost of goods.

Well I was the one who consolidated the numbers they put into the systems like [in the cases of] high volume, high promotion. I pulled the numbers from the systems that they played with and created the P&L. Actually the brand people they could see the rough P&L in the system but there were some limitations like the margin was not so precise, so we had to do some additional [manual] translation outside [the system] to have the actual margin to be shown in the budget meeting. For the advertising information or the factory expenses the brand [people] would not see them. They might know about the advertising of the brand but they did not know about the percentage [of other costs allocation] and others [relevant income/expenses] required in constructing the P&L. This information was not in the system but on Excel spreadsheets. I would pull it all together for the P&L upto the level of operating profit. In the system they would see only the margin after the product cost.

[Sometimes] it's about the factory expenses, for example: this year they had an improvement, they had [put in the budget] their own quality control issues. Our marketing [team] would be like not wanting to own so much of these, they would told us to just tell them what was the reason [for the additional cost] and they would explain it accordingly.

She made it clear that the marketing team owned the P&L, but she would help to advise them on how to present it to the management.

> They would come to me and my team saying how come the profit for this year for them was so bad. How should they explain it? Or [when the] profit was so good, where should they highlight? They already had it in their mind what they wanted to do for this year still they would like to do a little "dry run" with us, like this one was the main item, would it have [any] impact? If there was anything [unusual] please remind us of them. It's [because] we already had done the analysis and [saw that] it was like this/that.
>
> We let them change things so many times before it was finalized. Well in between the budget preparation they were like, they played with the numbers and found something was not normal. [In this case] they might run to us already like how come the margin was this bad? "Well it's because you put a lot of promotion." At this point there was not a final P&L. After they were done they would go to management for the first round [of discussion.] And when management rejected it saying that they were not satisfied with the P&L, that the margin was too low, there would be a revision round. In this revision round they [the marketing team] were already aware that they had low margin as there was too high promotion. They would go revise and revise so that it would be USD 5 million better, for example. When it became the "final" P&L it was like the management had approved the P&L. But when they went [further] to [get the approval from] the headquarters and wanted to make presentation in a more precise way they would ask like, "There was a selling price increase with impact from which month to which month, and what else? We spent too much on promotion, right? What was the impact? Which one is bigger?"

In no time, Anne found her marketing partners always sought her advice on the management view and the reliable detailed back-up analysis from her team.

> Yes, it was when they could not find it [the answer] and we had the analysis in hand. When they came over we could delve in point by point. The level of analysis we did was very precise and usually they would not argue they would listen and say, "Oh, oh, yes." It's like we were teaching them the analysis at the same time.

She also informed them if the number was not realistic.

> For example, when we did the [analysis to see the] financial impact in the case of building [sales] volume to [justify] spend promotion [and we have found out that] it [the sales number] was not realistic. The [sales volume] assumption should be lower. Like in the plan all of a sudden [there was] the promotion increase but we did not do [build in] any [impact from the]

cannibalization. We had the [increase in the] promotion item but the regular [sales] item should be gobbled up as well. When we told them that this should be the model to calculate the financial impact they would say, "That's it, yes, yes." I would say if you plan for a big volume I would not agree to it, if the assumption was not realistic. They would think about it and act accordingly every time.

At this point Anne was confident in the analysis element of her work. Dealing with this analysis regularly, she gradually learned not only how to quantify the overall impact to the P&L of the brand from the planned marketing activities but also how to evaluate if the numbers made sense. She had therefore become an expert in the area of brand profitability analysis, the one who people listened to.

From the heavy-hearted I began to feel like "having fun." I got the glimpse of the business and began to feel excited about it. In the case of promotion, for example, I felt like they had accepted me when they took in what I said and followed my advice. Basically they listened to what I said.

In any case she limited her role just to providing reliable information on the financial impact from the marketing decision.

We never said do this campaign, that campaign.

I felt I myself, not my team, I might not be that good. I was not able to say that this wouldn't work, and that finance did not agree. I felt I dared not say that. But I would say [instead that] this [particular item would make it worse off, worse off by USD X million. Without this one we would be USD X million better off. When we said this they would turn around and look at us like "Really? You think [it would go] this way?" They just took it for their re-consideration. We had already offered our recommendation. We only said that next year we would have only USD 5 million not as much as we [earlier] thought.

As for the planning process, Anne stressed the importance of an agreed timeline.

I would look at the budget process, [in terms of the] overall picture. This cycle we did the budget for two months. The first day for the budget meeting was to be on this [so-and-so] date. I would go ask for advice if they could manage within this date and would they be able to deliver the budget in time.

She credited her in-depth know-how about the planning process, acquired when she was the category analysis manager, for enabling her to coordinate all the necessary activities, something that sometimes required sidestepping some processes. Dealing with the budget process every year, she became an expert on the process who could advise those involved about what they should do.

> In the budget process there was a lot of people [taking part] in there but I could provide the whole picture. It was like if somebody could not do it in time [I know] how we could help. When someone wanted to know if we would help sidestep some of the budget processes he/she would come to me. I felt I had a specific knowledge for CONSUMCO-T's [budget process] and this might be because I liked to memorize the details [of the process]. So I could advise them if they would like to skip some of the processes.

She pointed to the importance of learning from details upwards and the benefit of being earlier engaged in the budget process herself.

> So it's not like listening about the process and you could do it, you had to go through it yourself so you would be able to do it. Pay a lot of attention to it and once you do the budget you remember forever and you [would have the] feel for like whether this one [person] had side-stepped something. And [whether] there would be a wide margin of error [from this]. You have to get involved [in the budget process] since being the analyst [when] you look after the whole picture. We would feel that we were still "in" with the budget process so much even though one year had already gone by. It [the experience] made us know our work quite well and enabled us to provide advice about these steps.

Anne's hands-on experience of the budget process informed her on how she could side-step to make the process go through according to the agreed timeline.

> Suppose the costing number wasn't available. Well prior to this I usually coordinated with the costing that the number would be available on so and so date. I told them ahead of time that we needed it to communicate with the marketing about the new cost.
>
> If it were like this I might have to use the previous given cost and tell the whole commercial team meeting that we would have to use the old costs as the new one would not be [available] in time and ask them [costing] to

advise the impact, like how many percentage or how many millions. We would ask them to give a rough estimate in percentage for the impact so we could tell the commercial team. Once we had the updated costs we would layer the new cost in and communicate the latest [cost estimates] to the commercial team once more.

Little by little, through daily coping, Anne became confident about her work knowledge. But most of all she was happy that she was accepted as the expert in her field of financial planning and analysis.

5.4.2 *Sharing the Practice*

Anne trusted her boss for career advice and relied on her boss for giving her new opportunities.

I had a boss who was knowledgeable and gave me opportunity to learn new things. I always looked at my peers and told myself if they could do it I could do it as well. I compared myself to others. I believed that my boss would take care of me, providing me with the opportunities.

Anne was relatively comfortable about her current work and did not proactively look for new opportunities, but then things changed after she took a short-term assignment to do a consolidation of reports from various countries for the Asia division. This experience broadened her horizons and opened her up to other career opportunities in finance.

But then I got a short-term assignment to go to Hong Kong which was not the kind of job I am doing. The scope was expanded. Those who were at the same position [as me] in other countries might have something not the same as mine, could be something more or less than me. When I did the assignment in HK I found that this point [for example] so far I did not know. People would always say, "how would you know [about it] when you have never done it before?" I would ask myself then how come I had not done that. Why [under] this role in other countries they had done it and they could answer it. Maybe they had not done it [before]. Maybe [it's because] they had come from another department and that's why they knew about this. When I was there I raised these questions [to myself] frequently. I then understood that the role of commercial finance did not end here. Something should be added on continuously. With the broader/bigger picture [involved], when we went for the assignment like this there were a lot of things I could not answer.

The experience of the bigger picture left Anne with the impression that there was still lots to be learned beyond the current commercial finance perspective that she was familiar with. And to gain that knowledge she might have to venture outside her current role. The quest to provide answers began again. She was now open to expanding her current role in order to gain a broader knowledge. But it seemed that she still did not know precisely what she would like to pursue.

> I worked in finance I knew the commercial [side] but I didn't think it's sufficient. I would welcome some of the exposure to other aspects of finance, say tax accounting but perhaps not full blown.
>
> I wanted to be a controller, something more, [perhaps in] costing, changing the role in the company, or changing the role in my life. Not like one day we just concentrated on promotion [activities], knowing only [about] promotion, every year there were just promotions. Maybe there would be some other changes but it was still in promotion area. I might want to know how the factory operates. These kinds of things are all interesting.
>
> If anything, I wanted to stay at the same level but doing a different job like costing, customer development finance, not [the analysis] at brand level. Not a manager [looking] at brand level like now.
>
> I think I should be doing some other thing and not what I am doing today. To prepare the statement, take the position that has more responsibility, [preparing] many [companies' statements at the same time. I see myself as a bit narrow in these areas.
>
> I just want to change my competency or move to the finance of the division looking over many countries, consolidating/combining numbers for the division. I am open for that. I just want to continue learning working in different [career] paths.

Anne was not afraid to move on. She believed that she would persevere and be able to cope with new challenges on her own.

> But I have one confidence in me that I would be able to learn progressively. I am not the kind of person when being taught … and when changing job struggles forever. I think I have the capacity to adapt enough. When changing the job to something I don't know … Now I think I am ready to [self-] learn whenever I am lost. When I said I was not able to answer and had a sense of failure, it's not that I stopped there at not knowing. It makes me want to know more. I still have a positive view of myself that I am not the kind of person that would not take anything new in life. I think even though

I do not know, but muddling through it every day I would be able to turn around. That's why I want to do something else. Even though it's new stuff or adapting anew I think I should be able to do it.

Taking stock of what she had learned besides the technical know-how, Anne mentioned how to manage work complexity.

Because the work at CONSUMCO-T is complicated the learning is about prioritizing, managing my work. There is a lot of work so if we continue learning we would know about the budget process. It's like how to shuffle it so that it goes smoothly. It's about how to prioritize the work.

She realized that she still needed to learn about how to adapt and get out of her rule abiding controller's mode, especially when dealing with "difficult" people.

I am the kind of person that ... if we are strict to our timeline we must be able to do it. I would be strong, saying it used to be fine doing this why should it not be this time. Is it that you go home too early? But I could not say that. So I would be upset all the time. I do not need to know he could not do it because he is lazy or is it because he is not interested in it. In this process how come he cannot do it? I don't know how to talk him down. I am not ready to make an argument with everyone like this.

Adapting, I would say, to the difficulty of the work like in the past when I did not know about the expenses, like when this expense item was high [and I could not explain why], this was no [longer a] problem. But when it came to people skill ... even if I worked in another department and had to face someone who had been difficult to deal with [again] I would still have a problem dealing with this person. This does not mean that having a problem here would prevent me from doing the job. I would continue talking uncomfortably [with him], [while] wanting to have my senior [manager] come help talk to this person, "Can I have my boss come talk with you?" At the end, I would be able to do it [the job]. But it's just that [when it came down to] the way to deal with the people, I could not deal with them all, they being at the same level or higher. Yet, it doesn't mean that I could not manage at all.

During this period her direct boss was taking up a new assignment at a regional level. With the new boss giving her the freedom to do things with minimum guidance, Anne missed the usual direct support and close working relationship, and began to contemplate on the future of her career. At the same time she was nominated to participate in a leadership development program, which was laid out to broaden her work perspective and help her progress further in her career with CONSUMCO-T. But not long after she came back from this training program, she resigned to seek a new job opportunity.

5.5 The Lifelong Self-Orienting Process

5.5.1 Self-Orienting Process, Teleoaffective Structure

In the same manner as in the case of Carol, through the BPDM lens, Anne performs four alternate key actions: acquiring technical knowledge and practical know-how, acquiring practical understanding, sharing the practice, and engaging in other practices relevant to her four key career milestones (Table 5.1). In the early stage of her career we see the prevalence of acquiring knowledge and practical understanding to build up the bench strength of the financial analyst. Later, when she has gained sufficient experience, she begins to share financial practices and engage in commercial practice, gaining additional practical understanding and winning acceptance to become the expert in her field of financial analysis and planning. All the actions and their related activities are geared towards a specific goal: for example, Anne joins the MBA program in order to gain a necessary knowledge and credentials to enter financial management practice; she works tirelessly on challenging Excel workbooks in order to gain an understanding of how they work, in order to master them so she can become a competent financial analyst; and she shares financial analysis practice in order to build an additional practical understanding or hands-on experience in order to perform her job satisfactorily and be accepted by her peers, in order to be promoted to finance manager. These key goal-oriented actions are organized into two micro-processes: becoming a finance apprentice and becoming a finance expert, forming an overall self-orienting process towards an end goal; that is, becoming a well-accepted high-ranking financial practitioner in an organization (Fig. 5.1). As in the previous case, in both of the micro-processes there appears to be the action of gaining (additional) practical understanding through sharing financial practice and engaging in commercial practice. This seems to be the crucial action in the self-orienting process of management accountants who are facing continuous changes and want to survive.

Table 5.1 List of actions and key milestones of financial planning and analysis career

Being credit assessment assistant	*Being credit assessment and control assistant*	*Being category analysis manager*	*Being financial planning and analysis manager*
Acquiring practical know-how	Acquiring practical know-how	Acquiring practical know-how	
Acquiring practical understanding	Acquiring additional practical understanding	Acquiring practical understanding	Acquiring (additional) practical understanding
	Sharing the practice	Sharing the practice	Sharing the practice
			Engaging in other practices

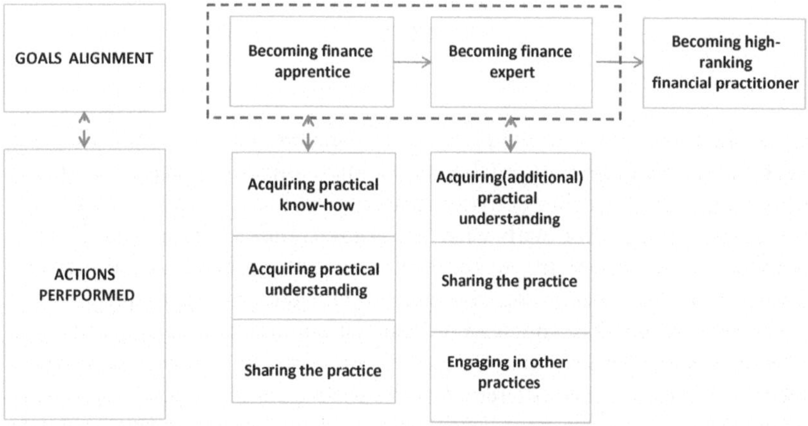

Fig. 5.1 Self-orienting process and goal aligning – financial planning and analysis manager

Unlike Carol, who is self-driven and knows exactly what she wants, and charts her own course accordingly, it is important for Anne to feel accepted and recognized by those around her, her family, her bosses, and her colleagues (Table 5.2). Her story has shown us that she is most happy when she is praised for her work accomplishments; for example, when she is able to provide answers to questions posted by her commercial counterparts or

Table 5.2 Self-orienting and teleoaffective structure – financial planning and analysis manager

Motivations, things that matter	*Affectivities*	*Self-orienting activities*	*Goals*	*Ends*
Security, being accepted, being "listened to"	Feeling comfortable under the wing of the mentor	Self-learning with guidance and strong support from supervisors, quitting when support disappears	Becoming financial manager	Becoming high-ranking financial practitioner
	Disliking confrontation	Arguing her case using rules, established procedure, referring to formal authority, muddling through, participating in the commercial meeting when requested		

when she is promoted to the position of manager at a relatively young age. Seeking security in terms of being accepted motivates her to align her purposeful self-orienting activities towards achieving a specific organizational position, in line with what she understands to be a typical career path of a financial practitioner of her time: getting an MBA, becoming a financial analyst, becoming a finance manager, and perhaps later on becoming the CFO or the head of financial operations of an organization. It is the sense of security that influences Anne's major career moves, which most of the time are associated with the withering or disappearing of support from her direct bosses. With support from her direct boss she stays for a long time in her assignment, muddling through all kinds of challenges without any problem. But when the support withers, such as when she joins OILCO for the second time or at a later stage in her career with CONSUMCO, she decides to leave and to take other job opportunities.

5.5.2 *Self-Orienting, Personal Characteristics, and Affectivities*

In the case of Anne, it is found that certain personal characteristics affect her degree of orientation towards business through "affectivities" (Fig. 5.2). Being perseverant, she has no problem dealing with tremen-

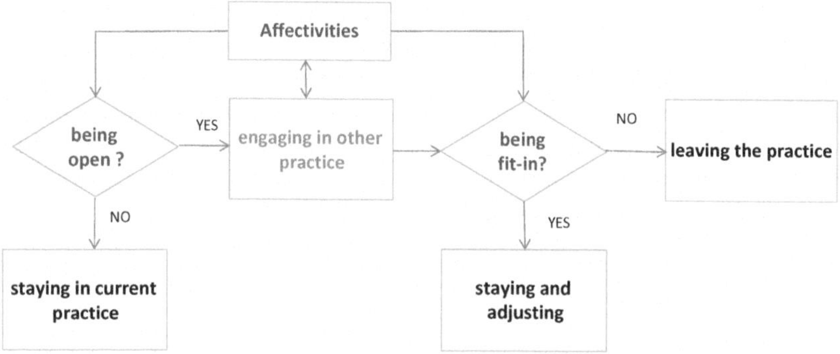

Fig. 5.2 Turning point—financial planning and analysis manager

dously detailed work. She has been willing to "suffer" learning about and mastering the challenging Excel workbook on her own for over six months, so she can prove herself to be as capable as her peers, and so she can set off on her path to become a well-recognized finance manager. On the other hand, not being assertive, abiding by the rules, and always avoiding confrontation, Anne limits her commercial engagement mostly to providing advice together with detailed analyses for budgeting and controlling purposes, such as the comparisons of actual performance versus the budget—including gaps that indicate areas that need to be addressed, such as trade spending, volume growth, and price increases, only when required. And even though she participates in the commercial meeting, she feels uncomfortable and that she does not fit in (Fig. 5.2), tending to sit quietly and providing financial information only when asked. This limited engagement in commercial activities leads to a lower degree of business orientation compared with the other cases discussed.

5.5.3 *Self-Orienting, the Cultural Context, and Affectivity*

Anne works in the same organization as Carol. Therefore they share the same supportive organizational culture and other site-specific elements such as an advanced information system, the availability of powerful analytics, and a cohort of experts from different areas. However, so far Anne seems to be relying more on the supportive culture in terms of mentoring and coaching and general support from her direct bosses than Carol. And while the support makes her feel comfortable and confident in meeting new challenges, it seems to prevent her from moving away from her comfort zone in the area of financial analysis and planning into a more challenging assignment, such as commercial practice. The lower degree of business orientation in her case when compared with the other cases is manifested in her reluctance to participate in the areas she is not familiar with, such as on-the-ground commercial activities and the uneasiness she feels while engaging in those activities.

CHAPTER 6

Commercial Finance Career

When you wake up every morning (think about) what value you will be adding each day. It does not have to be anything significant, it can also be very little things. This can be related to both work and personal life. Key is to keep this thought in mind and ask yourself every day. Don't let a day pass by without adding value. (Madelyn's comment on what she has learned from her boss)

Madelyn is a successful woman executive in her mid-40s. Her career path reflects a significant impact from change in work context from the stable "old world" of a manufacturing company to the ever-changing and highly dynamic "new world" of fast-moving consumer goods, in which information on the consumer's behavior and up-to-the-minute company performance become key success factors. It features the challenge of the new age of information in which "big data" has a significant impact on work life and mastering it becomes a prerequisite for today's corporate finance practitioners. It depicts the way in which she has successfully transformed herself to being the "business partner" over the course of her career to meet this new challenge, which is facing corporate finance practitioners today and will face them tomorrow. Besides the internal inherent elements, such as personal goals/end, personal characteristics, and motivation, this case highlights how the broader organizational culture and past practices influence the degree of business orientation.

P. Chotiyanon, V. Joannidès de Lautour,
The Changing Role of the Management Accountants,
https://doi.org/10.1007/978-3-319-90300-2_6

Madelyn was the commercial finance director-Asia of CONSUMCO, the parent company of CONSUMCO-T. She began her career at a young age of 19, fresh out of college, by joining the management accounting practice at MANCO-T, a subsidiary of a leading German chemical conglomerate. Over the course of her long career life she has had the opportunity to accumulate a significant wealth of experience in management control practices under different business contexts—within the manufacturing and pharmaceutical industries for about ten years and within the fast-moving consumer goods industry for another 15 years. At CONSUMCO she built on her previous experiences by establishing a solid planning and control system, expanding her role into commercial practice and engaging in domestic, regional, and global markets, and becoming an expert in commercial finance, being a recognized "business partner" for all her peers.

Madelyn was highly experienced, hands-on, and widely accepted as an expert in CONSUMCO's commercial finance practice, the advice of which is sought by colleagues all over the world. Her approach to work was analytical and detailed, yet also with an integrated or "big picture" view. When faced with obstacles she was determined and persevering. She was passionate about her work, dedicated, working her way from the ground up along her career path until she reached a finance pinnacle as finance director (FD) of one of the world leaders in the fast-moving consumer goods (FMCG) industry at a relatively young age and the first local member of staff to take on a regional position. She was adaptable and open both to opportunity and to the risk associated with engaging in other practices.

Madelyn described her career as a continuous improvement process, keeping on challenging herself to do things differently. Key success factor for her was the support from her bosses, "I learned that to do things differently and passionately you'd need a support from your bosses." In the following sections we trace her lifelong self-orienting process towards being business partner with four career milestones: being a controller, a budget manager, the associated director, commercial finance, and the commercial finance director, Asian division. This will allow us to understand the process through which she has developed her business orientation under a strong and supportive organizational culture.

6.1 Becoming a Controller (1990–1999)

6.1.1 Acquiring Practical Know-How and Practical Understanding

Madelyn had an outstanding educational background. She graduated in finance, with honors, from one of the top-two business schools. In her senior year she sent out a few application letters to some potential employers, as most senior students did. The first company that responded to her was MANCO-T. She recalled going for an interview with the "big boss," Alain, and his planning and budgeting manager, still in her school uniform. She was nervous, but formed a good impression of the company and agreed to start working as a financial analyst at MANCO-T right after she graduated.

At the time she joined MANCO-T in 1990 the planning and management reports were manually prepared. In those early days she pulled company financial information from a centralized electronic data processing system and manually draw up the business division's profit and loss (P&L) statement for both budgeted and actual numbers for management. To her it was adding numbers and reconciling the divisional P&L numbers to those of the statutory reports. This paper-based exercise was later replaced by the advent of Excel spreadsheets. However, the manual exercise provided Madelyn with in-depth knowledge about the reporting structure, including the accounting structure that enabled her to do her daily work. At the same time she was assigned to analyze development in the product's gross profit margin, the operating and non-operating expenses, and the inventory and accounts receivable movement. These detailed analysis exercises helped her to understand the whole planning and control system from the ground up. At the end she had gained not only an overall picture of the company but also the supporting details, such as the performance of major products that rolled up into the total company P&L, and the impact of inventory and accounts receivable management on financing cost and balance sheet position. This knowledge gave her an advantage over other accounting staff and her business counterparts, who usually specialized in certain areas of operation and had no grasp of the overall picture. During this period she was closely guided and coached by her planning and budgeting manager, who also acted as her mentor.

Looking back and comparing her current role with that of the early days, Madelyn saw her work at that time as stable, rather mundane, "nothing exciting." Nevertheless, it was the period in which she formed a solid knowledge about the planning and reporting practice, learning from MANCO-T's well-established system. It was also the period in which she began to develop her analytical ability, her fondness for details, and her overall view approach, which would greatly benefit her in the later stages of her career.

As the business expanded and planning and reporting activities grew, Madelyn was promoted to planning and reporting supervisor, with two subordinates to help out with her increased planning and reporting activities for all MANCO-T's subsidiaries. In 1998, after reorganization of the MANCO-T group, she joined MANCO-P, the group's pharmaceutical arm, to take over the management accounting activities of this former business unit. With her solid experience and her expertise in MANCO-T management accounting practice, she was promoted to the position of controller after about two years there.

6.2 Becoming a Budget Manager (2000–2006)

6.2.1 Sharing the Practice, Acquiring Practical Understanding

In 2000, David, the incumbent FD of CONSUMCO-T, was contemplating upgrading the capability of his budget team so that it was in line with the changes in business requirements. Exhausting the internal resources, he decided to bring in expertise from outside the company. He got Madelyn's name and her exceptional profile from one of his colleagues in his FD network, and decided to invite her over for an interview. Madelyn was interested in the job, although she admitted that it was a big challenge for her coming from a different business environment. They agreed that she should start as an internal auditor for a few months before getting into the budget area. This would provide her with an opportunity to learn about the business complexity and the people involved, so she was able to adjust to the new environment.

> Actually, the plan was to let me get into budget role post joining after two months, so that I could have a complete introduction to business. David said audit was the best place to start off, which was true, as during the two months I slowly had business feel of consumer goods which is totally different from pharmaceutical business.

Well, it's an entirely new business, both new people and new environment. New business was the key, as the pharmaceutical business was pretty stable and consistent, while consumer goods things were much more dynamic, with rapid changes all the time [as far as competitors/customers/market, etc. are concerned].

The work environment is also very different. In my prior company, I connected only with each business unit lead to get inputs, while in the new place I needed to connect with all cross-functional business counterparts at all levels. There were many meetings to attend, in order to understand business insights and link them back to internal financials. There was much more business exposure.

This role was only for two months. There was a good introduction planned by my boss. I slowly met all functional directors and had a brief session with all of them. It was not too much of an adjustment, as the exposure to commercial counterparts came later, when I moved into the budget manager role.

After a little over a month and about three hours of briefing from the incumbent, Madelyn took over the position of budget manager with two analysts to help her out. She was comfortable about the budgeting concept, having gained a solid foundation during her prior work experience. But she was a bit concerned about the complexity of the business and the related volume of activities.

To be honest, I was pretty comfortable getting into a budget role, as it's something I have sound experience in and I was pretty confident that I would be able to perform the job.

[After about] Only three hours [of] overview [introduction] and [job] hand over, she [the incumbent] then left for New York the following day. It was a challenge, but actually on the other side of the coin I drilled all details of every aspect of the work by myself and learned a lot. It took me some time to settle in and was very tough. One great thing was I had a solid foundation of the role from my prior company.

Key differences between the two places were scope, business complexity, and volume of work where in CONSUMCO-T [it] was much more than [in] MANCO-T. We planned 500+ SKUs [stock keeping units], and not only for local business but for all countries within Indochina (i.e., replication of the same process for planning/reporting five times for five countries.) We also got into customer dimension planning, in addition to product category/brand/SKU planning which led to further complexity. For example, each sub-category (SC1, SC2, and SC3) within product category1 had different market dynamics, different pricing, promotions, segmentations, etc. In addition, they also had different customer dynamics, with different promotion plans in different weeks for each customer. The same applied to product category 2, 3, and 4. Customer strategy also varied by sub-categories.

The key change for me was the scope/volume of work and complete understanding of the different trade channel/category dynamics that I needed to feel comfortable with at the soonest. It took me three to four months to get the true feel of business. However, the planning concept remained the same and could be applied to any international company.

6.2.2 *Engaging in Commercial Practice, Creating Value*

At the time the CONSUMCO-T budget was prepared on Excel spreadsheets. The input came in from various sources in different formats. The budget team input the data into separate Excel spreadsheets, again with different formats. These numbers were then added and rolled up; that is, adding numbers to get the profit margin and the P&L at brand, category, and then company levels. There were issues of inconsistency and data integrity. The whole process was cumbersome and time consuming, with the mid-year operational review taking about two months and the annual budget review about three months. The time was mostly spent on preparing the statements and the required "exhibits," which were templates of information for the annual formal budget review. As such there was little analysis done. Madelyn decided to make a change.

First, she started with the simplification of the internal budget process by standardizing the spreadsheet used in data consolidation by her team and then the marketing's input spreadsheet, enabling them to input the data in one unified format and see the number right away at their end—without the budget team rekeying the data and printing the spreadsheets again for them.

She referred to David's guidance for CONSUMCO's financial policy.

Getting started, David was my sound reference for all CONSUMCO's financial policies and KPIs (Key Performance Indicators), definitions/calculations, etc.

With the policy in place she implemented the standardized process and related workbooks.

Each of them was working in different Excel file formats, there was no standardization in planning working files, so company consolidation was a nightmare, i.e., absolute manual work, adding each sub-total of key P&L lines for each sub-category, to arrive at a consolidated total company picture.

> With this, I started to implement standard Excel working file formats, with modifications to both analysts' as-is files, in order to align all working files within the team for consolidation automation. Next, we then slowly standardized inputs templates provided by all marketing leads. Efficiencies were realized, thereby slowly influencing these small changes [so we] were successful.

The resulting standard Excel workbook was somewhat large but quite useful for the team. There was from that point onwards a single format for everyone. There was no more repetitive data entry and validation. This change in process resulted in an improvement in data quality, releasing time previously spent on keying in data twice to check and verify data for more data analysis. At first the marketing team refused to cooperate, asking the budget team to input for them as before. Madelyn convinced them to try the new template so they could see the benefits of the change.

> Yes, as we had data input from lowest level (SKU), to be able to roll up to size, brand, sub-category, product category and company. We also had monthly dimension integrated. Actually, we started the standardization/automation from scratch at the time.

David was happy with the change.

> He was impressed with the speed [with which] we could deliver brand operating P&Ls to management, with more accuracy levels than before. There were still minor errors at the beginning, as a result of inaccurate formula setups. However, significant human error of numbers not adding up from all dimensions did not recur any more. It was a great start, and this was mainly due to the solid planning foundation in my prior experience that could be applied to CONSUMCO-T.

After this, Madelyn worked on the standard report benchmarking the actual performance against the budget and latest estimates. In the budget review she insisted on using just one set of numbers, her numbers, instead of different sets of numbers from sales, marketing, and other departments.

> Next, I started to put presentations in place for brand operating P&L comparisons in one summary chart, one sheet per brand. We had year-to-date (YTD)/year-to-go (YTG) current year versus prior year same periods P&L comparisons, including current year, prior year, budget, and latest estimates. Commercial organization and management were thrilled with this output. I was a little surprised that these summary P&L charts were not available before. I guess it's more [about] having information of different periods in different places versus one snapshot summary.

Implementing these changes in the budget process, she received full support from her direct boss, David. The incumbent marketing director, Frank, who received the brand P&L prepared by her team for the first time, was quite impressed. He saw the benefits of this change in the budget process, and did not hesitate to provide additional support by enlisting all marketing managers' support in its implementation.

Going into details as she worked alongside her subordinates and her counterparts, sharing her prior experiences, Madelyn made sure that her numbers were valid and reliable, thereby gaining buy-ins from everyone involved. David was happy that Madelyn had won over marketing for their necessary support, and realized that they appreciated the finance team's contribution.

6.3 Becoming Associated Director-Commercial Finance (2007–2012)

6.3.1 Engaging in Commercial Practice, Acquiring Additional Practical Understanding

David introduced Madelyn to CONSUMCO-T's management by inviting her to the management committee (Mancom) meeting.

> I made my first presentation to Mancom after I joined for a month during my internal audit role. I presented an ABC simplification analysis (number of invoices, customer ranking, product ranking, etc.) and received very good feedback. Management was very warm and welcoming. I guess all credit went to David, as he was behind all this support and arranged for the great introduction sessions for me.

Afterwards she was to join the management committee meeting on a regular basis, presenting the commercial finance aspect of the business, the detailed profit development of the product categories, to the management. Being close to management provided her with opportunities to gain insights into the business from a management point of view, and this enabled her to prepare relevant information that met their requirements.

> David took me to the Mancom meeting regularly. I was the key member of Mancom even though I was not the director and was the first local staff member to attend the high-level meeting.

Madelyn kept abreast of business development with regard to other aspects of the operation by participating in a regular cross-functional commercial meeting, involving marketing, sales, supply chain, and finance teams. From both meetings she began to collect key questions about the main management concerns regarding ongoing business development, which would become a guide for her team's analysis and reporting. Learning gradually about the business, she was able not only to provide relevant answers to the questions being raised, but was also able to anticipate questions and challenge the operation team on certain issues. Her valuable contribution given in an honest manner won her admiration and respect from both her subordinates and her peers.

> However, after attending a couple of commercial meetings and reviews, I finally got hold of business and felt more comfortable to provide sound contributions, recommendations to management's discussions/decisions.

David was happy about Madelyn's performance. He continued to provide support by engaging her in Mancom as much as possible. Besides this, he also invited her to participate in the annual budget review, which involved the regional and global management teams as well as the local one. This helped provide her with an insight into broader management imperatives.

6.3.2 *Sharing Practice, Creating Value*

In her first budget review meeting which was just a few months after she joined the company, Madelyn got a chance to meet her role model, Shahan, for the first time. At that time he was a project manager in charge of implementing strategic planning process in Asia and was part of the visiting regional management team. She recalled the moment vividly.

> In July 2000, after two months in internal audit role I moved into the budget manager role. Around August and September was my first budget review. I prepared the budget after two months in the role and attended the official review with regional management.

She was scared of the meeting.

> Pretty scared and stressed, not much about delivering the numbers/decks in time, but stressed because I was afraid that I would not be able to answer

key analytical questions in the review, as at the time I still did not have a full "feel" of complete business portfolio dynamics within CONSUMCO-T. Brand strategies, customer strategies, pricing, spending, margins, etc. varied across sub-categories, and the size of each product. It's pretty detailed.

I remembered Shahan asking me, "What was the margin of product X?" I was shocked. I could not answer that. I'd just been there for a few months. No way could I provide the answer. At the same time I was thinking they did go to this level of detail!

It was a wakeup call for her. Madelyn realized that from that point onwards she would have to get to the deepest details, at SKU level. The overall picture was necessary, but one also needed the full supporting details.

In response, she came up with a summary of brand performance in a standard report called "brand snapshot," her first reporting innovation. This report was part of a comprehensive standard workbook which included the P&L of a brand according to its budget and actual performances, including an estimate for the current year with details by product category and the summary sheet, the "brand snapshot," which showed the net sales, operating profit, and the brand KPIs, such as selling price, material cost, and trade spending and advertising. She designed the report and implemented it within her team. Each brand analyst was to regularly update his/her work book with the information drawn from the main SAP system (an enterprise resource planning software developed by a German company, SAP, SE). The up-to-date and relevant data was automatically fed into the summary sheet upon which the analyst prepared the analysis and provided the relevant comment on the brand performance. This workbook provided for the first time all the relevant key management information in a standardized snapshot, with a level of detail that had never existed before.

There were different charts for different information/updates in place here and there, but there was not a summary high-level business snapshot for management's review, covering all aspects within commercial finance in an integrated manner, both category and customer highlights.

Management was very happy with her contribution.

Yes they were, as once tools for automation and standardization were completely in place, it led to efficiencies, allowing time savings which were then reinvested back into elevating analytics we had at the time to the next level. All company's key KPIs movements were closely monitored and reviewed, leading to early gaps/opportunities identification. The ability to foresee gaps and opportunities upfront early enough led to in-time key decisions required to turn around business plans and reprioritization of investment allocations.

Madelyn gave the credit to Shahan as the one who challenged her to do things differently and to come up with a way to do things better. She recalled his mantra about being different and creating value.

> When you wake up every morning [think about] what value you will be adding each day. It does not have to be anything significant, it can also be very little things. This can be related to both work and personal life. Key is to keep this thought in mind and ask yourself every day. Don't let a day pass by without adding value.

Not long after their first meeting, in which he challenged Madelyn on the level of detail in her analysis, and thus its validity, Shahan was assigned to succeed Frank as the new marketing director of CONSUMCO-T. Within a year he became the company's managing director (MD). Shahan was analytical and loved details. During this period Madelyn worked closely with him on various projects, during which she learned about management KPIs. She made sure that those KPIs were incorporated into the "brand snapshot," thereby making the report relevant and meaningful for management decisions.

During this period David gave her a free hand as far as commercial finance was concerned. He was happy about her accomplishment and continued to provide her with support and to look for opportunities to broaden her exposure to business whenever it arose. During his tenure he arranged for her to join an international internal audit team as a guest auditor for about three weeks, auditing one of CONSUMCO's subsidiaries in Europe. On another occasion he put her on an eight-week short-term assignment at headquarters, working with the international team in consolidating the financial reports of the Asian region. These assignments were aimed at broadening Madelyn's exposure to other CONSUMCO operations in other countries and allow her to build up a global financial network.

> It was my first time traveling for a long trip away from home, but he told me that it's a must for my future career advancement.
>
> Big learning for me, I had an opportunity to see the bigger picture beyond my country, with fifteen countries within divisional consolidation. It broadened

my business perspective. This was more a high-level view, of looking at key countries with key contributions to division's goals, both top line and bottom line. The work covered consolidation and analysis of division's key KPI movements, driven by different countries' business dynamics and mix. I built strong network/relationships, working closely with budget managers across subsidiaries within division and corporate finance. It was a unique eye opener experience for me, as every country had its own business challenges. It was a great opportunity to learn more about CONSUMCO's business from both scope and complexity aspects.

Attending Asia division's budget review with the corporate team was great exposure for me. I had the opportunity to meet CONSUMCO's senior executives. They were very warm and welcoming. It was interesting to see how the real review happened at corporate level versus at subsidiary or division levels, i.e., with different sets of presentations, types of questions asked and key points discussed, etc.

In the meantime she began to think about the customer dimension of the brand analysis.

It [the idea] came across with more frequency of attendance at commercial meetings, reviews, trade visits, customer meetings, etc. This led to full understanding of an external view impacting internal business. The turning point was my first attendance to meeting with one of our key customers, i.e., joint business plan meeting.

David invited Madelyn to join a top-to-top meeting with a key customer who was a market leader in the hypermarket segment. In the meeting she was impressed by the quality of data and analysis that was presented. Basically, the customer ran a thoroughly detailed comparative analysis on all of their suppliers including CONSUMCO-T. It was an eye opener. Not only was she meeting the management team of the key customer for the first time, but she was also gaining an insight into their views and how they regarded CONSUMCO-T.

This was a true eye opener for me. I realized that we were too internally focused. What matters to customers is their category growth, and CONSUMCO-T only represents a certain percentage of the total market within each of their categories. If our product ran off the shelf quickly, we got more space on shelf and thereby shares, and faster shipments. However, as category leaders, we needed to have joint plans with customers, to help them drive growth of all products on the shelf, using category insights we held, and not just CONSUMCO-T's products. It's creating a win-win scenario for both us and our customers.

She began to wonder why CONSUMCO-T did not have the mirror analysis on the customer as well. She decided to change this.

This customer concept was then soundly in my mind, and thereby I started to think how we should start to review each customer, their P&Ls with integration to their product mix, etc. separately, in order to propose different commercial plans, aligning ours and customers' strategy.

Madelyn began by assigning Star, a new analyst, to do the customer analysis in the same manner as the analysis on products. The idea was to replicate the P&L of the products on to the customers. The outcome, the integrated customer and product P&L, was considered a major CONSUMCO-T reporting breakthrough. For the first time CONSUMCO-T's management had an integrated view of products and customers upon which they could promptly react.

It was a revolution. We were then in a position to identify exact gaps/opportunities by brand by each customer, including a specific gap resolution plan to be developed.

With an integrated planning tool in place, we get automated reports generated. The report in place includes integrated information in standard format, i.e., actual and plan data. This leads to efficiency in validation, reporting consolidation and a basis on which second level analytics can be performed. All parties can view same data, same budget numbers, latest estimates in an integrated manner, i.e., both brand P&Ls and customer P&Ls are readily available in the same system.

Significant time savings as a result of simplification in business process and tools automation have been invested back into developing the quality of analytics. We have enriched detailed analytics in place at size/mix level by brand and by customer dimension. Analytics has been enhanced. We can quantify selling price and percentage margin movement points by drivers which are key KPIs in the brand and customer P&Ls.

Madelyn moved on to recruit another analyst, who was assigned to gather information on key customers by trade channel. This marked the birth of the customer development finance function under the umbrella of CONSUMCO-T. Her expanded team could provide not only an integrated view on customer/brand performance but also detailed supporting analysis by trade channel. Her rich integrated reporting tool was recognized as

Asia's best practice, bringing her wide recognition in CONSUMCO's financing community and winning her promotion to the position of associated FD, the first local staff member to take such a high position in the local organization.

6.4 Becoming Commercial Finance Director, Asia (2013–Present)

6.4.1 Sharing the Practice, Creating Value

Shortly after Madelyn's promotion, David retired and Bert arrived from head office to take his place. Being the new FD, Bert continued to give Madelyn a free hand on the commercial side of finance that she had pioneered in CONSUMCO-T. She continued to work closely with Shahan. From the "brand snapshot" they developed a presentation chart depicting an overview of key KPIs. "Shahan's chart," as she fondly referred to it, became a highlight in the local management committee meeting and the semi-annual performance review meeting with the global management team.

> Actually, I did not report directly to him (Shahan). However, he supported me and always respected me and my opinion in front of local management division and global teams. Some examples, normally only functional directors attended and shared presentation in [the budget] review [sessions]. However, he requested me to present a section on GTN (gross to net sales development) overview during Fabrio's (the global chief operating officer) visit and also attend and present commercial finance overview in all Mancom meetings. There was no other local associate director attending or presenting in these meetings.
>
> I would cover commercial finance overview, including company, categories and key customers' key KPIs movements, relationships, business implications of these KPIs (volumes, net sales, selling prices, trade spending, percentage margin/mix), and trends, including risks and opportunities identification. Shahan was impressed with these charts being developed, thereby requesting me to present to Fabrio and incorporate this as standard Key KPIs chart, to be reviewed by management on a monthly basis.

Together they also introduced more financial disciplines into the commercial operation.

> During Shahan's time, we also implemented the ROI (return on investment) concept. We set up quarterly ROI day and key KPIs to be reviewed in

> these meetings, for key customers and key brands. This led to significant savings and efficiencies, with focus reviews of KPIs, taking into consideration external inputs (market shares, competitors/ customers activities, etc.). There was a lot of learning and best practice sharing across customers and brands which helped in improving company's top line and margin. The credit goes to Shahan as he provided great detailed inputs all along and took full accountability.

During his time, Madelyn came up with a another major planning tool, "what-if modeling," which was a planning tool in which the marketing and sales teams could do their own P&L simulation based on changes in sales and other KPIs without having to submit the data to the budget team to prepare for the P&L again. This new tool completely changed the way CONSUMCO-T did its planning and budgeting. Instead of working separately, each of them, being a member of a cross-functional team, worked closely together on the plan and the budget. Shahan gave his full support to implementing this tool at CONSUMCO-T.

> Actually, Shahan came over to my office one day and told me to develop a simplified tool that could drive efficiency in commercial meetings preparation, as he saw the marketing team spending a lot of time to come up with financials of different business scenarios and proposals for meeting discussions and decisions. In addition, there were different formats being presented by each marketing lead. He was looking for both standardization and efficiency.
>
> With this request, I then thought of developing an automated Excel-based financial tool to generate P&Ls for different business scenarios. It was a big change for the commercial team and his full support to kick off the new tool and the new process within the commercial team would be required. He really backed me up, therefore the implementation was a success and finally all parties realized the benefits of the tool.

At about the same time, global CONSUMCO came up with the idea of a standard business planning tool for all its subsidiaries. There was to be a global rollout of the new tool, led by a global project team. This team's initial task was to gather input from all operating companies. Shahan nominated Madelyn as the area expert providing the input for the global team. Reviewing the scheme of the new tool, she found out that her "real-time" "what-if model" was far superior to the global model, which relied on sequential data processing. Madelyn saw the opportunity to improve the global tool by incorporating her "what-if model" into it. She took this up with Shahan. He agreed with her, and decided to make a proposal to the global team to adopt the local model in their impending rollout. To make this happen, he sent her over to the head office with one assignment; to convince and win over the global team.

> After this self-developed tool implementation in Asia, there was a global tool with the same objective, to be developed for CONSUMCO business planning, and Shahan sent me to the US to attend this meeting (on the tool implementation). It was a very stressful time for me as the global bundle shared with me prior to the visit was not a true "what-if modeling" tool, compared with the tool we developed in Asia. I shared this assessment with him before I left, and he said this was actually even better, that's why he wanted global to listen to our inputs, as we were much advanced in automation than the rest of the divisions and he wanted global to build Asia's request as part of the standard global bundle.
>
> Well, a small person like me with a small position at the time would not be able to convince global, especially to suggest changes to be made to global design. However, before I left he told me to call him any time for any support required, which I did.
>
> After my presentation, global team just said no to the requested change proposal from Asia. I then asked them to set up a teleconference with Shahan to hear his inputs before a final decision was made. This call was roughly around midnight local time, and he did call in. He said that he reviewed the proposal personally and the tool was successfully implemented in Asia. This was a great support to me as it was the right thing for CONSUMCO-T and it was about time for the change and finally it was approved. He told me later that prior to my call, one of the global executive committee members called him and said what I presented was valid and they would perform feasibility assessments with IT [information technology] before a final decision could be made. I guess people saw the true benefit. However, this involved change and most of the time change was always difficult to convince. Key learning was to strongly believe in yourself and that what you were doing was the right thing.

With strong support from Shahan, Madelyn successfully convinced the global team to incorporate her "what-if model" into the new tool. The global tool implementation was on a grand scale, involving not only finance teams from around the world but all other functions engaging in planning and budgeting activities. It also affected the way CONSUMCO companies all over the world did their planning and budgeting.

> It took them around two years to build the final global solution, called CONSUMCO Business Planning Tool. It took a longer time, as inputs from the rest of the divisions were also assessed and incorporated. The lucky part was the "what-if modeling" tool was a consistent requirement across the globe.

She became part of the leadership team implementing the new global tool in Asia. The project implementation was a success, with Madelyn and her team's contribution winning global recognition. They were flown into headquarters to receive the award from CONSUMCO's chief executive officer (CEO) in a grand annual corporate event. At this time, Madelyn began to gain not only global recognition but also became a member of the global finance network, as a subject matter expert in commercial finance.

> Yes, I was a member of a global community, referred to as Asia's subject matter expert in the area, and was also finance implementation lead of the global tool.
>
> Absolutely, this was one of the biggest achievements in CONSUMCO where we (cross-functional project team) won an achievement award for Asia's successful pilot implementation.

As mentioned earlier, the change was not only related to the tool but the whole planning and budgeting process.

> Key benefits include online live data automation, integration, simplification, and standardization, leading to efficiencies and time savings within the commercial process.
>
> In the new process, each month we have three critical cross-functional team meetings where output from one meeting feeds as inputs into the next meeting. The first meeting is where we identify business gaps by brand and by customer, then we get into a second meeting where we align the solutions to close gaps among the team, and the last meeting is where we propose and get management's approval on gap closure solutions.
>
> As with the integrated tool being in place, each function accesses data to identify gaps by itself, mainly top line; e.g., marketing identifies gaps from brand aspect, sales identify gaps from customer aspect, etc.
>
> This is not one function deciding. All gaps are put on the table and we all as cross-functional commercial team members look into the significance/implications of each gap to business, and align on the prioritization of gap closure solutions which we further propose to management for a final decision.

In the second meeting, once we know where the gaps are, a couple of solutions will be proposed and aligned among the commercial working team. Each solution proposal requires financial implications, thereby the what-if scenarios come into the picture.

Based on the final decision in the last meeting of the month, for approved items, cross-functional team members then get back and update data directly in the system, and not-approved items get dropped.

It's both top line and margin at company level. We consolidate a list of gap closure solutions across all sub-categories/brands, and many times sub-category mix helps contribute to company margin gap closure, thereby the consolidated gap closure lists get adjusted and once again aligned.

In all her recent initiatives, Madelyn gave credit to Shahan, who gave her both the opportunity and provided full moral support and recognition. He was her role model from whom she learned the importance of detailed analysis, challenging the status quo, and doing things differently and better.

He is very detail oriented and gets into the root cause of things (more or less the same as me). He keeps challenging me all the time. He is satisfied by accomplishments from my side, but he is always full of energy and the mind-set of raising the bar. For any request, his statement always starts with, "How can we do this differently?" and "How can we get even better?"

I have raised my own bar automatically, working closely with him. I start to think of the same questions and get prepared to answer these questions to him upfront for any assignments given.

Madelyn's experience of working closely with Shahan informed her of the importance of the role of the mentor in challenging and providing support to shore up confidence, enabling one to go beyond the normal frontier and raise the bar.

The best lesson learned from him is that I have learned to believe that there is nothing that we cannot do. To make any change, you yourself need to have complete faith that it will take you to a better place first. And then another critical path to achievement is the strong support from your boss who believes in you.

After about a year as MD, Shahan was promoted to regional president role. He relocated but kept in contact, calling Madelyn once in a while for her opinion on various matters. Vincente, the succeeding MD, was given a good brief on her profile and accomplishments from Shahan. He had also seen her presentation and was pleased with the quality of analysis from the budget team. He was also much impressed by the integrated customer and product P&L and the level of detailed analysis, saying he had not seen this anywhere else.

> I am lucky, I must say. I would give all credits to Shahan, as he was behind all this. He gave an orientation about each of his best people upfront to Vincente, and I was part of the name list.
>
> I made my first presentation in the Mancom meeting to Vincente and he was very impressed. He mentioned that he had never seen a complete integrated commercial presentation before and this was "one stop shopping." He said this in front of the management team, although he was meeting me for the first time. I was pretty surprised and very happy, as having a supportive boss was key to career success.

Vincente completely trusted Madelyn and relied on her in the area of commercial finance. He made her a permanent member of Mancom. He also invited her to join the official annual budget review. At one time he asked her to present CONSUMCO-T's budget to CONSUMCO's global CEO when Bert had not yet arrived to take up his new position.

> I recall, there was a review, and we were missing FD (during new FD transition phase). Vincente told me to present on FD's behalf. To be honest, I told him that I could comfortably present commercial finance section but not the operations finance aspect. He told me in a very confident manner that "I believe you can do both." With that said I was stressed out, but finally prepared thoroughly and went through the presentation smoothly. I guess the key to success was the faith leadership had in you. This made you try to be exceptionally perfect not to let him down.

Vincente had a background in sales. He was keen on the selling activities and looked for ways to improve their efficiency. He and Bert supported Madelyn in firmly establishing and expanding the role of her customer development team in providing support to CONSUMCO-T's sales team. The establishment of a customer development function in finance represented a breakthrough in CONSUMCO-T's finance function and was another of Madelyn's major contributions to CONSUMCO-T. It marked one of her major achievements in her long career life.

> I set up the finance department to support the sales team by channel, i.e., direct trade and indirect trade. The setup also included process simplification and standard analytics. I mirrored critical analytics and reporting in place from category/brand aspect (marketing support) to customer aspect (sales support.) As a result, we are now at the point where we are able to review a complete picture of brand P&Ls and key KPIs movement within key customers.

In the meantime, Bert gave Madelyn a free hand and necessary support. He initially invited her to join another two internal audit trips in Europe. However, these trips were different from her previous one. This time she was more confident about her area of expertise, and was able to recommend solutions and improvement that were relevant to the local management. They all appreciated her inputs. It was the first time they had met someone from finance who was highly knowledgeable about the business and commercial process. She began to build a strong network with these MDs and FDs, assisting them by providing advice whenever they called for help. By this time she was recognized within CONSUMCO's finance community as someone who was knowledgeable in commercial finance, and whose advice everyone sought. To expand Madelyn's network and firmly establish her position in the customer development area, Bert arranged for a personalized leadership learning program involving the US customer finance operation. This trip not only enriched her US business operation exposure but also provided her with an insight into the on-ground customer development supporting practice at the global office.

6.4.2 *Engaging in Commercial Practice, Creating Additional Value*

This period was when Madelyn firmly established the commercial finance function under the umbrella of CONSUMCO-T. She became a strong business partner for her local counterparts, and was widely recognized as an area expert in the CONSUMCO world. She enjoyed her daily activities. She found the customer and consumer aspects of commercial finance exciting compared with the traditional finance activities. One of the most memorable moments in her career was when Vincente nominated her to be the first CONSUMCO-T women's network leader, Asia chapter, thereby expanding her global networking beyond the finance community and firmly establishing her among Asian leadership communities.

One of the most memorable times with him (besides work in which he strongly supported me in everything I did, always put my name as the lead to any new global initiatives to be implemented) was when he proposed to global to let me lead the local CONSUMCO women's network establishment and be part of the division and global teams.

This was a very big event around CONSUMCO world, where women's leadership and career enhancements were the focus. For the launch, the worldwide CFO and COO came for a visit and Vincente asked me to make a presentation to both of them during the official kick-off.

To be honest, this was great respect that I had been given, as there were a couple of key women leaders in the company and he chose me. I did ask him again, "Are you sure you have finalized your decision?" I even proposed a name of one person (I thought was) appropriate to him (i.e., my commercial counterpart in customer development) as I felt she was a better fit. However, he said he had thought it through from all aspects and his decision was final. It was the greatest feeling being selected as a successful woman leader in the CONSUMCO world.

Vincente and Bert completed their local assignment and left at about the same time. Wake took over as the new FD, while Bill took over as the new MD. During this period Madelyn's engagement with local management became limited. She spent most of her time delving into the commercial side of business, engaging in various global and regional projects that represented not only the local country but also Asia as she was an expert in this area, and she built a stronger commercial network.

With my firm credibility built over years, global has always been referring to me to be part of all key future global finance initiatives, i.e., future 2020, new CONSUMCO integrated business planning process & tool, commercial analytics and management decks design: global bundle, etc. So I was pretty occupied with these global initiatives, representing Asia.

She began to be more interested in the regional role, working closely with Arne, the new regional finance vice-president, who incidentally reported to Shahan, her former boss who was at that point in time the leader of the Asia region.

There was a new regional finance vice-president, Arne. He came to one of the local reviews, and as part of one of the finance breakout sessions, there was a request to review the commercial finance overview. Assuming the role, I was assigned to do the presentation.

Arne saw my presentation for the first time and he was very impressed. He then requested me to help him implement my presentation deck in all Asian countries across the region, as he wanted to review exactly this presentation in all locations he landed. I finally fulfilled his wish with the implementation by connecting to each country's commercial finance lead and the FDs. Since then, we were connected and I felt all the support from behind the scenes to global was actually coming from him. By the way, the world is round, as Arne at the time reported to Shahan who was division president for Asia.

Arne was impressed with what Madelyn had prepared for him and decided to approach her to work for him.

We were pretty connected. After the first task, he then connected to me all along, working on a couple of regional projects whereby he asked whether I would mind helping him out (though not reporting to him). I told him that I was truly happy to do so, as I was actually receiving the best learning opportunity and this helped broaden my business perspective, having a broader view of different business processes and dynamics across different countries in Asia.

He also asked me whether I would like to work for him in a regional role and I said yes right away on one condition, i.e., I needed to be based locally, and he accommodated my request. After a year and a half I then moved into regional division as he created a role for me as finance director—commercial finance for Asia division.

After this appointment, Madelyn continued to participate in global projects and lead the regional ones. She assisted in establishing a commercial finance function in all Asian countries, thereby gaining wider recognition and expanding her network to an even wider extent.

For the first time in Asia we implemented customer development team for finance organization being set up across all countries within Division. This covered all aspects, starting with people, process, and tools. We started off with thorough as-is analysis of what level of support was provided on the ground in each country. This was a critical foundation to be further built upon. We then designed the goal, i.e., the ideal to-be stage of what we wanted to achieve in future, within the next three years.

This firstly involved aligning the organization structure and reporting line, roles and responsibilities alignment across all countries, standardization of reporting tool and elevating analytics. In order to get to the ideal stage, we implemented the change via a roadmap approach with local management's support. This was a big success and involved significant change management. In a year and a half, we were actually tracking ahead of the roadmap and were recognized by global finance as best in class division in terms of progress and success in place versus the rest of the divisions.

In her role as Asian commercial finance director, Madelyn had transformed herself into a strong business partner for her commercial counterparts in all countries, regionally and globally. Her finance network became even stronger.

From her long experience, she summed up what it was to be a business partner and an active member of the commercial practice:

Being a true commercial person is how you get accepted within commercial organization, management, and global level. We need to have solid finance ground which is the foundation; however, the key is the ability to communicate, negotiate, influence the team with commercial language and not finance language.

One critical ability required is (the ability) to be able to link external information/data into internal financials. Understanding different business scenarios on the ground, in different locations (being realistic) is another key success factor in making successful decisions/implementations in a regional role. There is no one rule that could be applied to all. Understanding details of how the business is run in different locations, the trade dynamics, etc., will help contribute to quality assessments and resolution/recommendations.

Networking is another important factor that leads to successful implementations ... Sharing of best practices in order not to reinvent the wheel ... Once people know you and your reputation, they are much easier to convince.

On communication, she placed importance on presentation skills, in other words the ability to present information from the management's angle. She said that hers was much improved under Arne's guidance.

I also learned to upgrade my presentation skills. This is another very important skill set. Arne really spent time with me and taught me how the presentation should be completed for different audiences. He requested me to present in Asia's FDs meeting, Asia's commercial directors meeting (marketing and sales directors), regional management meeting, etc. Once

I went through all these meetings' presentation a couple of times the confidence became firmly established.

He was also satisfied with the outcome, and later comfortably asked me to prepare different presentations for him. I still remember he said to me, "If in one slide you cannot deliver three key messages, you lose the attention of management."

Her experience also confirmed her honest approach.

Being yourself, being honest is also very important. Facts need to be communicated to the leadership; no matter it is good news or bad news. Having the mindset of celebrating success and at the same time looking into further enhancements for opportunities is a required attitude for success.

After Arne was promoted to the global role and relocated back to headquarters, Jeane succeeded him as the new regional finance vice president. Having seen Madelyn's presentation for the first time, after being briefed about her by Arne, he formed a complete trust in her and continued to give her a free hand, providing her with all the necessary support she needed.

Jeane was my next boss. He was a very quiet/polite character but a very sincere and nice person. He trusted me starting day one as well. He spoke very little and gave me all the liberty to do the right thing, as he believed in my expertise in the area. I think Arne was behind this strong support transition. Therefore, I exercised all my skill set built over the years even more and more.

Besides the support of her bosses, support from her own team was also important. Madelyn supported internal on-the job training for her team members in the same manner that she herself had been trained. She personally and closely trained most of her team members, in effect becoming not only their direct boss but also their mentor.

After she became the budget manager of CONSUMCO-T, Madelyn recruited two Masters of Business Administration (MBAs) with prior experience in financial analysis to join her team, Star and Jane. Star was a certified public accountant (CPA) and an MBA, with the benefit of knowledge of detailed analysis and the bigger picture. She was assigned to oversee reporting at company level, the company's P&L and operating expenses, for example, including monthly estimates. She also took care of analysis of one of the product categories. She worked closely with Madelyn on the monthly estimate. Jane, on the other hand, came with an MBA and detailed analysis experience from a food retail environment. She was analytical and highly skillful in the art of Excel spreadsheets. It was Jane who used these skills to build the standard worksheets used by the finance analysts and the standard input sheet used by marketing. She also helped to build the standard workbook that consolidated the "brand snapshot," with an underlying macro mechanism for Madelyn.

> They all have solid Finance background, MBA with honors with GPA [grade point average] 3.5 and more from abroad and Bachelors from the local first-tiered business school.
>
> Training depended on which role they came into. For example, Star, she came into a reporting role and was responsible for divisional and corporate reporting. In this role, you needed to have a bigger picture of things, for example, performing total company's estimated P&Ls, spending analysis, and general ledger reconciliation for auditors both external and corporate. She had CPA and therefore the job fit her educational background and expertise.
>
> After she settled in, [I] expanded her assignment to cover customer P&Ls key KPIs analysis, customer spending analysis, etc. (more or less mirroring analysis completed from category/brand dimension). She did a good job, as this was still the big picture but applying logical thinking and an analytical skill set. It's critical to have the team member understanding the big picture and at the same time be able to get into details, to understand key drivers behind the numbers.
>
> Another example, Jane, who was the opposite [of Star], very detail oriented, logical thinking, holding strong analytical and computer skills. So she came in as category manager, in charge of analytics from all category/brand perspective. She developed a great excel tool that could link different sets of data from SAP system, [and build a] key database to further perform second level analytics. She enhanced the tool even further by putting all automated formulas, to calculate key KPIs movements between any comparison periods automatically, e.g., quantifying average selling price points, percentage margin points splits, etc. This role was a tougher role, as for category/brand dimension in order to be able to identify mix movements between periods, we needed to get down to the lowest detailed level which is SKU.
>
> In terms of scope, this was much bigger, as this covered all category/sub-categories we had in the CONSUMCO portfolio … In addition, there were several brand splits within each sub-category as well…

> We were lucky to have her; she had strong analytical skills coming from a major US quick service restaurant chain.

While Jane provided support for the product analysis Star covered the customer front. They both assisted Madelyn in the implementation of the standard planning tools and system.

> After a year or a year and a half of joining CONSUMCO-T, we implemented budget and planning, for the first time with a standardized planning tool within SAP.

This new tool was an integrated tool within SAP, so both actual and planning data were available and could be accessed within this same tool, by copying actual data in.

> It led to standardization having all inputs with one same number reference across functions in one tool, a lot of time savings from prior process in gathering data with (no more) different formats, different source templates in the rollup P&Ls, as the new tool provided integrated information.
>
> Yes, we developed standard upload templates for different lines of P&Ls assumptions to be provided cross-functionally. At least now within cross category marketing teams, we had one aligned template in place to be used by all.
>
> Based on all key assumptions uploaded into the system, we then had the system perform a valuation to arrive at complete brand P&Ls. It's all automation, no need for manual calculations generating each line P&Ls and KPIs formula as in the past. However, inputs were critical as the system only did processing work. We needed to ensure accuracy and quality of inputs across functions or else it's garbage in garbage out.

With this tool in place, time was freed up to be spent on more value added analysis. Madelyn was proud of her team's quality and power of analysis, and it was recognized as the best in Asia.

After the global budget and planning was rolled out, she recruited Julie and Anne into the team to help Star and Jane cover the increase in business activity. The new recruits came in with less experience and required more training. Madelyn took part in this training. In the same way that she had coached Star and Jane, she first gave them a category to analyze, then moved them cross-category to learn about the complexity of the business. After that it was the broader picture of the whole company. In the process she was able to identify who was more analytical and suitable for the category analyses work, for example. In the process Madelyn emphasized detailed analysis. She insisted that analysis had to go down to the level of SKUs, so they would understand the business complexity.

> The lucky part was (that) the automation and analytical reporting tool was already firmly in place. Therefore, basic analysis could easily be completed by any analyst. However, more time was spent coaching them on delivering quality top line/key bullets/key drivers analysis. I always read each and every analyst's analyses completed and provided them all with prior analysis in place as reference materials, so they had a feel on what could be key drivers to KPIs movements in the P&Ls. I tried to let them stand on their own and be independent. After one round of detailed explanation coaching with each by myself, I then started to have them complete analysis on their own, and then I reverted to many detailed questions when their analysis performed was not on track. Also, I requested them to send off their analysis directly to management without my prior review. They got many questions at the beginning and I helped guide each of them in the right direction. This direct connect to management helped them become more careful and ensure their analysis was sound before releasing it. Though I had direct reports, I still connected with each analyst directly with any specific questions I had and always spent time to coach them for better quality outcome (monthly basis).
>
> I encouraged/forced all analysts to attend commercial meetings of their own sub-categories in their charges, also to get external with sales team to see and understand our 5Ps strategy on shelf. In addition, I had them lead mini projects, task force, STAs [short-term assignments], do presentations in monthly meetings, etc., in order to let them have business exposure and become more confident.
>
> My own experiences, attending all commercial meetings, business reviews, Mancom meetings, etc., helped, plus I am detailed oriented myself. Actually, questions being asked in the meeting by top management are the best insights to elevate quality of analytics. I slowly absorbed all these business questions and each time ensured we prepare a couple of steps ahead as solid back up in case any questions got repeated, which most of the time they did. Shahan was the best source of all great questions that could come up in reviews, and we had to be prepared for them.

In Madelyn's view, to be a good business partner one would need to be good at numbers (analytical), knowledgeable about financial reports, open and willing to learn new things, and be flexible enough to adapt to changes.

It would be helpful if one had a prior financial analysis experience in the same business environment.

> Besides, numbers/internal financials (P&Ls), another key learning is to open up and learn, get updates/inputs on what is going on in the market (growth, shares, trend), our competitors'/customers' performance/promotion plans, and link them back to our internal (CONSUMCO's) KPIs, in order to understand different implications to our business across categories and key customers.
>
> Solid finance background is (the) key, with MBA abroad. The latter leads to openness to learn new things/new ways and being flexible to adapt to changes.

After gaining enough experience, one was ready and confident. All one needed was the opportunity to shine. Madelyn was happy to oblige, providing one would go an extra mile the same way she did.

> It comes with experiences and knowing firmly your own stuff, with thorough analysis as backup in place. The acceptance will be gained when you slowly start speaking up with confidence in the meetings, leading to the next level of confidence being built, being able to do finance presentations in meetings. It takes time to build credibility over years and needs to be earned. Providing opportunity for team members to speak up when they are ready is critical.
>
> Another tip, you must coach your team members to always go an extra mile in working with commercial cross-functional counterparts or management.

6.5 The Lifelong Self-Orienting Process

From a Business Partner Development Model perspective, Madelyn's lifelong self-orienting process is about continuous improvement and adding value towards the end of being a "true" business partner, in her words a member of the commercial practice who is recognized and accepted by commercial peers. Among other key actions, there features the (additional) acquiring of practical understanding, which is prevalent throughout most of the management accountants' career, being the typical action of the self-orienting processas continuous change is faced; and creating value action that has not been observed in the previous cases. The latter represents the hallmark action indicative of being the business partner and occurs later in the career, after one has gained sufficient practical knowledge and skill in sharing financial expertise while being actively engaged in commercial practice (Table 6.1).

Table 6.1 List of actions and key milestones of commercial finance career

Being controller	*Being budget manager*	*Being associated finance director*	*Being commercial finance director-Asia division*
Acquiring practical know-how			
Acquiring practical understanding	Gaining practical understanding	Acquiring additional practical understanding	Gaining additional practical understanding
	Sharing the practice	Sharing the practice	Sharing the practice
	Engaging in commercial practices	Engaging in commercial practices	Engaging in commercial practices
	Creating value	Creating additional value	Creating additional value

All of the actions related to the self-orienting process contain various activities that are aimed at specific goals. These include willingly joining the initial short-term local audit assignment in order to gain an understanding of the overall local operation and the nature of the FMCG business, thus being able to effectively apply the budget and reporting knowledge and skill acquired from previous work experience to the new business context, thereby improving the current budget system and adding value and winning acceptance from new peers as a highly competent budget manager. These purposeful actions are aligned through short-term goals forming a lifelong self-orienting process geared towards the end goal of becoming a business partner (Fig. 6.1). Compared with the previous two cases of Carol and Anne, Madelyn's lifelong self-orienting process is distinguished by the crucial action of creating additional values that are found to be associated with a high degree of business orientation and a hallmark of becoming a business partner.[1]

6.5.1 *Self-Orienting Process, Teleoaffective Structure*

For Madelyn, what matters most (motivation) is continuing to add value to her organization. At CONSUMCO-T she capitalizes on her wealth of knowledge and experience and innovates in terms of a new reporting system,

[1]Chotiyanon, P. (2018). Becoming A Business Partner, a lifelong self-orienting process. (Doctoral dissertation) Grenoble Ecole de Management, Grenoble, France.

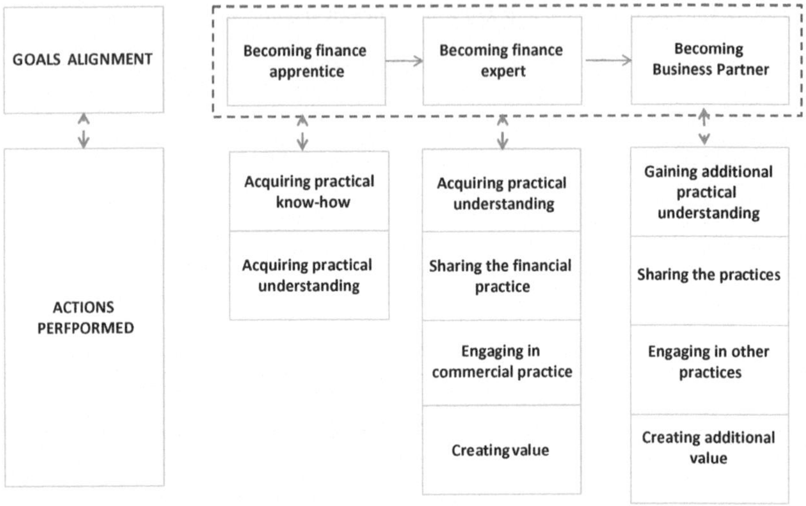

Fig. 6.1 Self-orienting process, commercial finance director

new analytics, a new way of doing things in various sub-practices, such as budgeting, commercial finance, and customer development, in order to add value to the new organization that she joins, in order to win acceptance and trust from her colleagues, in order to open more opportunities for further improvement, in order to add value, and so on. By always looking for ways to do things better, she leads a life of continuous improvement, seeking to constantly add value to her organization and thus incrementally increasing her wealth of experience on her way to becoming business partner, her end goal. These purposeful initiatives are associated with certain emotions-in-action or "affectivities" (Schatzki 2001, 2002). From her story, Madelyn is proud of her achievements, exhilarated when what she believes in and has been working for materializes and is well accepted. She is most happy when winning trust and respect. Her long career is dotted with several moments of pride, jubilation, and elation when her many accomplishments are being recognized and celebrated, for example when she successfully implements her first breakthrough in the area of management reporting: the "brand snapshot" capturing the gist of the market operation vis-à-vis strategic and operational plans with underlying details about the brand's actual performance versus the plan in key dimensions, such as sales volume, price, trade promotion, media spending, and cost of materials, which has been recog-

Table 6.2 Self-orienting and teleoaffective structure – commercial finance director

Motivations (things that matter)	*Affectivities (emotions-in-action)*	*Self-orienting activities*	*Goals*	*Ends*
Continuous improvement Adding value	Being excited about commercial initiatives	Getting actively involved in commercial activities	Being commercial finance manager	Being business partner
Being recognized, accepted, winning trust	Pride, love, joy	Innovating in terms of process, tools, and people		

nized as the best in class and is widely used in global corporate reporting, regional offices, and many countries in the CONSUMCO world solidifying her position in the global commercial finance community; the roll-out of the global planning tool with her initiative in the as-if modeling; the establishment of a global women network; and most importantly the establishment of a customer development function in CONSUMCO-T, which became the roll-out model for other countries. All these initiatives, which were aimed at making the lives of her commercial peers better, are imbued with Madelyn's love and joy in engaging in commercial practice, and the pride of being recognized and accepted as one of the key members of CONSUMCO's commercial practice has led her on the path to become a well-accepted and well-recognized business partner, her ultimate goal (Table 6.2).

6.5.2 *Self-Orienting, Personal Characteristics, and Affectivity*

Compared with the previous two cases, Madelyn seems to have a significantly higher degree of business orientation, which is manifested in the manner in which she engages in commercial practice. Madelyn is open to new opportunity, as in the case of Carol and Anne, but she is also more proactive, seeking to add value by innovating in ways that make things better in terms of process, tools, and people. Besides this she is detail oriented, hands on, and most importantly honest and straightforward. These personal characteristics are reflected in the way she provides realistic recommendations or advice, which are supported by solid detailed analysis that makes sense under current market conditions, in an honest manner, thereby winning respect and acceptance from her peers. She also has an

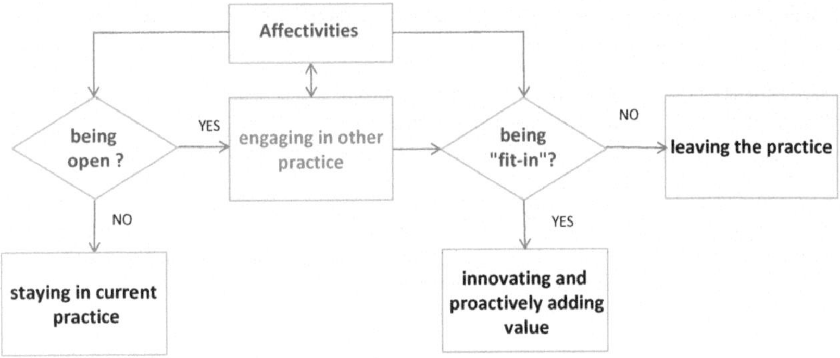

Fig. 6.2 Turning point: Asian commercial finance director

overall perspective, gained from her years of experience doing bottom up analyses at MANCO-T (past practices), which is helpful when negotiating or orchestrating contesting goals in the commercial meeting in which experts from different practices, such as sales, marketing, supply chain, and finance, participate. Most importantly she is passionate about commercial activities. These personal characteristics distinguish her from our other cases and contribute to her high degree of business orientation.

To Madelyn, moving from MANCO-T to CONSUMCO-T is to move from a relative "boring" and stable industrial goods market in which drastic changes, such as the oil price shock, are rare, to the exciting FMCG market where changes are the norm. Within this new dynamic business context, "fitting in" (Fig. 6.2) to her is more than adjusting to the status quo but rather involves taking initiatives to innovate, to change the way in which things relate to market development. This includes being external oriented, and having regular meetings with customers to align goals and coordinating activities. It is this passion for commercial activities as manifested in her proactive commercial engagement that contributes to her higher degree of business orientation than her colleagues in the two previous cases (Fig. 6.2).

This passion for commercial activities is manifested in "affectivity" (Table 6.2) while engaging in the commercial activities. For example, she is always excited about new product launches, new sales deals, and so on. The positive "emotions-in-action" drive her to take the initiative to pay regular visits to retail stores to see the uptake of newly launched products and competitors' reactions to the launches, or to go to convenience stores to check on competitors' pricing campaigns. Gathering market intelligence on her own, out of her own interest and beyond the call of duty, is aimed at being "on the ground," keeping herself fully abreast of the current market situation. The acquired knowledge in combination with learning about non-financial KPIs such as "share-of-voice" or "share-of-the-wallet" from regular participating in the commercial meetings enables her to talk the "commercial talk" in a convincing manner, thereby winning respect and acceptance from her peers and putting her on the path to becoming a "true" business partner, one who is recognized as an equal member of the commercial practice and not an outsider from financial practice.[2]

6.5.3 *Self-Orienting, Cultural Context, and Affectivity*

In the same manner as previous cases, Madelyn's business orientation is positively influenced by the supportive culture of CONSUMCO-T in terms of mentoring and coaching from her direct bosses. This supportive organizational culture makes her confident enough to take on new challenges related to commercial practice. Madelyn is fortunate in the sense that she has had successive support from her direct bosses, which is not always the case. This support comes in the form of mentoring and sponsoring. David, her first direct boss, recruited her into CONSUMCO, arranged for her to get oriented to the CONSUMCO-T business through a short internal audit assignment, and encouraged her to engage in commercial practice. He gave her a free hand in budgeting and planning as well as commercial finance. He was happy that she worked closely with both local management and Shahan in providing a financial planning and controlling service and developing new tools for management. However, it was Shahan who shared the passion for analytics and taught her about focusing on details, providing her with new challenges and the necessary support and recognition. In this sense Shahan was her mentor and role model whereas David was her sponsor, taking care of the formal career plan administration and providing supports in daily life. Later, Vincente and Bert took the roles of mentor and sponsor respectively. After Vincente

[2] In her words, it's about "how you are accepted" by your commercial team. This has a very important implication. First engaging in the commercial practice does not guarantee that one is a business partner (Morales and Lambert 2013). Second, how one is being accepted indicates various degrees of being the business partner, which in MM's case seems to be very high. In fact, she is accepted as an equal member by her peers.

and Bert she found both sponsor and mentor in Arne, the regional vice-president and her direct boss. Having gained a solid ground with a substantial level of experience, becoming the expert in her area of practice, Madelyn became less and less dependent on her mentor. Thereafter, Jeane, the successor of Arne and her direct boss, became her sponsor, and he continues to support her in everyday life—but he is not a mentor in the sense of Shahan, Vincente, or Arne.

With strong support and inspiration from her direct bosses, in particular David and Shahan, Madelyn has been one of the leading forces towards a new commercially driven culture at CONSUMCO-T. In the past, it was normal for the sales function just to focus on sales numbers using all available means to reach an annual sales target, with the marketing function thinking only about launching new products according to planned schedules within planned media spending, and supply chains and other supporting functions focusing on watching their respective costs in line with the allocated budget. These actions were formerly coordinated through the strategic plan and operating budgets. Each functional leader had to meet target performance as measured by specific KPIs that were related to the approved operating budget, such as target sales and overall level of profit. On a monthly basis the management committee reviewed the performance against the budget. Usually there was no major adjustment to the plan during these monthly reviews, as long as the overall target profit and sales levels were being met. Major adjustments to the plan might occur during the mid-year review when actual performance was compared to the budget across the regions. This top-down approach changed when Shahan became the MD and implemented the so-called "commercial discipline." This was all about "breaking the silos" and forcing organizational members to think in terms of commercial success, or "profitable growth," for example, no more high sales growth with heavy trade or media spending. Supporting this move, Madelyn and her team drew upon their financial knowledge and skill and introduced to the sales team the concept of return on investment for trade spending. Most importantly, the commercial-driven culture was facilitated by one of Madelyn's major reporting innovations, the three-dimensional P&L statement, with supporting details by products, customers, and trade channels, which provides the picture of how all actions are integrated in delivering the top and bottom line. In the current monthly commercial meeting, key players from sales, marketing, supply chain, and finance, refer to this P&L statement in discussing the market situation, with its gaps and opportunities, agreeing on joint actions before moving on to make proposals to the management committee in the monthly management meeting.

Madelyn's case highlights the influence of not only a supportive organizational culture but also the change in management philosophy on her business orienting and her related degree of business orientation. It demonstrates how the change in management philosophy (Granlund and Lukka 1998; Burns and Baldvinsdottir 2005) from product oriented at MANCO-T to customer oriented at CONSUMCO-T gave her an opportunity to engage more in the business, leading to a higher degree of orientation towards business. On the other hand, the way she works, collaborating activities across functional lines and adding various initiatives, has also contributed to changes in corporate culture at CONSUMCO-T, from functional oriented to commercially driven, leading all organizational members to be more business oriented, to the degree that is indicated by their level of engagement in commercial practice. In addition, the way in which Madelyn works demonstrates how past practice guides present practice, in her emphasis on detailed analysis together with the "big picture" view, which is the approach she has been using since her early days at MANCO-T.

In Madelyn's lifelong self-orienting process, the highlights have been innovation and the creation of value (in terms of process, tools, and people) as the hallmark of being a business partner. It also demonstrates that besides the internal inherent elements, such as personal goals, characteristics, and motivation; the external elements, such as organizational and corporate cultures, can significantly influence the self-orienting process towards business in terms of its direction as well as its extent. Finally, this case suggests that a passion for commercial activities and other positive "emotions-in-action", that manifest themselves during the time when the management accountants engage in commercial practice, are the key indicators pointing to the potential of becoming a business partner with a high degree of business orientation.

References

Burns, J., & Baldvinsdottir, G. (2005). An institutional perspective of accountants' new roles – The interplay of contradictions and praxis. *European Accounting Review, 14*(4), 725–757.

Granlund, M., & Lukka, K. (1998). Towards increasing business orientation: Finnish management accountants in a changing cultural context. *Management Accounting Research, 9*, 185–211.

Morales, J., & Lambert, C. (2013). Dirty work and the construction of identity. An ethnographic study of management accounting practices. *Accounting, Organizations and Society, 38*, 228–244.

Schatzki, T. R. (2001). Practice theory: An introduction. In T. R. Schatzki, K. Knorr Cetina, & E. von Savigny (Eds.), *The practice turn in contemporary theory* (pp. 1–14). London: Routledge.

Schatzki, T. R. (2002). *The site of the social: A philosophical account of the constitution of social life and change.* University Park: Pennsylvania State University Press.

CHAPTER 7

Management Control Career

> *...logic and adaptability ... are the most important... You adapt. You must have logic to be able to convince [the people].* (Alain's comment on "Adapting")

Alain is a retired managing director (MD) of MANCO-T, a subsidiary of MANCO one of the top-three German chemical conglomerates. He has been practicing finance for twenty-five years. He is a highly knowledgeable finance practitioner who is passionate about his work. He is logical and adaptable as well as a strategic thinker with a long-term view. In telling his story he is candid, open, and honest.

Unlike other cases Alain has neither formal financial education nor any kind of business training prior to embarking on his financial career. As such he views his career as a lifelong adapting project. In order to adapt to the new and changing environment he orients himself toward management, alternately acquiring the technical knowledge, practical understanding (Schatzki 2002), sharing the practice, engaging in other practices, creating additional value until he finally becomes a key member of the management committee up to his retirement in late 1990s. In this chapter we follow the key actions taken along his four major career milestones: as planning manager, as finance and account manager, as deputy administration manager,

P. Chotiyanon, V. Joannidès de Lautour,
The Changing Role of the Management Accountants,
https://doi.org/10.1007/978-3-319-90300-2_7

as CECO director in order to gain an understanding about his lifelong self-orienting process towards business.[1] Based on the Business Partner Development Model (BPDM), this process can be organized into three micro-processes: becoming a finance apprentice, a financial expert, and a business partner. At the same time we demonstrate how his lifelong self-orienting is influenced by changing management philosophy and business contexts, and also motivated by his concern for business continuity through teleoaffective orchestration, highlighting the extended role of a financial practitioner beyond business partner to change agent. We finally show how corporate culture influences Alain's course of action, and how his course of action in turn contributes to a new corporate culture.

7.1 Becoming a Planning Manager (1973–1975)

7.1.1 Acquiring Technical Knowledge

Alain spent almost ten years studying in the southern part of Germany until he graduated magna cum laude with a Master's in Mathematics from the famous University of Munich. With this educational background, he began investigating career opportunity in the assurance business. Earning a perfect 1.0 point under the German educational performance measurement system meant he was offered a job with a prestigious insurance company in the southern part of Germany. Unfortunately he had to turn it down as his father asked him to return home, which he did in 1973. He was invited for interviews with some big local insurance companies through his family's business network, and, wanting to find out more about the companies and the people he was going to work with he went along to the interviews and looked around.

> I went to TS Assurance ... I went to visit their office opposite the main railway station. When I saw tons of documents piling around and there was an "old man" taking care of the computer [department] I gave up ... There was a woman, a graduate from a very famous local university, talking to me. Her English was not very good ... The [TS] owner had asked me to start the next day. But I felt I'd better not.

Alain found himself more attracted to well-established international companies. After a few more job applications he was offered a good job by

[1] Central Executive Coordinating Office, an equivalent of German "Zentraldirectionabteilung".

a local subsidiary of one of the American assurance companies. However, the position they offered him was based in Hong-Kong. Again, he had to turn this down owing to his family obligations. As he was not very mobile, he also tried to find a job outside his area of expertise. He found teaching at a local university interesting, but unfortunately the pay was not sufficient for a young graduate who was trying to make a living in the capital city. In the end he went for an interview with another big local insurance company, which was located in the central business district. Arriving a bit early, he looked around. There in the same building was MANCO-T, a subsidiary of MANCO, one of the top three German chemical companies. He walked in, made a few enquiries, dropped a copy of his résumé with their human resources (HR) department, and left. And that was how his long work relationship with MANCO-T began.

At that time Podi, a delegate from MANCO, was MANCO-T's administration director. He was in charge of all supporting functions for local sales and production, including finance and accounts. Alain's outstanding academic profile from one of the most famous universities in Germany caught his attention. Seeing his potential contribution to the company, Podi decided to persuade him to work for MANCO-T. He invited Alain over for an interview. During this, Alain brought up his concern about his lack of a relevant business background, to which Podi responded that in his opinion Alain could literally do anything with such an outstanding educational background. They then discussed the four jobs that MANCO-T was willing to offer: assistant to the MD, assistant to the sales division manager, Electronic Data Processing (EDP) department head, and an assistant to Podi in the administration division. Afterwards he arranged for Alain to meet the MD. After this meeting Alain felt good about the company and accepted the job as Podi's assistant. When asked why he had chosen this particular job, he simply said, "I thought he [Podi] was a nice person."

For Alain the first month at MANCO-T was rather quiet. The incumbent assistant briefly showed him the report he manually prepared for Podi: the departmental income statement. Alain helped with some of the manual calculations. Occasionally he helped out with the translation of the report instructions from German to English. He kept his German fluent by socializing with his German boss, the secretary, and other German managers in the organization.

In the first month with MANCO-T, he found himself having "nothing much to do," so he began perusing the German operation manuals and some of the accounting reports sent to Podi's office.

> I was assisting Suchart [the incumbent assistant]... We prepared an income statement on a long sheet of paper, preparing a report...
>
> ...I read all the books [manuals]. Suchart did all the work. Suchart gave me a little brief. I talked with Sani [the secretary] in German all the time.
>
> When there was a new [reporting] requirement coming in, at that time in German, I translated it for Suchart. I read all the books [manuals] of MANCO. I read [about] "class-4" [operating], "class-2" [non-operating] income/expenses, stock reports every day until I got tired. What I was helping Suchart with was adding the numbers. I was so bored.

Among the operation manuals he found one, *Handbuch des Auslandesgesellschaft*, containing important information about MANCO's management and control system. From this Alain learned about the legal structure governing the relations among companies within the MANCO group; that is, how they were organized into subsidiaries and associated companies, including the decision rights and reporting requirement. He also learned about how businesses were grouped in business divisions (*Bereiche*), cutting across the boundary of the legal entities, and what groups of products went into each business division. In short, the manual helped him to understand MANCO's control matrix, its company and divisional structure, which governed the activities of all the legal entities and business divisions that spread all over the world. For example, the MD of the local operation was accountable for the overall performance of all companies located within the country. At the same time, each divisional head in MANCO-T who reported directly to the local MD also had a dotted reporting line to his/her head of related division in Frankfurt. In addition to the company's controlling structure, Alain also learned about planning and control process from the manual. He studied the planning cycle in detail, learning who was to do what on which timeline together with the related performance monitoring process, in other words the comparison of the actual with the budget numbers, as well as the reporting system, including specimens of reports to be prepared and submitted, together with the detailed description of all reporting lines.

From another document, MANCO's chart of accounts manual or the *Kostenrechnung Handbuch*, Alain learned about MANCO's cost structure and the definition of each individual account. He gained knowledge about how individual accounts were grouped into accounting categories, such as sales, cost of goods sold, operating and non-operating expenses, inventory, and accounts receivable (AR), and how each category was classified in the financial reports, the income statement and the balance sheet. Having learned accounting by himself, he was able to distinguish between accounting for management purposes (management accounting) and financial accounting for external statutory reporting, and he focused his attention on the former.

> Know a little about the balance sheet, know about the profit and loss. The balance sheet is the most important, then the profit and loss.
>
> For practical use, you take the numbers for practical use.
>
> Take them in managing.
>
> Right … How to make the balance sheet look nice and stable.
>
> The balance sheet will tell us … how much AR or stock we have… We have bad customers, other liabilities … we can see everything.
>
> The accounting system is about booking in and out, we have no interest there. But we have to understand the system of profit and loss and the balance sheet, that's all.

Going through the manual several times on his own, Alain had gained a great deal of knowledge about MANCO's accounting structure for reporting purposes. He was well equipped with all the necessary technical knowledge and was waiting for a chance to use it.

7.1.2 Acquiring Practical Understanding

In the early days, noticing that Alain was beginning to get bored because he had nothing specific to do, Podi began to assign him some tasks that he believed would require Alain to apply his mathematical skill to practical ends. First he asked Alain to prepare a simple price index for the stationery supplies.

> He asked me to study purchasing … I studied the buying of box files. How many [were bought], [same for] pencils, etc. I did a comparison to show where we bought the stuff from and how much [we pay for it]. Most of the time there was only one supplier. I showed statistics to see how prices varied.

With this exercise Alain demonstrated how to use an index as a new way to monitor the purchasing activities. Unfortunately it seemed that no one took his report seriously. He felt frustrated that he was not able to contribute to the maximum of his potential and so decided to leave.

> I wanted to resign because I had no work to do. Podi was concerned. I said I had no work and was so bored. I had studied so much and I had nothing to do. Crow [the current MD who] was about to leave came into the room and tapped on my shoulder, saying, "Take it easy!"

Crow not only managed to persuade Alain to stay but also gave him some of the most important career advice: the importance of obtaining detailed practical knowledge and understanding from the ground up.

> Learn all the small things ... You must learn from the bottom up before you can manage.

He began to follow this advice by spending his free time reviewing all kinds of reports that were sent to Podi's office.

> [I gained] experience from Podi. At the beginning Podi asked, "Why you did not question these three [items]?" After one month Podi stopped questioning. I did not have to ask him again as I knew it all. I became an expert on class 4 [operating expenses], income statement.

Practicing analyzing, Alain gained a deeper understanding about the nature and behavior of the accounts, which when combined with the knowledge he had acquired earlier about the management reporting system, enabled him to fulfill a planning report requirement that had been an issue at MANCO-T for quite a while.

> ...at that time there was Forms 72–75, new forms for budget planning. Susan [finance and account manager at the time] did it but it was incorrect.

Alain saw this issue as a simple mathematical problem of "balancing the pluses and the minuses" and a perfect opportunity to apply the technical knowledge that he had acquired through self-studying. He offered to help.

> ...we needed to close its pluses/minuses. Susan did this but she could not close it: the pluses were not equal to the minuses. I did it and it was correct. We submitted it to headquarters.
>
> Once they saw that I was capable they threw it all to me, including the planning job. Even though I had not obtained an official position I helped out.

Being knowledgeable, open, and ready to help with the "problematic" planning reports had opened an opportunity for Alain to engage in MANCO's reporting practice. With his acquired technical knowledge and practical understanding of the nature and behavior of the accounts, he was able to prepare a realistic forecast before taking over the whole of MANCO's reporting requirement.

> ...in five days we have actual sales [numbers] so we [could] estimate the profit and loss and submitted it over. ... Little by little after that we took over all of the reporting requirements.

At about the same time Stolzen, the new MD, began to ask Alain to prepare for ad hoc analyses that would aid in the decision-making process. This kind of exercise not only helped in developing his keen analytical skill but also prompted Alain to delve deeper into the business operation to get more information, thereby enabling him to gradually learn about the ongoing business.

> Stolzen started to ask me to do stuff.
>
> From having nothing much to do but wanting to learn I had learned a lot. You learned about the inside [operation] of the company...
>
> ...you knew the on-going of each department...
>
> ...what they sold, how many people they had, how much the gross margin was, what product was the most important for them in order to make a profit.

Alain always made himself ready and available to help out even when it was not in his domain of work. By being "open" and "ready" he was able to expand his work horizon, learning more about other practices and broaden his career opportunity at the same time.

Performing ad hoc analyses for the MD he was able to detect the gap in the management information needs, and was able to fill it with the most relevant and realistic data, thereby opening the way for him to play a role in the management control practice.

Schummer was very weak. When there was any question in the MK meeting he could not answer it at all. King [an industrial sales division manager] could not answer the question either. So Stolzen said, "Let's have Alain join in the meeting."

So I went into the meeting. [In there] I had become somewhat of a hero. Whatever they asked I could answer.

7.1.3 Creating Value

Alain felt good about being involved in the management control practice. He became passionate about his work and began to create value in the form of new analytic tools. Besides sales information, Stolzen was also concerned about the cost of products, in particular those of locally manufactured goods. However, the relevant data was not readily available. To get the needed information from the existing data processing system was rather complicated. Alain decided to do this manually. Applying his mathematical logic, he built a simple calculation model to forecast future product cost, based on the variation in the raw material prices. He called his piece of paper a "pre-calculation sheet," and it was the first break-through in the management reporting system at MANCO-T.

I knew the [production] formula of each product. So if you had 20 products you had 20 formulas. I [For example], Mowil 135 [a finished product]... used VAM [main raw material] 70% overhead fixed [at] 15%. If the price of VAM went up by 5% the total product cost would rise by this much. At that time there was no PC [personal computer] ... Wanda [data processing manager] did not want to run [prepare] the [simulation] reports. [She said] she had to run [process] all the data for all of the seven plants at the same time...

I asked ... Suda [a cost accountant], "For 20 products you could do it in half a day." I did not have to depend on Wanda...

The same for Agricultural [products]... We have to watch Delta-M prices.

Podi was happy about Alain's accomplishments and arranged for a short visit for Alain to the headquarters in order to acquaint himself with MANCO's system and culture. At the headquarters there was a high level of concern about the fact that MANCO-T seemed to be struggling with meeting their reporting requirement. However, this was of no concern to Alain. With his newly acquired knowledge he was quite confident that he could deliver whatever was required.

...It was a big problem for other people but not for me. No problem. ...the costing department [in headquarters] said to me, "You know all the stuff already, why are you coming?" And I said, "They gave me a free ticket!"

Although Alain played down the visit as not significant to him, it provided an opportunity for him to confirm the relevance of the knowledge that he had acquired on his own during his early days with MANCO-T and his status as a competent member of MANCO's global management accounting practice. He proved this standing by demonstrating his ability to prepare a new set of planning reports, Forms 72–75, the planned divisional profit and loss statement and balance sheet, according to the new reporting requirement from MANCO, an exercise that the finance and accounting staff struggled with because of their unfamiliarity with looking into the future, as opposed to the past, which was required in the preparation of the forecast. This was coupled with a lack of understanding about MANCO's reporting structure, including the relationship between local statutory numbers and divisional numbers.[2]

Alain's expertise in planning and reporting was widely accepted and recognized by the management, in particular the MK. In fact, the management was so pleased with his reports and analyses that they began to think of ways in which they could retain him within the organization. The MD expressed his desire to appoint him a "delegate."[3]

But I said no because being a delegate they could send you anywhere. Schummer ... was dumbfounded. He did not understand why I did not take it. I said [if I took it] they could send me anywhere. My children were still young. [And] you could say no once but not the second time.

7.2 Becoming Finance and Account Manager (1976–1978)

Less than two years after his first promotion, Alain was promoted again to the position of finance and account manager of MANCO-T.

After a few years, in the third year, they appointed me finance account [manager]. I said I would die. I did not know how to talk with the Revenue Department [the local tax authority] on tax matters.

[2] For example, the divisional profit is calculated before tax but after the "notional interest," which is a theoretical interest charge based on the capital employed times the required rate of return; whereas the net profit for the statutory report is after the interest and tax expenses.

[3] This means he would have an employment contract with a better global benefit package, like those of his German colleagues.

Having neither formal background in finance nor financial accounting, this episode, to Alain, represented the most challenging period of his work life. At the same time it demonstrated how being open to new opportunities and being ready to help allowed him to engage in the accounting and finance operation prior to taking the position, thereby helping him gain the relevant knowledge and skill and enabling him to be accepted as a competent member of the finance and account practice, even before he was officially appointed.

7.2.1 Engaging in Other Practices, Gaining Additional Practical Understanding

During Schummer's time, when Alain was the newly appointed junior planning manager and Susan was the senior finance and accounts manager, both reporting to Schummer, there was a significant accounting issue of long overdue outstanding accounts; these were reported in MANCO-T's balance sheet as "other accounts receivable." Among the miscellaneous receivable accounts reported under this category there was a significant long-overdue balance from MANCO and an unsettled balance of advances given to local salesmen as an allowance for traveling expenses related to customer visits. Settling the balances of these two outstanding accounts had become a problem for the accounting staff, resulting in an increasing outstanding amount at the end of each closing period. Alain took the initiative to resolve this issue.

In settling the outstanding balance of the local salesmen's travelling expenses, he established an advance settlement policy. This stipulated that each salesman had to settle the balance of the advance made under his/her name by the end of the month before the new advance for the next trip was approved.

> I said, "You had to settle it first. Then you can ask for advance again on the following day." I was the one who managed it [the policy]. At that time Pharmaceutical [people] hated me so much for this.

Asked why he "volunteered" to solve this issue even though it was not in his line of duty as a planning manager, not to mention the risk of creating enemies in the sales teams, at first Alain said he did not know (Schön 1983); but later he added that he simply wanted to help Susan, the incumbent senior finance and accounts manager, to resolve the issue and to help make things run smoothly.

> When I did it I was not thinking [about] anything ... If we let things be the way they were, i.e., no system, this could create fraud.

Settling another type of outstanding account was much more complicated. The balance in question had to do with expenses related to compensation and the fringe benefits for expatriates. At the time, the information regarding their compensation package was shared locally only between the MD and Mariah, the MD's secretary, who arranged for payments to and the tax filing for all the expatriates in MANCO-T, whereas the accounting department processed the transactions as approved by the MD. After a few successions of the MDs there was no one in MANCO-T who had a full understanding of the matter, so the balance was left alone until it became sizable, posing an issue not only for MANCO-T but also for MANCO's account closing process. The current MD wanted to settle the issue before leaving for his next assignment, but it seemed that no one wanted to have anything to do with the matter.

> No one wanted to do it. ... Accounting, they did not take care or pay attention to the matter.

Determined to make himself useful, Alain delved into the accounting practices and helped to solve the issue.

> I contacted the equivalent of the accounting department [in Frankfurt]...
>
> ..."Kunderbuchhaltung." I said the money should have come. We have an outstanding over here so we should do this/that. I proposed and they accepted...

After discussion with the responsible parties in Germany, Alain advised the local management on how to proceed. The MD agreed:

> He agreed and asked me to proceed. We added 10% to the price to compensate for this amount. Gradually the account is settled. Big problem like third party like ... in Sweden whom should we make the contact? After a few failed correspondences I wrote the balance off.
>
> It's not that I just asked for a price increase.... Indirectly I talked to them [sales department] first and advised them of the 10% price increase ...
>
> ...It took us one to two years to settle.

Alain "volunteered" his services and was soon engaged in other practices even though they did not directly fall into his accountability. In settling the long outstanding accounts of MANCO-T he had learned how to coordinate internal activities and proved to the management that he was capable of settling an accounting issue that was rather complicated, requiring not only knowledge of the accounting system but also practical understanding about how to settle intercompany accounts. In addition, he demonstrated the capability of negotiating and convincing the counterparties in Frankfurt and local divisional managers that they needed to support him.

7.2.2 Sharing the Practice, Creating Value

While he was a planning manager, Alain participated in the off-site annual budget review. His main task was supplying planning information for MK members, but he also took the opportunity to "educate" them about financial discipline as well.

> At that time it was —three to four days at a seaside resort so there would not be anyone interrupting. I prepared and took with me GP by product so I could refer to it. They asked what the plan for fertilizer sales was. King could not answer; Alain could. [There was] discussion for half a day about the share of administration [expenses], i.e., the "admin key"...

The "administration key" was an administrative cost allocation rule that stipulated a certain percentage of administration costs should go to companies or sales divisions that used the services and support of MANCO-T,[4] which Alain implemented for MANCO-T. Applying the knowledge of MANCO's cost allocation rule from self-studying of MANCO's accounting manual, together with his acquired understanding of the nature of the local business operation, he made some adjustments to the global standard rule to suit the local business situation and made a proposal for the MK's review and approval. He took the opportunity of participating in the bud-

[4] The administration division of MANCO-T provided services to all sales divisions under the umbrella of MANCO-T and two production companies within the local MANCO group of companies. The administration costs were allocated to the sales divisions and those companies according to the agreed "admin. key."

get review meeting to explain the general principle of cost allocation to MK members, proposed the adjusted allocation rule, and managed to convince them with business logic to agree to his proposal.

> Aber did not agree. King did not agree. They got into arguments. …it was the biggest issue for every country: how to allocate [the costs]. I said the guideline from MANCO was not bad. [For] AR we used the number of invoices. EDP we could use the number of hours in printing [for] allocation [bases]…

In the same manner, Alain established an "interest key" for the interest cost allocation. Studying the MANCO accounting manual, he gained knowledge about financing and the link to cash flow. He used the relationship therein as the basis for interest cost allocation argument.

> …we used the assets as basis [for allocation], assets of each department. Assets and AR, plus stock minus AP [accounts payable]. That's all. How much of these were for each department? Take [only] the marketing's, exclude the administration's and then allocate [accordingly].

However, the way in which he convinced MK members that they should approve was not by explaining to them about the calculation method but by highlighting how to manage cash flow better in order to reduce interest costs and increase the profit.

> …how we saved the money for you …[in terms of interest/administration costs saving]… Take 365 days [for the year] if we could help each other to collect [from the customer] faster by one day… At 15% interest we got a couple of 100k per day." They were shocked.

Alain continued to provide assistance to Susan whenever he could, becoming her trusted assistant. When Schummer left and Susan became the administration manager, Alain took over her position and became the new finance and account manager. Again, being open and having proved himself capable of handling some of the most challenging finance and account issues earned him the promotion in less than three years.

While fully engaged in the finance and account practice as the department manager, Alain did not intervene in the routine daily operations. Instead he delegated as much as he could to his capable subordinates by providing accounts and finance policies, then standing by to provide help whenever needed. On the accounting front he provided policy on the general provision, administration, and interest cost allocation, booking of the expatriate expenses allocation, and provisions for AR and inventory, for example. He made sure that MANCO's accounting policy was adhered to and that the company's practice was also in line with local accounting practice at all times. For example, he liaised with both local auditors and accounting departments in Germany and decided upon the amount of general provision to be made.

> It was part of the routine. … I was the one who made provision much more than what they wanted. I did not recall now, 2% [of] finished goods or…

Learning from the earlier mentioned long-overdue accounting issue, Alain made sure that he had no issue with account closing.

> My true aim was to have the balance sheet system of the company clean and tidy… "Clean" meant there was nothing fishy, covered, something like that. Having everything in order.

On the finance front, Alain studied MANCO's financing policy to learn about the financial risks and how to deal with them. While he left the finance manager to carry on the daily finance operations, he helped to make decisions on loan agreements and foreign exchange risk cover.

> Most of the time [when] I looked after finance Jane [the finance manager] would be [handling] the operation. When we were to make a decision on borrowing Jane would run to me.

During this period Alain began to establish a strong finance and accounting network within MANCO's finance and accounting organizations (*Finanzswesensabteilung*) as well as in the outside communities, the external auditor bankers, and the tax authority. He was recognized by them as a strong and competent member of the finance and accounting practice.

7.3 Becoming Deputy Administration Manager (1979–1981)

Alain had been providing assistance to Susan, the administration manager, since the day he became planning manager. Being ever open and ready to help. he had the opportunity to get more and more involved in the administration and financial management practice using his expertise in planning and reporting (being future oriented) and his growing understanding about the business operation. He found himself most of the time coordinating the vast activities within and outside the administration division. It was a period during which he built up his organizational skills, drawing upon a strong network within MANCO and external communities.

7.3.1 *Sharing the Practice, Building on Practical Understanding*

When Stolzen, the MD, left at about the same time as Schummer, Warten succeeded him as the country manager: he was in charge of the operations of the MANCO group, which consisted of three local legal entities: MANCO-T, MANCO-P, and MANCO-C. He was in post for about two years before Hilkesohn, the next MD, succeeded him. During this relatively short stint, Warten made some significant changes to the local organization. First he appointed Susan as the first local administration division manager, replacing Schummer. According to Alain, he wanted to make the division even bigger, creating an administration division manager who counter-balanced the powerful divisional sales managers. So in addition to the usual finance and accounts, the electronic data processing and the purchasing departments, Susan was also in charge of order processing services, warehouses, and shipping. In other words she was in charge of all functions besides production and sales. During this period, Alain continued to provide her with whatever assistance he could, even though this involved working outside the area of his responsibility. Doing so he became her most trusted assistant and the person she always turned to when she encountered any problems. In fact, he was acting as her deputy even though he had not yet been promoted to the position.

> I was finance account manager who looked after everything: purchasing, finance, DP [data processing], everything.

After a while the workload proved to be too much for Susan. So Warten promoted Alain to be her deputy.

> But this was too much for her. There were 300 people under her. Way too many. So they appointed me ... so I could help take away the reporting part and Susan could concentrate on other stuff like IBM.

Susan was viewed by the sales division managers as overpowering as she controlled all the service and support functions of MANCO-T. According to Alain she was a nice person but rather "inflexible," strictly abiding by the rules and regulation. In no time she became a target for attack from the sales division managers. Unfortunately two of her managers became the victims of this attack: Wanda, the EDP manager, and Poon, the purchasing manager. They were both attacked for being "stubborn", "inflexible," and "difficult to work with."

> These people attacked Poon because Poon picked on small things. You ordered stuff with the purchase order and if you did not indicate the color he would not buy it for you. And Wanda got a problem because she stuck with the [legacy] IBM system but we had decided to use Siemens Nixdorf's ... In fact the issue is small. Poon's can be resolved. Simply put they attacked them because they did not like Susan being too powerful. Warten made her too powerful...

After Warten left, Hilkesohn arrived to take over the position of MD overseeing the local operation. He put a lot of pressure on Susan on many issues, in particular the number of employees in the administration division.

> Hilkesohn asked her to reduce the headcount. He insisted that we use Siemens Nixdorf's, let Wanda go and find a replacement.

Finally both managers were forced to leave during Hilkesohn's time. They were replaced with one manager who was transferred from inside the company and a new manager hired from outside.

As time went by Susan became more and more involved with the SAP (an enterprise resource planning software developed by a Germany company, SAP SE) implement project, and Alain continued to provide support and assistance to Susan in all other matters. As her deputy he found himself spending more time on coordinating activities within the administration division and between the administration divisions and other divisions. Through this, he had a chance to practice and build on his coordination and organizing skills.

7.3.2 Engaging in Other Practices, Creating Value

Alain believed in the value of good teamwork and practiced it. On this he referred back to an incident in the early 1980s, which he recalled as the proudest moment in his career life. This involved him taking a proactive action in helping the company settle a fire insurance claim successfully within a record time. He attributed this success to the readiness and availability of competency from a cross-functional team that came together for one common purpose: to put the company back into business as soon as possible.

The fire accidentally broke out in one of the warehouses that stored pharmaceutical finished products in the early hours of one morning. Alain recalled that Susan came by very early in the morning to pick him up from his house. They went together to the warehouse to investigate the damage the fire had done to the property. He remembered getting there and seeing two production managers crying at the site. A number of the people at the factories who were starting their shift had witnessed the fire and were crying at the sight of the partially burnt down warehouse.

> In the morning a guy called from the factory and cried. Early in the morning about 4–5 am. Schultz [factory and manufacturing division director] was crying. They felt sad. They lost all the goods. When I arrived they all were crying.

Alain recalled that Susan was due to attend a training session in Germany immediately afterwards and that Hilkesohn was also away. Being the deputy administration division manager, it was clear to him that it was his duty to coordinate the activities and put forward an insurance claim for the burnt finished goods as soon as possible, so that the company could quickly got back to business.

He consulted Schultz and arranged for a meeting with all concerned to coordinate the activities. He worked closely with Savvy, the head of logistics, who was a very knowledgeable person on insurance matters. Savvy took care of the local insurance companies while Alain took care of the reinsurer representative from Germany.

> We split the work. It was clear [that the] settling of the insurance claim was mine. The only thing I needed was the numbers from Vicha [the cost accounting manager] and DP: how much the stock in warehouse at that moment was. I got the link to the insurance through Savvy... but most important was Weiss [the representative from the reinsurer].

He realized the value of timely, accurate, and relevant numbers, and used his reporting expertise in preparing the insurance claim in no time.

> I took care of Weiss. I took good care of him, whatever [information] he needed I asked Vicha to prepare for him.
>
> ...we had to prove the value of the stock that we had. How much got burnt down? How much were the goods in transit? We could prepare that in just a few days and also proved that the numbers were correct.

Based on the calculated numbers, Alain negotiated in a direct, honest, and fair manner.

> ...it was proven that DAXA that we were about to export, goods in transit, we claimed them at selling prices. [However] they found some in production. They said these ["work-in-process" stock] cannot be claimed at the selling price. They had reasons. We discussed clearly and formed a common agreement, i.e., fairness.
>
> Honestly, insurance people they wanted to have the thing settled as soon as possible. ...they would like to have reliable information that they could use. In that case they would close the case easily. But if they had to ask for this for that and we did not have it they could not do anything.

Together they managed to settle the claim in record time, under 30 days.

> Weiss liked me so much. He said it was perfect, everything was ready ...In thirty days we got the money ... If you asked me I was proud ... I felt good.
>
> I was proud because there had not been a case where you could claim the insurance within 30 days. [Here in] 30 days you got the money!

In addition, this experience helped Alain learn and develop what he called "my way of negotiation," which was basically obliging (to "reasonable demand") and negotiating in an honest and fair manner based on the agreed numbers.

...They fed me with the numbers and I negotiated. My way of negotiating was better. That's all.

He [Weiss] wanted this/that. I gave them to him next day from DP, etc. In addition as I mentioned earlier when he disagreed I changed it right away.

Weiss was happy that things got settled quickly. They just wanted proof, facts, and numbers to confirm. Easier to talk now that the numbers were ready everything was ready.

His way of negotiation with the support of solid numbers proved to be useful and effective in other negotiation rounds and established him as a strong but fair and honest negotiator.

As the deputy to the Administration Division manager, Alain was in charge of maintaining the balance sheet structure, including the dividend payout policy. Every year he contacted his counterpart in MANCO's Finance Division to negotiate for the amount of dividend payout.

... let's say they demanded from Hilkesohn this much. They [other local management members] would oblige but I would not. I would try to tell them that this could not be. One, you had to make the balance sheet look nice so we could borrow the money from the bank easily. Two, as a good company you had to pay tax to the local country.

They listened.

Alain argued logically, citing the potential tax and financing implications on the business operation costs; this reflected his knowledge of local tax and financial practices.

Everything I said was backed up with reasons. We had to be a good tax payer. We had to pay tax here. Otherwise there would be a problem about the [tax] audit on this/that. It was not about being afraid that the revenue department would audit us. But we tried to refer to the fact that we traded locally, we had to show profit for them and pay tax. We [also] referred to the case of other German companies like BAY [a local subsidiary of another big German chemical company] who transferred all the profit they made to overseas and let there be a loss over here. Or in the [other] case of SMN [a local subsidiary of a big German industrial goods company] who had loss.[5]

[5] Alain was a member of the local German Chamber of Commerce. He had built a strong network and had an opportunity to share best practices among finance directors and other executives of German companies operating locally.

In the end, he said it was for the good of the company as a whole, and everybody agreed.

> ...he [Wien] knew that whatever I said it was for the benefit of the company and nothing else.
>
> Say if you got good performance, your company was good. Your employees were good. Everyone got benefit. Everything was good.
>
> Everyone was happy.

He negotiated for an intercompany transfer price using the same logic.

> ...when they would like to transfer [profit] such that the local company would have a loss I would not oblige. I would argue that we had to keep the company [as] ... What is the word? Good ... Good citizen... for we paid the tax.
>
> We had to pay tax. I would argue this way.

Being knowledgeable, honest, fair, and respectful of others while being able to oblige what he called "reasonable" demands at the same time, during negotiations and normal contact with his counterparts won him lots of goodwill and support from MANCO.

Besides engaging in insurance, dividend payouts, and transfer price policies, Alain was also involved in a broader strategic finance practice: a restructuring of MANCO-C, one of the two production arms of the local group of companies. It was an opportunity to gain knowledge about financial valuation practice and build a relationship with consultants. Using his expertise in forecasting, he developed a valuation model that met the requirements of MANCO and helped to solve a dispute between local and German consultants.

> ... MANCO-C got partners: DEG [German Development Bank], who had a policy that they would pull out once the company was earning a profit. They would withdraw from shareholding. That's when we sold [the share of] DEG to BBank, IInsurance, and asked Theepa [a local consutant] for valuation of selling price. Theepa had come up with a price which was 13 to 15 times something. PM [a consulting company retained by MANCO] in Germany sent a letter complaining about Theepa.
>
> [They said], "How could you come up with this [number]?" Theepa came and consulted with me. He said according to market we needed to price at 13–15 times. I told him this was only an internal matter. ... [Finally], we took the past five years and the five-year planning to compute the value. Then we sent it over to overseas and that was the end of it.

7.4 Becoming Central Executive Coordinating Office (CECO) Director (1982–1997)

In his last career stage as a financial practitioner, Alain firmly established management and control practice in MANCO-T. This materialized in an organization called the Central Executive Coordinating Office (CECO), which was established in 1982. Alain was promoted to be the first CECO division director and a member of the management committee in the same year. According to him this was the longest and "smoothest" period in his career life, a period in which he was "having fun" working. He had become a powerful MK member, with the source of his power being mainly the work knowledge, practical understanding, and work connections/networks which he had accumulated over a long period of time.

7.4.1 *Sharing the Practice, Building on Practical Understanding*

As mentioned earlier Alain became a strong MK member. He sustained his standing by sharing and engaging others in the management control practice. He taught the cost accountants to prepare management reports for the management committee. He educated the sales departmental/divisional and other functional managers about the planning process, how to prepare their own budget, and how to monitor their own business through it.

> ...we didn't just teach them. We gave them information so they know how to run the business. If we said business it's a lot [of things].
>
> It's not that we just sell and [think] that collection, stock and everything else were not related to it.
>
> ...we wanted to teach them to take care of these things. [Imagine] how much the delay in payment of one day would impact our profit situation. Something like this we taught them. Besides this we trained their people...
>
> ...in doing the planning, cost control, costing... Marketing did not have any idea about this.[6] What we tried to do was to appoint the management accountant in every division. We trained their people. We taught them and trained them.

By sharing the practice, Alain aimed to have the divisions control their own fate, while CECO provided the overall control and monitoring.

[6] Alain used "Sales" and "Marketing" alternately when referring to the local business divisions.

> If they were able to do it [the planning] then they would be able to look after their own profit and loss. Their planning would be realistic not just something that was done carelessly. How should we control the stock? How should we control the customer?
>
> This is very important.
>
> If they ordered too much stock we would warn them. From our work unit we would tell them that this could not be and we would ask the business controller on their side why they allowed such a thing to happen.

Alain emphasized teaching and sharing to create practical understanding and willingness to join the practice, as opposing to imposing the practice—which would result in others rebelling against it. He mentioned the case of the newly acquired company, MANCO-D, in which he and Susan had sent in Supa in as "MANCO-T's controller" to establish a new controlling practice, without success.

> The original idea was that they wanted me to become the MD, which I declined. I did not take it. I said I would help by being a director and also in building up the reporting system. That's when I dragged Supa into it as I did not know Yani [MANCO-D's incumbent financial controller at that time]. And that's the problem. Supa was a problem as he was not flexible and Yani was more capable. Supa was not flexible. He said, "MANCO-T did it this way, you would have to do the same." There was no compromising. He was the kind of person who insisted that things got to be in this/that way.

Without cooperation from Yani, Supa had no chance of gaining any understanding about MANCO-D practices or sharing those of MANCO-T. He became frustrated and decided to leave the company, putting the integration of MANCO-D at risk. At this point Alain stepped in to help. He began by regularly participating in the monthly management meeting at MANCO-D's site, thereby gaining understanding about the company and its people. He also brought along one of his managers as a consultant for MANCO-D to provide assistance and to advise Yani on how to fulfill the reporting requirement of MANCO-T. By teaching and sharing, he gradually engaged the MANCO-D controller in MANCO-T management control practice. He also developed a close relationship with MANCO-D management, which finally resulted in the smooth integration of MANCO-D into MANCO-T's group and established good cooperation between the two companies in daily business operations.

By this time, Alain's advice was sought after not only within the MANCO-T organizations but by local external parties, such as the auditors, the tax authority, the banking community, as well as other German subsidiaries. People came to him for advice related to various fields: accounting, finance, sales, inventory, AR management, tax, and employee benefits. The more issues he faced the more experience he gained. With this wealth of experience he was known as a financial expert not only in management planning and control matters but also in strategic finance, tax, employees' benefits, and other administration matters.

7.4.2 *Engaging in Other Practices, Creating Value*

At this time one of the local business divisions was making such huge losses that MANCO contemplated shutting it down. Before doing so a divisional controller was sent over to investigate. Alain was ready for the visit: he knew what was required for the discussion. Using his expertise in management accounting practice, he guided his team in preparing a profitability analysis by product. As this report was not part of the standard reporting requirement, the MANCO controller was surprised and quite impressed to see it. With this much-needed information ready at hand, his task was much easier than he had predicted. The meeting turned out to be fruitful, with further discussions leading to a favorable outcome for the local operation.

> They wanted to know why we had a loss. So they came to analyze [the situation] ...We were prepared... I asked Peony [a planning manager] to prepare the GP by product... the allocation of interest, allocation according to stock, etc. ...till the bottom line.
>
> They never looked at each single product the way we did.
>
> Hans [the division controller] got overseas' [profit] number [of the product in question]. And he said overseas got so much profit [out of it].
>
> ...this product, after adding [back] the profit transferred [to overseas] is actually making profit.
>
> When he [Hans] got back [to HQ] he reduced the price and transferred the profit [back] to us.

Getting involved in this case, Alain had won acceptance from the MANCO controller. To the sales division manager, he had become not only a trusted advisor but also a true partner who would be ready to help out when needed.

Alain used the experience gained from this episode to negotiate in the case of price increases for pharmaceutical supplies from headquarters. He rallied his course through Wien, the head of MANCO's finance division.

> In the case of Pharmaceuticals... I told them to make provision for non-collectibles ... It was the provision so the profit would be less. This was because [MANCO's] Pharmaceuticals would jack up the prices right away if you showed too high a profit, more than 5% for example.
>
> My aim was to maintain the profit within the company...
>
> I told him [Wien] we had investment here. We had confidence [in the country] so we had to have profit here [for reinvestment].
>
> So our status was solid. When I went talking to the bank we could borrow with a good interest [rate]. Aim was here.

Discussing the matter with his counterpart in the head office, Alain persuaded them to look at the satisfactory dividend payment record from a production unit rather than risking a tax audit at the selling unit. His counter-proposal made a lot of sense and was therefore accepted by all parties involved.

Being a member of the management committee, he came across various operational issues. He began to get involved in "everything," solving several problems and setting various policies without delving into the daily operation.

> I got involved in everything. I got all the information. I knew everything. Personnel policy I had the knowledge. Investment policy, dividend policy, social security policy, I also knew. Only the routines of the personnel I did not look after. Routines of the finance and account I did not look after. Basically I involved myself in all.

During a preliminary budget review with the cosmetic product department head, Alain noticed a high employee turnover over the previous two years. He was concerned that the business could not be sustained because of this and raised the issue with the department head. He found out that the culprit was the relatively low salary that was paid out to the purchase consultants (PCs) who worked at supermarkets, discount stores, and so on, promoting the company's hair care products. In order to retain employees for longer, Alain suggested that their salaries be increased and that the department included this increase in the budget for the next year.

What I am most proud of is when I adjusted [the salary] for the PCs ...

...the turnover of PCs was rather high. A lot of people left. Why, the salary was so low. Commission included, it was only a little more than USD 9000...

We had discussion in a meeting, might have been in a small group not a big one. During the planning session I said, "You could not do like this. You've got to find out why the turnover rate was so high" ... Hilkesohn and everyone else agreed that we could not go on like this...

The one who got the problem was Sakda [the head of cosmetics product department]... he wanted to ... make a high profit, which was not right. It was not for the top guy to get paid high and the lower ranks get little. We'd got to be fair.

Arguing his case, Alain pointed to the alternative scenario of higher costs of training for the new staff, the higher salary to be offered in the job market, and the loss in sales owing to inexperienced staff. To add to his point, he did a quick calculation to show that the impact from the salary increase could be comfortably absorbed by the projected profit level for the department. In addition, the current departmental profit was "huge," making the salary adjustment even more feasible.

Alain also justified his recommendation by referring to the precedent case.

In former time ... we adjusted the wages up. This was because in the long run we wanted the workers to stay with us for a long period of time. So many times we had people who stayed with us for ten years and [when] we hired new people in [we found that] the salary gap was small. We needed to adjust the payroll many times in the past ... We made the adjustment to the salary. In one year let's assume we wanted to give 8% increase: we said we gave more to the less paid and less to the higher paid. For the lower paid we might give them 10% or 11 to 12%.

Alain got engaged in personnel management practice first by recommending the salary adjustment to the cosmetics products department's PCs, followed by proposing to the MK that they should establish a provident fund with contributions from both the employer and the employees. This was another accomplishment he was proud of.

The idea of social security for employees at that time was relatively new. There was no legal obligation to provide this and most of the local companies did not. At MANCO-T, besides the basic salary and bonus and company cars for the salesmen, there was no other significant fringe benefit available to the employees. Learning from his MANCO counterparts in Germany, Alain proposed to the MK that local companies should set up a provident fund to provide for employees' long-term security. He liaised with the headquarters in Germany in order to set up such a fund. At first there was some resistance to the idea. Some people argued that the majority of the factory workers could not afford the monthly contribution. In response, Alain suggested an increase in the basic salary so that the fund could be established, and so the staff could benefit from the fund in the future.

> They said the workers did not have the money. I said it was fine. We'd pay for them through salary increase. From 3% we increased it to 5%. Pay them salary.

He managed to convince the MK to go for this as a logical solution to alleviate the high rate of worker turnover and retain employees in the long run. In addition to his expertise in assurance mathematics, Alain could easily help HR to overcome the hugely complex calculation mechanism that was necessary in the implementing process. The fund was finally established with full support from all concerned in Germany.

> I had an advantage … Schuss [who was in charge of] social security, provident fund matter … was very impressed about me. I could talk to costing … Hans [the MANCO's controller] … the Marburg manager. All of them respected me.

To Alain, this last episode of his financial management and control work life represented the time he was enjoying it the most. His knowledge and practical understanding reached their peak. He became an expert in corporate financial management and control, and the MD, other MK members, and divisional managers always sought help and advice from him. Through the years, he had gained a complete "feel" for the business.

> …we planned for USD 400 million in profit. In January alone we made USD 100 million. I was so very happy. It's that we said we would make 400 [USD million] and we did. It's like riding a horse. You pull to the left, it goes to the left.

After Hilkesohn retired in 1993, Schmolz succeeded him as the new MD of MANCO-T. During 1994–1997 there was a major organizational restructuring in MANCO-T, with the result that each division was spun off to become an independent legal entity. Applying his prior knowledge in corporate restructuring, Alain assisted the MD in the restructuring process until it was complete. Finally, he became the MD of MANCO-T in 1998.

7.5 The Lifelong Self-Orienting Process

For Alain, his career is about constantly adapting to changing business contexts by learning, gaining the necessary know-how, and building on practical understanding about financial/management practice in different contexts. In learning about the new craft of finance and adapting himself to the world of business, he orients himself towards management, in other words each individual MD that he works with, drawing upon them for management imperatives and specific goals, for example the target overall profit for the year. Different set of actions at specific points in time as marked by major career milestones (Table 7.1) are aligned and directed towards assisting the MDs to achieve their specific short- to intermediate-term goals.

From the narrative, the constant transitions of various MDs with related changes in goals, policies, or even management philosophy teaches Alain that it is important to have the business continue to run smoothly during

Table 7.1 List of actions and key milestones of the management control career

Being planning manager	*Being finance and account manager*	*Being deputy administration manager*	*Being CECO division manager*
Acquiring technical knowledge			
Acquiring practical understanding	Gaining additional practical understanding	Building on practical understanding	Building on practical understanding
	Engaging in other practices	Engaging in other practices	Engaging in other practices
	Sharing the practice	Sharing the practice	Sharing the practice
Creating value	Creating additional value	Creating additional value	Creating additional value

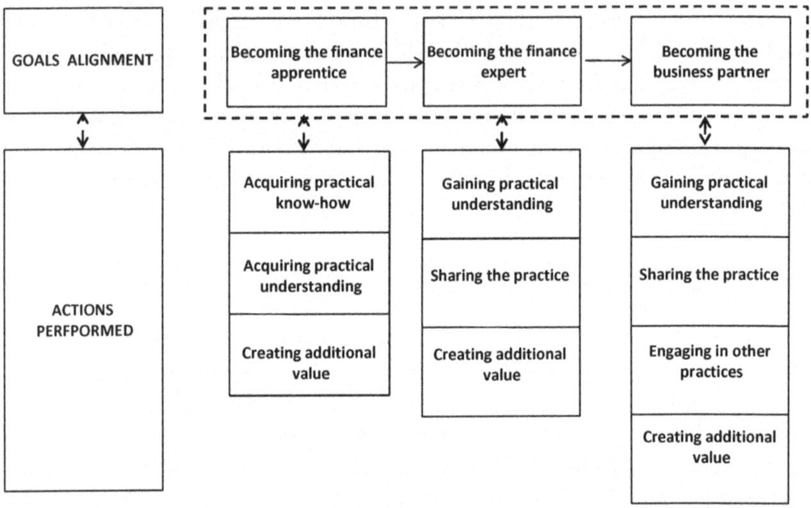

Fig. 7.1 Self-orienting process and goal aligning-CECO director

the transition period and in the long run. This concern for the ongoing business becomes his main motivation in aligning his courses of action over the years (Fig. 7.1). Alain's self-orientation process over the years emphasizes the creating of value action, a hallmark of business orientation, from the very beginning throughout every phase of his career.

7.5.1 Self-Orienting, Teleoaffective Structure

Being self-driven, Alain sets his own goals in line with those of management and keeps challenging himself. For example, he sets a target for insurance claim settlement at 30 days, a target that no one in the insurance industry has ever achieved; but he achieves it. In another case he sets a personal goal to help the company achieve a challenging annual profit of USD 400 million. And once it is achieved he is very happy and proud about it, saying it is such a joy to achieve this target. He feels as if he is in complete control of the business. "It's like riding a horse. You pull to the left, it goes to the left." Always raising the bar, he is happy and proud of his own achievements, and is content with this (Table 7.2).

Table 7.2 Self-orienting and teleoaffective structure – CECO director

Motivations (things that matter)	*Affectivities (emotions-in-actions)*	*Self-orienting activities*	*Goals*	*Ends*
Concern for the ongoing business	Pride associated with his own achievements, joy/ excitement in meeting the challenge	Coordinating cross-functional activities, creating value in terms of new tools, new processes, new practices	Achieving the short-term profit target	Overall well-being of the company as well as his own
Family value	Feeling concerned	Declining job that does not suit the lifestyle of the family	Building a career locally	

7.5.2 *Self-Orienting, Personal Characteristics, and Affectivity*

Compared with the other cases, Alain attributes his long career to his being adaptive and logical.[7] In building a long career at MANCO-T, Alain takes on a continuous process of adapting towards different management styles and philosophies and proactively creating additional value for the organizations. Being adaptive to new management styles and imperatives, he displays his sense of logic, arguing his case with reasons in a straightforward manner, winning trust and acceptance from his peers. Unlike others, he does not hesitate to say no when the situation calls for it. He is also systematic, having an integrated view: he knows how to link each organizational activity back to the overall goal, such as the target profit of the company. These personal characteristics are manifested in his daily engaging in business: the course of action on which he decides is driven by his concern for the business (motivation) (Fig. 7.2).

Alain's family (motivation) is important for him in making a career choice. In considering whether he would "fit in" (Fig. 7.2), he also thinks about how this will affect his family life. The story shows how he turns down his "dream job" in Germany in order to oblige his father's request, and that he declines to be appointed a delegate because he sees that mov-

[7] Alain refers to the German words of *Anpassungsfaehigkeit* as "adaptability" and *anpassen* as "adapt." In this study the words adapting, fitting in, adjusting, being flexible are used alternately as having the same meaning as these German words. His idea of adapting is like, as he has mentioned, "be in Rome, act like a Roman".

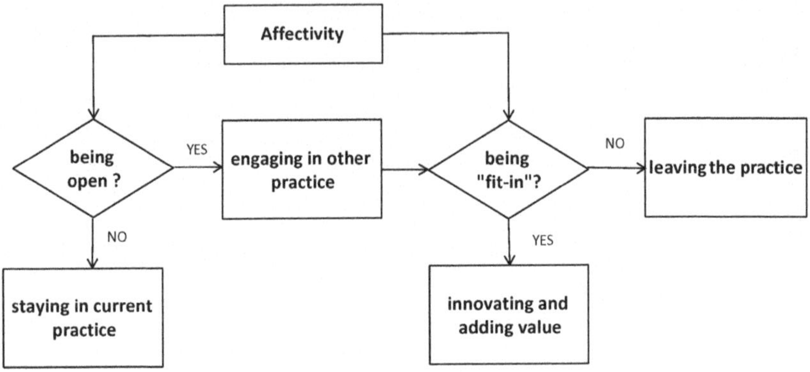

Fig. 7.2 Turning point – CECO director

ing around is not suitable for his young family. Knowing his limits and being honest with himself, he also rejects a promotion offer to be the MD of MANCO-D, saying he "does not like" the sales aspect of the position. His work inclinations or disinclinations are also logically related to the acquired practical understanding that he has gained from his first-hand experience of being actively engaged in the related business contexts.

7.5.3 *Self-Orienting, Cultural Context, and Affectivity*

From his own account, Alain has spent his formative years in the southern part of the Germany. During his time there he has learned about being punctual, being direct, and other cultural aspects. Working at MANCO-T, which is heavily influenced by the German way of management, with a German management committee and a majority of German managers (both in MANCO-T and its local associated companies), he feels almost at home. He is comfortable arguing his case with his local and overseas counterparts, whereas his other colleagues seem to be reluctant to do so. He adapts well to the top-down management philosophy, which accords accountability to the functional leads. In daily business engagement Alain respects the expertise and accountability of the functional leaders, a feature of organizational culture that is related to the German management style (Ahrens 1996). For the sake of having business continuity in the long run and helping each MD achieve specific intermediate goals, he gets engaged in business, helps solve problems, and makes sure that things go well in day-to-day operation. Many times he goes over his line of duty to help resolve issues which no one seems able to resolve. In all cases, he makes sure that he leaves the decision-making and the execution, and thus the accountability, to the functional leads.[8] Working in this favorable cultural context has been an enjoyable experience, making him feel he fits in (Fig. 7.2), and he decides to make his whole career at just one company.

Nevertheless, this does not mean that Alain prefers the status quo. On the contrary, and in the same manner as Madelyn, Alain always looks for ways to do things better. Despite the clear line of responsibility and accountability Alain realizes the importance of coordination as the business expands and the companies become bigger. "Bridging the silos," he goes out of his domain, drawing upon his wealth of know-how and expertise in providing support to his business counterparts so that that the business operation can continue smoothly in a changing environment. As with Madelyn, Alain adds value to the organization by solving issues that require coordination/collaboration across functional line of duties, winning acceptance from his peers. His major breakthroughs are the setting up CECO to coordinate cross-functional activities, and the establishment and dispersion of management accounting practice for the first time in MANCO-T's history. His efforts significantly contributed to an open collaborative culture within the existing functional organization setup.

In all, this case demonstrates how Alain's lifelong self-orienting is influenced by the changing management philosophy and business contexts and motivated by his concern for business continuity through the teleoaffective structure. It also highlights an extended role of a financial practitioner, beyond being business partner to becoming a change agent, and how corporate culture influences his course of action and how his course of action in turns contributes to a new corporate culture.

References

Ahrens, T. (1996). Styles of accountability. *Accounting, Organizations and Society, 21*(2–3), 139–173.

Ahrens, T. (1997). Talking accounting: An ethnography of management knowledge in British and German brewers. *Accounting, Organizations and Society, 22*(7), 617–637.

[8] This is consistent with the German corporate practice in which organizational members tend to respect functional accountability and rarely go beyond their own domains (Ahrens 1997; Ahrens and Chapman 2000).

Ahrens, T., & Chapman, C. S. (2000). Occupational identity of management accountants in Britain and Germany. *The European Accounting Review, 9*(4), 477–498.

Schatzki, T. R. (2002). *The site of the social: A philosophical account of the constitution of social life and change.* University Park: Pennsylvania State University Press.

Schön, D. A. (1983). *The reflective practitioner: How professionals think in action.* New York: Basic Books, Inc.

PART III

Crafting an Orientation Program

CHAPTER 8

Business Partner Development Program

Besides external elements, such as corporate and organizational cultures or the management philosophy, the internal inherent elements such as personal goals and ends, motivations and personal characteristics, significantly influence the self-orienting process toward becoming business partners. Both elements can simultaneously affect the direction as well as the extent of business orientation at the turning point where management accountants engage in commercial activities. Capitalizing on this knowledge, we propose an internal business partner development program which emphasizes on building a supportive organizational culture, found to be the crucial element that positively influences the decision towards becoming business oriented as well as the relevant technical knowledge base and practical skills from "on-the-ground" commercial engagement, which we believe would help in guiding future management accountants towards becoming relevant business partners.

8.1 The Crucial Role of the Mentor[1] and the Sponsor

The four narratives (Chaps. 4–7) have demonstrated how management, including direct bosses, plays a significant role in the self-orienting process

[1] From the narratives in the chaps. 4–7, we see a few cases of "mentor-cum-sponsor" role. In those cases the mentor is usually drawn from within finance practice, and performing the role of the sponsor as well.

P. Chotiyanon, V. Joannidès de Lautour,
The Changing Role of the Management Accountants,
https://doi.org/10.1007/978-3-319-90300-2_8

of management accountants (Burns and Baldvinsdottir 2005; Hopper and Macintosh 1993). They can act as role models (Goretzki et al. 2013) as well as provide opportunity and support. Having in place mentors and sponsors, providing a training program that involves engagement in commercial activities, helps management accountants gain the necessary practical understanding about commercial practice and build up their confidence to carry out related activities.

Although the narratives have suggested that gaining the necessary understanding of the related practice is accomplished through self-learning, they also point to the important role of both mentors and sponsors in the planning and executing of the career development program in facilitating the self-learning process. The support of mentors and sponsors is crucial in the early stages of the career, in particular at the very beginning. The case of Madelyn shows that the self-orienting process towards business is of most benefit when the commercial mentor shares understanding of the financial practice and the added benefit from an economic perspective. Hence it is suggested that the mentors be identified and work closely with the training candidates and the sponsors from the very beginning of their career development.

While the role of sponsors is formally established in organizations, mentors are not formally appointed but are recognized as those holding a stake and sharing a keen interest in the work effort of the candidates. Ideally, the mentor should be someone who is usually two levels up the reporting line from the training participants. This person could be someone within the finance practice, but for the business partner development program, preferably from commercial management practice. On the other hand, a sponsor is drawn from within the finance practice and most of the time is the direct boss of the participant. The sponsor administers the career of the participant, pays for the costs, and shares the stake in the outcome of the participant's work effort. Nevertheless, both the mentor and the sponsor need to work together in planning and executing the career of the business partner.[2]

[2] The "business partner" here refers to being business or commercial oriented, having a significant level of engagement in commercial/business practices, and being accepted as a value-adding member by peers.

8.2 Planning and Executing of the Career Development Program

Based on the Business Partner Developing Model (BPDM) in Chap. 3, a career development program for the business partner is built. This program begins with the crucial role of the finance sponsor in identifying a candidate who already possesses analytical skills or has the potential to develop them. In any case the candidate should have a proven track record of learning ability. Depending on the candidate's style, as manifested in daily activities, the sponsor then identifies a mentor, who works closely with the sponsor and much more so with the candidate in planning and executing the career development program during the career stages. The sponsor–mentor–candidate financial career development program for a business partner could be designed and executed in three phases (Table 8.1).

Table 8.1 Business partner development program

Key actions	*Phase I: pre-managerial (becoming finance apprentice)*	*Phase II: managerial (becoming finance expert)*	*Phase III: post-managerial (becoming business partner)*
1. Acquiring financial know-how and understanding	Training on the analytical tools		
2. Sharing the practice and acquiring practical understanding	Comprehensive analysis assignment	Cross-functional team assignment	Financial leadership in key global/regional organization
3. Engaging in commercial and other practices			
Internal	Collaboration with business counterparts	Mandatory participation in commercial meeting	Integration of the finance and commercial practices project
External		Mandatory participation in meeting with external partners	Joint decision-making with external partners
4. Creating additional value	Leader in financial training program	Leadership in cross-functional team project	Leadership in game-changing project

8.2.1 Pre-managerial Stage

The first phase of the career development emphasizes training in technical knowledge and understanding of site-specific analytical tools: how the tools work and how to use them. At the same time the aim is to build an attention to detail, which is important in analytical work. For a big organization or a complex business the training is facilitated by a solid accounting information system, such as the SAP system (an enterprise resource management software developed by a German company, SAP SE), together with the sound management accounting system. In addition there exists an operation manual and/or financial policy as a general guideline and reference.

The training program includes various comprehensive analysis assignments from a detailed level up. The assignment can run across the breadth of products or customers dimensions but focuses much more on the depth; that is, detailed analysis in order to develop the keen analytical skills that may be directly applied to a specific business context. In Chap. 6, we gained an insight into how Madelyn trains her team members. Learning on how the analytical tools work, they are assigned to delve deeply into the detailed product analysis down to the level of sales keeping units. Once they have mastered the deep product analysis, she would give a new assignment in customer analysis, involving a new dimension/perspective and thereby expanding the breadth while maintaining the same level of detail. After this it would be an overall corporate profit and loss (P&L) analysis to get to the integrated "big picture." Along the way they would be gradually moving from working in isolation as analysts, learning how to operate the analytical tools, to finance area experts, members of the cross-functional commercial team who own specific product/customer P&Ls, share knowledge about the analytical tools, teach others how to use them properly in making sense of commercial decisions, and thus demonstrate their understanding of the practices in the later stages.

At the beginning of the career the involvement of both mentor and sponsor are crucial. It is found that to execute the development plan well it is helpful if the sponsor is not only a competent member of the financial practice, with a significant level of experience in managing the tools in various business contexts, but is also a competent business partner him/herself. Besides providing the necessary training pertaining to the analytics, it is important that the sponsor identifies and establishes a commercial mentor for the business partner development program participant at the earliest opportunity. The role of the commercial mentor at this stage is to foster and nurture a passion for the commercial aspect of financial practice and an openness to opportunity and risk that is related to participating in the commercial side of the business from the very beginning. Besides being a competent member of the commercial practice, the mentor should share the understanding of financial analytics in the commercial context, including their economic perspective. But most importantly the mentor is able to influence the career of the training program participant.

In the case of Alain, we see the significant role of Podi as sponsor-cum-mentor, who provides not only a career opportunity but also the chance to learn new things and gain continuous career support. It is Podi who introduces Alain to Stolzen, his first commercial/management mentor. It is Stolzen who not only appreciates Alain's work but also challenges him and shows him the management's angle on financial practice. Podi and Stolzen provide strong support for Alain's overall fast-track career development until he has mastered his craft and is able to stand firmly on his own. For his part, Alain adapts quite well to his new environment and continues self-learning/adapting and winning trust from succeeding MDs, who are to become his subsequent sponsors.

In the case of Madelyn, it is David, her official sponsor, who sees her potential value and introduces her to the management committee and to Shahan, her commercial mentor in the early stage of her career. In the same manner as Alain's Podi, David is open to Madelyn working directly with Shahan in order to gain a broader perspective and an understanding of management requirements. From there on, building on solid experience with a well-established management information system at MANCO-T, Madelyn is able to gain broader and deeper practical understanding, establish a firm ground on her own, and win over her future sponsors without any difficulty. Working closely with Shahan, Madelyn learns about the commercial aspect of finance practice and becomes passionate about it. In turn, Madelyn is mentor and sponsor to both Carol and Anne during the time she is their direct boss.

8.2.2 *Managerial Stage*

The second stage of career development stresses the gaining of practical understanding, the know-how, in order to apply and make sense of analyses in broader business contexts through engaging in "on-the-ground" commercial practice. This is about extending the scope of work, beginning with regularly participating in commercial meetings with both internal and external commercial partners sharing know-how with the aim of becoming part of the cross-functional team that makes joint commercial decisions. By being active and providing sensible input and guidance from the financial angle, the participant demonstrates his/her understanding of the commercial finance practice.

The role of the sponsor and mentor at this stage is to challenge the participant to step beyond his/her financial domain into other practices. Examples are Stolzen challenging Alain to explain the raw material price variance or to simplify the annual budget review process, or Shahan challenging Madelyn on the depth of an analysis, a new angle of the profitability analysis, or the simplification of the budget process. In order to encourage the participant to engage in other practices, this development stage could involve a short-term assignment in financial areas such as internal audit assignment in another organization in order to gain understanding of the business process, discovering how to solve broader operation issues and build a business network at the same time; or preparing a management/financial report consolidation assignment in order to gain an understanding of the overall corporate picture. These assignments, which Carol, Anne, and Madelyn have done, mainly help in broadening perspective or adding emphasis to working with cross-functional team members in preparation for an active role in the cross-functional commercial team.

As indicated by BPDM, besides the support from the mentor and the sponsor, the level of commercial engagement depends on the personality of the participants as well. For example, in the case of self-driven Alain and Madelyn, who have strong support from their commercial mentors and direct bosses, they become passionate about their work and more open to opportunity and risk. In such cases there is a higher level of engagement in commercial practice than in the case of Carol and Anne, who unfortunately do not have the benefit of a commercial mentor and prefer to stay in their comfort zone within the financial practice. In the latter two cases there is a higher level of engagement in the financial practice than in the commercial practice (Fig. 8.1). This inclination has implications for the preferred career choice of the participants, given the same opportunities.

BPDM implies a significant role for the sponsor and the mentor in identifying the appropriate career choice for the participant, by observing his/her style/personality, these being manifested in the way he/she engages in commercial practices. For example, in the cases of Carol and

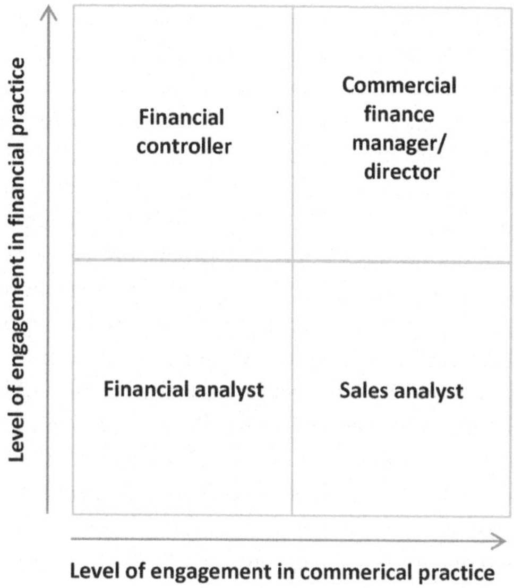

Fig. 8.1 Level of engagement in practices and career choices

Anne, who prefer less risk and are more rule abiding, when given the same opportunities as Alain and Madelyn, they are inclined to stay in their comfort zone close within the traditional financial practice, opting to be perhaps a financial controller rather than venturing into commercial practices and becoming a commercial finance manager/director.

8.2.3 Post-managerial Stage

At this stage the participant has accumulated a wealth of experience and is accepted as one of the leaders in finance practice. This stage involves continuous learning and sharing best practices to meet the challenges of the changing business context. It is also about managing relationships, and creating and maintaining wider internal and external networks across the practices and across the organizations.

The key development area at this stage is an involvement in key decision-making, involving both internal and external partners as leader of financial practice in the global or regional leadership team. This includes the establishment of a dedicated commercial finance support function, as in the cases of Alain and Madelyn. It might involve leadership in key financial projects with a significant impact on the business process, such as revamping or upgrading analytical tools and the reporting system, or financial support reorganization. This stage could be preceded by an assignment to represent the organization to external parties in preparation for the active financial "ambassador role" in the leadership team. The role of sponsors in career development continues during this stage, while the role of mentors becomes less prominent and in some case non-existent as the participants themselves become mentors to other members of the practices.

At this stage there is a possibility of career development beyond financial practice, such as in general management,[3] provided that the business partner is "open and ready" when the opportunity arises. Alain's career branches out from financial management practice to general management practice when he becomes the MD of MANCO-T and a member of the board of directors of MANCO's local group of companies, overseeing the operation of all of the local subsidiaries. Besides being passionate about what he does, he is open to opportunity and risk and always happy to be engaged in other practices outside his domain. He also seems to possess a strong sense of logic and a systematic approach, which is not apparent in the other cases.

8.3 Management Consideration and Challenges

In this chapter we have proposed an internal business partner development program built on BPDM's premise that to be a business partner one needs to be engaged in commercial practice. This means a high degree of risk, going beyond the comfort zone of finance practice into the new terrain of commercial practice, requiring one to be open and passionate about the new area. In this respect the program highlights a crucial role for the commercial mentor in fostering passion about engaging in commercial practice and opening up opportunities by inviting the program participant to work closely with the mentor in solving commercial issues through a combination of financial and commercial logic. By engaging in commercial practice, the financial practitioner gains both a general understanding about what it is to be a member of commercial practice, the specifics of commercial practice, for example, the difference between trade environments (e.g., retail and wholesale, different trade deals), and how to

[3] Ahrens and Chapman (2000) have suggested the German formal educational background that prepares management accountants for commercial and/or managerial practices in addition to the financial control practice.

apply financial disciplines to the commercial context. Once this understanding is established, the participant becomes confident in carrying out daily activities in close cooperation with commercial partners, and is able to challenge them on commercial decisions, winning their acceptance as a competent member of the commercial practice. The most important aspect of the proposed three-pronged (mentor–sponsor–participant) approach is to develop an environment that will foster and nurture the passion for commercial practice, which seems to be the critical factor deciding the degree of business orientation.

Our BPDM has suggested that external elements such as a broader culture and management philosophy can influence career decisions as well as the internal elements that are inherent to management accountants, such as personal goals and ends, motivation, and certain personal characteristics. In this respect, in fostering and nurturing the passion for becoming a business partner in addition to capitalizing mainly on internal resources, the program can benefit from collaboration with external professional and academic communities as well. Prior research has shown that professional management communities such as the Controller Verein and the Controller Akademie in Germany or the Chartered Institute of Management Accountants in the UK can help provide not only the necessary technical knowledge but also and more importantly promote the new role, thereby inspiring future management accountants to embark on a career as business partners (Ahrens and Chapman 2000; Goretzki et al. 2013). These professional organizations play a significant role in spreading the business- or management-oriented "philosophy" through various workshops and seminars, in which the participating management accountants have the chance to familiarize themselves with the "philosophy" of being business oriented while acquiring knowledge about the necessary tools at the same time.[4]

On the academic front, companies can collaborate with business schools in designing the curriculum for the management accounting program, incorporating elements of, and direct links to, such subjects as strategy, hands-on information technology, change management, and other aspects of business life that have previously been viewed as "someone else's domain" (Burns and Vaivio 2001). In addition, part of the program should include activities that mimic real business practice, having the students

[4]See Heinzelmann, R. (2016). Comparing Professions in UK and German-Speaking 10.1080/17449480.2016.1143560.

practice working with students from other disciplines, for example in project works that involve providing consulting service to small enterprises or entrepreneurial organizations under close supervision of the academic advisor and in collaboration with professional or practitioner communities. This approach aims to create awareness and interest in management accounting practice as a career choice by providing an insight into the subject, allowing students the opportunity to draw upon their technical knowledge and apply it in a broader context in real life situations. Working closely with other students in a cross-functional team and under close supervision should help them to feel comfortable and ready to work with people from other disciplines in the future. In addition, by working closely with professional and/or practitioner communities in administering the program, the academic advisor would be able to gain insights into business practices that would be beneficial for further program development.

References

Ahrens, T., & Chapman, C. S. (2000). Occupational identity of management accountants in Britain and Germany. *The European Accounting Review, 9*(4), 477–498.

Burns, J., & Baldvinsdottir, G. (2005). An institutional perspective of accountants' new roles – The interplay of contradictions and praxis. *European Accounting Review, 14*(4), 725–757.

Burns, J., & Vaivio, J. (2001). Management accounting change. *Management Accounting Research, 12*, 389–402.

Goretzki, L., Strauss, E., & Weber, J. (2013). An institutional perspective on the changes in management accountants' professional role. *Management Accounting Research, 24*, 41–63.

Hopper, T. M., & Macintosh, N. (1993). Management accounting as disciplinary practice: The case of ITT under Harold Geneen. *Management Accounting Research, 4*, 181–216.

CHAPTER 9

Conclusion

This book has taken the readers on a journey in time that explores the diverse work life experiences of four finance practitioners. At the end of this journey we hope that readers will have a richer knowledge of practitioners in general and management accountants in their continuously changing role in particular. At this point we would like to take stock of what we have learned and recommend the steps forward for future researches, which should help further the building of a knowledge base about practitioners in the context of practices, while also contributing to the broader research area of the sociology of professions.

Our journey begins with the phenomenon of the emerging new role of management accountants as business partners, with its associated strikingly diverse activities. Tracing the professional life journeys of these finance practitioners through the theoretical lens of Schatzki (2002, 2005b, 2010), we begin to gain an understanding of the emerging business-oriented role in terms of its dynamics as well as its diversity. This knowledge crystallizes in the Business Partner Developing Model (BPDM), which explains the changing role of management accountants through their lifelong self-orienting processes. For the first time we have provided a deep insight into how and why the role emerges from the lifelong self-orienting process. As such, we have contributed to the scarce literature on the "making" of management accountants that places emphasis on the purposeful actions of the organizational players (Burns and Baldvinsdottir

P. Chotiyanon, V. Joannidès de Lautour,
The Changing Role of the Management Accountants,
https://doi.org/10.1007/978-3-319-90300-2_9

2005; Goretzki et al. 2013). Ours represents one of the rarest accounts and perhaps the only one that shows the agency of management accountants at the micro-level. In addition, by mobilizing Schatzki's theoretical concept, we have brought to light for the very first time not only the self-orientating process of management accountants but also additional insights into and understanding about the dynamics of the external and internal elements that influence the varying degree of business orientation that has been found in earlier research (Järvenpää 2007; Friedman and Lyne 1997; Burns and Baldvinsdottir 2005; Bryne and Pierce 2007; Morales and Lambert 2013).

BPDM has extended the notion of agency (Ahrens 2009; Mouritsen 1996; Burns and Baldvinsdottir 2005; Fauré and Rouleau 2011; Morales and Lambert 2013) to cover the influence of past activities on management accountants' present roles (Ahrens and Ferry 2016). Delving into the past, we have found that development in business orientation over the years takes place in tandem with changes in business contexts (Granlund and Lukka 1998; Burns and Baldvinsdottir 2005; Järvenpää 2007; Bryne and Pierce 2007; Goretzki et al. 2013), which transpire from the organizational culture and the management philosophy. From these narratives we can see the influence of organizational culture and management philosophy in the case of Alain, who began his career in the 1970s in a company which was at the time characterized by a centralized top-down management control approach with a clear functional accountability. His corporate culture-attuned activities focused on providing useful advice and relevant reports geared towards management control and decision-making, while leaving final decisions to the line functions. However, in the 1980s and 1990s, when business expanded and the organization became more complex, prompting acquisitions and spin-offs, and related organizational restructuring and the need for coordinating various internal activities became apparent, the narrative shows him getting more involved in the business, coordinating cross-functional activities while still respecting the functional accountability. We can also use Madelyn as an example: she carried the centralized product-oriented management control practice from MANCO-T over to CONSUM-T in the late 1990s and adapted it to the new customer-oriented management philosophy to cope with the increasingly complex business environment.

These site specifics, such as organizational cultures and management philosophy, not only influence the day-to-day activities of practitioners in the self-orienting process (Granlund and Lukka 1998; Järvenpää 2007), but also affect the degree of business orientation as manifested in the way they engage in business. From the cases of Alain and Madelyn it seems that the notion of "business partners" arises from management's efforts to break away from a "working in silos" organizational culture to adapt to the increase in size and business complexity. In Alain's case he feels the urge to "bridge the silos". His way of being a business partner involves coordinating activities and providing advice and support beyond his line of duty, for example by settling the insurance claim matter, protecting a sales division from being shut down, and advising the sales department to increase the salary of the sales staff beyond the given guidelines. In so doing, he "feels right" but never interferes with the execution or normal operation of other functions. Rather, he respects their functional accountability, leaving his counterparts to decide whether or not to follow his advice and giving them leeway in how to execute them. This is more or less in line with German management control practice and culture (Ahrens 1996; Ahrens and Chapman 2000), in which organizational members tend to respect functional expertise and accountability. On the other hand, for Madelyn, being a business partner means "breaking the silos," and getting involved in both the strategic planning and the detailed day-to-day execution. This includes challenging the marketing team about whether a promotion campaign (such as "buy two get one free") would make economic sense, or the sales team about whether deep trade spending (in a particular trade channel) would meet the return on investment criteria. Being passionate about marketing activities she also enthusiastically seeks on-the-ground marketing intelligence informally on her own. This deeper involvement in commercial execution seems to be supported by the customer-focused management philosophy that is associated with highly dynamic fast-moving consumer goods markets with constant changes as the norm, compared with the relatively stable business environment of the chemical industry in which Alain works. In "bridging the silos" or "breaking the silos," being business partners in their own ways, both Alain and Madelyn have demonstrated a relatively high degree of business orientation. Furthermore, their activities as influenced by the broad culture and management philosophy have significantly contributed to a change in the management control practices and the broader organizational cultures at MANCO-T and CONSUM-T, respectively.

While some contemporary management accounting research has associated the emergence of the new role to the "abrupt" change (Nor-Aziah and Scapens 2007), following the purposeful actions of key organizational players, such as chief executive officer (Hopper and Macintosh 1993), senior finance manager (Burns and Baldvinsdottir 2005), and chief financial officer (Goretzki et al. 2013), in response to external forces; we highlight here the gradual nature of the process in which management accountants "internalize" their new role. This process of change "from within" focuses on continuous learning to acquire financial knowledge, relevant practical know-how, and practical understanding in order to apply them in various business contexts, thereby adding more and more practical know-how and understanding in order to master the craft and becoming able to adapt to changing business contexts while creating additional value in the process. These emotions-imbued actions are aligned by personal goals and driven by motivation towards an ultimate end, forming a lifelong self-orienting process. Carol is open and happy to learn new things in order to gain relevant knowledge and skills, so she can become a knowledgeable finance practitioner. She dislikes work-related traveling and decides to choose a career in corporate finance over auditing. Alain is concerned for his family, so he declines his promotion in order to become a delegate working outside his home country and builds a career with a local subsidiary instead. Madelyn is driven on by the continuous improvement that is important for her and engages enthusiastically in commercial activities. We can see her being excited about new commercial activities, learning more, gaining deeper understanding about commercial practice, and creating additional value in terms of new tools, new systems, and new people on her way to gradually becoming a business partner.

In addition to the empirical contribution, in terms of a deep insight into the phenomenon through life experiences, theorizing the BPDM enables us to explain the changing role of management accountants through their lifelong self-orienting process. BPDM establishes relationships between activities across time through a teleoaffective structure. It argues that each activity is associated with specific personal goals and imbued with the affectivities (Schatzki 2002) or "emotions-in-action." Through the underlying short-term and long-term goals aligning process the purposeful actions are aligned and driven by motivations (what matters) towards an ultimate end, such as becoming a business partner, by forming a lifelong self-orienting process that is made up of three micro-processes: becoming a finance apprentice, a finance expert, and a business partner. In addition, BPDM points to creating value and the associated positive emotions-in-action as the hallmarks of business orientation. This model is robust enough to explain and predict the varying degree of business orientation. It postulates that macro-level elements such as the culture as well as micro-level elements such as personal goals/ends, motivation, and personal characteristics can simultaneously influence the degree of business orientation through the affectivities (Schatzki 2002). Furthermore, it suggests that a high degree of business orientation is manifested in being proactive in engaging in commercial activities and in the associated positive emotions-in-action, such as being happy, joyful, and excited, at the "turning point," which is when management accountants engage in commercial activities and "feel" whether they fit in or not.

Earlier research has informed us of the variation in degree of business orientation (Bryne and Pierce 2007; Morales and Lambert 2013). BPDM associates this with "what matters" (motivations), personal goals and ends, certain personal characteristics, and specific site contexts, such as the corporate or organizational cultures and the management philosophy, that reside in general understanding (Schatzki 2002; Jørgensen and Messner 2010). These internal elements inherent to management accountants as well as external elements can simultaneously affect the manner in which management accountants orient towards business through the emotion-in-action at the "turning point," which is the point when they are engaging in commercial practice. The high degree of business orientation is found to be associated with certain personal characteristics, such as being open to new opportunities and related risks, and being proactive, which is manifested in the manner of business engagement and the related positive "emotions-in-action," such as being happy, joyful, and excited.[1] In terms of the personal characteristics, besides the importance of being open and proactive there are others that seem to be associated with a varying degree of business orientation, such as being self-driven and an excellent learner, being detail-oriented with an overall/integrated view, and being honest and straightforward. Nevertheless, these characteristics do not pre-prescribe being a business partner, rather they constitute being a business partner at the moment of business engagement (Schatzki 2002).

[1] As opposed to negative emotions such as unhappy, uneasy, frustrated, bored, which are found to be associated with the lower degree of business orientation.

Adding to the earlier mentioned empirical and theoretical contributions, we have proposed an internal career development program for future management accountants, highlighting the significant roles of mentors and sponsors in creating and nurturing a passion for commercial practice. Such a program should be beneficial not only for the individual practitioner embarking on building a career in management accounting but most importantly for the management, contemplating on establishing a new role for management accountants in their organizations, as well as for the educators planning the corresponding program changes. We also suggest capitalizing on external networks, such as professional associations and educational programs, in order to inspire future management accountants to embark on a management accounting career path, in addition to mobilizing internal resources.

Another area of our contribution lies in our longitudinal approach to the study of practitioners in the context of practices, in the tradition of the oral history.[2] In general there are three approaches to study these practices (Hui et al. 2017) and practitioners: conversation analysis (Ahrens 1997; Fauré and Rouleau 2011), ethnography (Morales and Lambert 2013), and oral history (Ahrens and Ferry 2016). By design, they all offer a deep insight and understanding of the phenomenon by having the researcher actively take part in the experiences by living them, in the case of ethnography, and by reliving them together with the research participants, in the case of oral history and conversation analysis. While ethnography and conversation analysis are mostly mobilized to study the "present" as experienced by the researchers, the oral history approach can offer a longer view, incorporating a much longer time span to include entire life experiences, in other words the past as well as the present aspects of the phenomenon. The other benefit of the oral history approach, besides providing a deep insight from the past, is that it is a collection of history of many people who have had a first-hand experience of the same phenomenon (Janesick 2010). In this respect, and pioneering this approach, we have opened up a new venue of research which has the potential to help enrich the history of the making of management accountants, contributing to the knowledge base with additional validity and reliability at the same time.

[2] Used in many disciplines, oral history is the collection of stories, statements, and reminiscences of a person or persons who have first-hand knowledge of any number of experiences. It offers qualitative researchers a way to capture the lived experiences of participants (Janesick 2010, 2014).

Drawing upon the narratives of the four finance practitioners about their lifelong self-orienting processes towards becoming relevant business partners, we can see each emerging "new" role of management accountants as marking a new phase in the movement in time that spans one's entire career. From the past we have seen a movement from the role of "reporter," providing reports and analyses, to "navigator," doing score-keeping, directing attention, and problem-solving for management, facilitating the controlling and decision-making processes to create a more active role of "business partner" with a high level of engagement in the business at present (Simon et al. 1954; Mouritsen 1996; Ahrens 1997; Goretzki et al. 2013). In this sense, the present emergent role of "business-oriented" management accountants (Granlund and Lukka 1998; Ahrens and Chapman 2000; Burns and Baldvinsdottir 2005; Bryne and Pierce 2007; Goretzki et al. 2013), generally referred to as the "business partner" role type (Järvenpää 2007), is not the end but rather the beginning of a new phase in the continuous self-orienting process, through which being a management accountant (and the meaning thereof) transpires and perpetuates in many variations (Schatzki 2005a, 2006). As indicated in the narratives, being a "business partner" today has already evolved to include not only being the partner to internal clients such as sales teams and marketing teams (Granlund and Lukka 1998; Ahrens and Chapman 2000; Burns and Baldvinsdottir 2005; Järvenpää 2007; Bryne and Pierce 2007; Goretzki et al. 2013), but increasingly becoming a partner to external clients, the customers, as well. We can see examples of a broader external orientation with Madelyn's participation in regular meetings with key retail customers and Alain's visits to key customers to solve credit issues. In this respect the emerging of the new role signifies the continuous self-orienting process that perpetuates management accounting practice within the changing business context (Schatzki 2005a, 2006).

Being business partners today is not the end but perhaps a beginning of another phase in the progression towards the yet-to-emerge state of management accountants/finance practitioners. In other words, today's business partner could become a past phenomenon, which future researchers, adopting the BPDM model, can study in order to build on their knowledge of practitioners as they continue on their path of "constant becoming" (Schatzki 2002, p. 189). Following the oral history tradition, we would like to invite future researchers to join in building the life histories of those practitioners who have shared the same experiences.

New avenues of research could include management accountants working in different "sites," such as in small versus large organizations, in different industries, in profit versus non-profit organizations, or in different cultural contexts. Adopting this historical approach should be beneficial in terms of contributing not only to the scarce knowledge about practitioners in general, but also to a richer and more robust history of practitioners than before. In addition, BPDM and its underlying concept of the "turning point" can help future research gain a better understanding of the dynamics of the micro- and macro-elements and their effects on practitioners' volition. This implication is particularly beneficial for practice research under Schatzki's lens, which attempts to make sense of the broader "beyond-practice" elements in the context of change (Hui et al. 2017; Nama and Lowe 2014).

References

Ahrens, T. (1996). Styles of accountability. *Accounting, Organizations and Society, 21*(2–3), 139–173.

Ahrens, T. (1997). Talking accounting: An ethnography of management knowledge in British and German brewers. *Accounting, Organizations and Society, 22*(7), 617–637.

Ahrens, T. (2009). Everyday accounting practices and intentionality. In C. S. Chapman, D. J. Cooper, & P. Miller (Eds.), *Accounting, organizations, and institutions* (pp. 30–47). Oxford: Oxford University Press.

Ahrens, T., & Chapman, C. S. (2000). Occupational identity of management accountants in Britain and Germany. *The European Accounting Review, 9*(4), 477–498.

Ahrens, T., & Ferry, L. (2016). Institutional entrepreneurship, practice memory, and cultural memory: Choice and creativity in the pursuit of endogenous change of local authority budgeting. *Management Accounting Research*. https://doi.org/10.1016/j.mar.2016.11.001.

Bryne, S., & Pierce, B. (2007). Towards a more comprehensive understanding of the roles of management accountants. *European Accounting Review, 16*(3), 469–498.

Burns, J., & Baldvinsdottir, G. (2005). An institutional perspective of accountants' new roles – The interplay of contradictions and praxis. *European Accounting Review, 14*(4), 725–757.

Fauré, B., & Rouleau, L. (2011). The strategic competence of accountants and middle managers in budget making. *Accounting, Organizations and Society, 36*, 167–182.

Friedman, A. L., & Lyne, S. R. (1997). Activity-based techniques and the death of the beancounter. *European Accounting Review, 6*(1), 19–44.

Goretzki, L., Strauss, E., & Weber, J. (2013). An institutional perspective on the changes in management accountants' professional role. *Management Accounting Research, 24*, 41–63.

Granlund, M., & Lukka, K. (1998). Towards increasing business orientation: Finnish management accountants in a changing cultural context. *Management Accounting Research, 9*, 185–211.

Hopper, T. M., & Macintosh, N. (1993). Management accounting as disciplinary practice: The case of ITT under Harold Geneen. *Management Accounting Research, 4*, 181–216.

Hui, A., Schatzki, T. R., & Shove, E. (2017). Introduction. In A. Hui, T. R. Schatzki, & E. Shove (Eds.), *The nexus of practices, connections, constellations, practitioners* (pp. 1–7). Oxon: Routledge.

Janesick, V. (2010). *Oral history for the qualitative researcher choreographing the story*. New York: The Guilford Press.

Janesick, V. (2014). *Oral history interviewing: Issues and possibilities*. In P. Leavy (Ed.), *The Oxford handbook of qualitative research* (pp. 300–314). New York: Oxford University Press.

Järvenpää, M. (2007). Making business partners: A case study on how management accounting culture was changed. *The European Accounting Review, 16*(1), 99–142.

Jørgensen, B., & Messner, M. (2010). Accounting and strategising: A case study from new product development. *Accounting, Organizations & Society, 35*(2), 184–204.

Morales, J., & Lambert, C. (2013). Dirty work and the construction of identity. An ethnographic study of management accounting practices. *Accounting, Organizations and Society, 38*, 228–244.

Mouritsen, J. (1996). Five aspects of accounting departments' work. *Management Accounting Research, 7*, 283–303.

Nama, Y., & Lowe, A. (2014). The 'situated functionality' of accounting in private equity practices: A social 'site' analysis. *Management Accounting Research, 25*, 284–303.

Nor-Aziah, A. K., & Scapens, R. W. (2007). Corporatisation and accounting change: The role of accounting and accountants in a Malaysian public utility. *Management Accounting Research, 18*(2), 209–247.

Schatzki, T. R. (2002). *The site of the social: A philosophical account of the constitution of social life and change*. University Park: Pennsylvania State University Press.

Schatzki, T. R. (2005a). The sites of organizations. *Organization Studies, 26*(3), 465–484.

Schatzki, T. R. (2005b). Where times meet. *Cosmos and History: The Journal of Natural and Social Philosophy, 1*(2), 1–14.
Schatzki, T. R. (2006). On organizations as they happen. *Organization Studies, 27*(12), 1863–1873.
Schatzki, T. R. (2010). *The timespace of human activity: On performance, society, and history as indeterminate teleological events.* Lanham, MD: Lexington Books.
Simon, H. A., Guetzkow, H., Kozmetsky, G., & Tyndall, G. (1954). *Centralization vs. decentralization in organizing the controller's department.* New York: The Controllership Foundation.

References

Abernethy, M., & Stoelwinder, J. (1995). The role of professional control in the management of complex organizations. *Accounting, Organizations and Society, 20*, 1–17.

Ahrens, T. (1996). Styles of accountability. *Accounting, Organizations and Society, 21*(2–3), 139–173.

Ahrens, T. (1997). Talking accounting: An ethnography of management knowledge in British and German brewers. *Accounting, Organizations and Society, 22*(7), 617–637.

Ahrens, T. (2009). Everyday accounting practices and intentionality. In C. S. Chapman, D. J. Cooper, & P. Miller (Eds.), *Accounting, organizations, and institutions* (pp. 30–47). Oxford: Oxford University Press.

Ahrens, T., & Chapman, C. S. (2000). Occupational identity of management accountants in Britain and Germany. *The European Accounting Review, 9*(4), 477–498.

Ahrens, T., & Chapman, C. S. (2002). The structuration of legitimate performance measures and management: Day-to-day contests of accountability in a U.K. restaurant chain. *Management Accounting Research, 13*(2), 151–171.

Ahrens, T., & Chapman, C. S. (2007). Management accounting as practice. *Accounting, Organizations and Society, 32*(1–2), 1–27.

Ahrens, T., & Ferry, L. (2016). Institutional entrepreneurship, practice memory, and cultural memory: Choice and creativity in the pursuit of endogenous change of local authority budgeting. *Management Accounting Research*. https://doi.org/10.1016/j.mar.2016.11.001.

P. Chotiyanon, V. Joannidès de Lautour,
The Changing Role of the Management Accountants,
https://doi.org/10.1007/978-3-319-90300-2

Ahrens, T., & Mollona, M. (2007). Organisational control as cultural practice – A shop floor ethnography of a Sheffield steel mill. *Accounting, Organizations and Society, 32*(4–5), 305–331.

Allsop, D., & Calveley, M. (2009). Miners' identity and the changing face of the labour process within the UK coal mining industry. *Qualitative Research in Accounting & Management, 6*(1/2), 57–69. https://doi.org/10.1108/11766090910940665.

Assmann, J. (2011). *Cultural memory and early civilization: Writing, remembrance, and political imagination*. New York: Cambridge University Press.

Bailyn, L. (1989). Understanding individual experience at work: Comments on the theory and practice of careers. In M. Arthur, D. Hall, & B. Lawrence (Eds.), *Handbook of career theory* (pp. 477–489). Cambridge, MA: Cambridge University Press.

Barley, S. (1989). Careers, identities, and institutions: The legacy of the Chicago School of Sociology. In M. Arthur, D. Hall, & B. Lawrence (Eds.), *Handbook of career theory* (pp. 41–65). Cambridge, MA: Cambridge University Press.

Barnes, B. (2001). Practice as collective action. In T. R. Schatzki, K. Knorr Cetina, & E. von Savigny (Eds.), *The practice turn in contemporary theory* (pp. 25–36). London: Routledge.

Baxter, J., & Chua, W. F. (2003). Alternative management accounting research-whence and whither. *Accounting, Organizations and Society, 28*, 97–126.

Baxter, J., & Chua, W. F. (2008). Be(com)ing the chief financial officer of an organisation: Experimenting with Bourdieu's practice theory. *Management Accounting Research, 19*, 212–230.

Beard, V. (1994). Popular culture and professional identity: Accountants in the movies. *Accounting Organizations and Society, 19*(3), 303–318.

Bentham, J. (1995). In M. Bozovic (Ed.), *The Panopticon writings*. London: Verso.

Berland, N., & Chiapello, E. (2009). Criticisms of capitalism, budgeting and the double enrolment: Budgetary control rhetoric and social reform in France in the 1930s and 1950s. *Accounting, Organizations and Society, 34*, 28–57.

Bougen, P. D. (1994). Joking apart: The serious side to the accounting stereotypes. *Accounting Organization and Society, 19*(3), 319–335.

Bourdieu, P. (1990). *The logic of practice* (trans: Nice, R.). Stanford, CA: Stanford University Press.

Briers, M., & Chua, W. F. (2001). The roles of actors-networks and boundary objects in management accounting change: A field study of an implementing of activity-based costing. *Accounting Organizations and Society, 26*, 237–269.

Burns, J., & Vaivio, J. (2001). Management accounting change. *Management Accounting Research, 12*, 389–402.

Byrne, S., & Pierce, B. (2007). Towards a more comprehensive understanding of the roles of management accountants. *European Accounting Review, 16*(3), 469–498.

Burns, J., & Baldvinsdottir, G. (2005). An institutional perspective of accountants' new roles – The interplay of contradictions and praxis. *European Accounting Review, 14*(4), 725–757.

Chandler, A. (1962). *Strategy and structure.* Cambridge, MA: MIT Press.

Chen, C. C., Jones, K. T., Scarlata, A. N., & Stone, D. N. (2012). Does the Holland model of occupational choice (HMOC) perpetuate the Beancounter-Bookkeeper (BB) stereotype of accountants? *Critical Perspectives on Accounting, 23*(4–5), 370–389.

Chotiyanon, P. (2018). *Becoming a business partner, a lifelong self-orienting process.* Doctoral dissertation. Grenoble Ecole de Management, Grenoble.

Chua, W. F. (1995). Experts, networks and inscriptions in the fabrication of accounting images: A story of representation of three public hospitals. *Accounting, Organizations and Society, 20*(2/3), 111–145.

DiMaggio, P. J. (1988). Interest and agency in institutional theory. In L. G. Zucker (Ed.), *Institutional patterns and organizations: Culture and environment* (pp. 3–21). Cambridge, MA: Ballinger.

Dimnik, T., & Felton, S. (2006). Accountant stereotypes in movies distributed in North America in the twentieth century. *Accounting Organizations and Society, 31*(2), 129–155.

Dreyfus, H. (1991). *Being-in-the-world. A commentary on Heidegger's being and time, division I.* Cambridge, MA: The MIT Press.

Fauré, B., & Rouleau, L. (2011). The strategic competence of accountants and middle managers in budget making. *Accounting, Organizations and Society, 36*, 167–182.

Foucault, M. (1979). *Discipline and punish: The birth of the prison.* New York: Vintage Books.

Friedland, R., & Alford, R. R. (1991). Bringing society back in: Symbols, practices, and institutional contradictions. In P. J. DiMaggio & W. W. Powell (Eds.), *The new institutionalism in organizational analysis.* Chicago: University of Chicago Press.

Friedman, A. L., & Lyne, S. R. (1997). Activity-based techniques and the death of the beancounter. *European Accounting Review, 6*(1), 19–44.

Friedman, A. L., & Lyne, S. R. (2001). The beancounter stereotype: Towards a general model of stereotype generation. *Critical Perspectives on Accounting, 12*(4), 423–451.

Giddens, A. (1984). *The constitution of society outline of the theory of structuration.* Cambridge: Polity Press.

Glaser, B. G., & Strauss, A. L. (1967, reprinted 2006). *The discovery of grounded theory strategies for qualitative research.* New Brunswick: Aldine Transaction, Transaction Publishers.

Goretzki, L., Strauss, E., & Weber, J. (2013). An institutional perspective on the changes in management accountants' professional role. *Management Accounting Research, 24*, 41–63.

Granlund, M., & Lukka, K. (1998). Towards increasing business orientation: Finnish management accountants in a changing cultural context. *Management Accounting Research, 9*, 185–211.

Guo. (2017). The odyssey of becoming: Professional identity and insecurity in the Canadian accounting field. *Critical Perspectives on Accounting*. https://doi.org/10.1016/j.cpa.2017.10.008.

Heidegger, M. (1962). *Being and time* (trans: Macquarrie, J. & Robinson, E.). Oxford: Blackwell Publishers Ltd. (Original work published 1953).

Hopper, T. M. (1980). Role conflicts of management accountants and their position within organisation structures. *Accounting, Organizations and Society, 5*(4), 401–411.

Hopper, T. M., & Macintosh, N. (1993). Management accounting as disciplinary practice: The case of ITT under Harold Geneen. *Management Accounting Research, 4*, 181–216.

Hopwood, A. G. (1987). The archaeology of accounting systems. *Accounting, Organizations and Society, 12*(3), 207–234.

Hoskin, K. W., & Macve, R. H. (1986). Accounting and the examination: A genealogy of disciplinary power. *Accounting, Organizations and Society, 13*(1), 37–74.

Hughes, E. C. (1951). Mistakes at work. *Canadian Journal of Economics and Political Science, 17*(3), 320–327. (Reprinted in *The sociological eye*. Selected papers, New Brunswick: Transaction Publishers, pp. 316–325).

Hui, A., Schatzki, T. R., & Shove, E. (2017). Introduction. In A. Hui, T. R. Schatzki, & E. Shove (Eds.), *The nexus of practices, connections, constellations, practitioners* (pp. 1–7). Oxon: Routledge.

Janesick, V. (2010). *Oral history for the qualitative researcher choreographing the story*. New York: The Guilford Press.

Janesick, V. (2014). *Oral history interviewing: Issues and possibilities*. In P. Leavy (Ed.), *The Oxford handbook of qualitative research* (pp. 300–314). New York: Oxford University Press.

Janin, F. (2016). When being a partner means more: The external role of football club management accountants. *Management Accounting Research*. https://doi.org/10.1016/j.mar.2016.05.002.

Järvenpää, M. (2007). Making business partners: A case study on how management accounting culture was changed. *The European Accounting Review, 16*(1), 99–142.

Jeacle, I. (2008). Beyond the boring grey: The construction of the colourful accountant. *Critical Perspectives on Accounting, 19*(8), 1296–1320.

Joannides, V., & Berland, N. (2013). Constructing a research network: Accounting knowledge in production. *Accounting, Auditing & Accountability Journal, 26*(4), 512–538.

Joannidès de Lautour, V. (2017). Etics, emics and ethnomethodology in accounting research. In Z. Hoque, L. Parker, M. Covaleski, & K. Haynes (Eds.), *Qualitative accounting research method* (pp. 463–482). New York: Routledge.

Jørgensen, B., & Messner, M. (2010). Accounting and strategising: A case study from new product development. *Accounting, Organizations & Society, 35*(2), 184–204.

Kuhn, T. (1970). *The structure of scientific revolutions*. Chicago: University of Chicago Press.

Lambert, C., & Pezet, E. (2010). The making of the management accountant, becoming the producer of truthful knowledge. *Accounting, Organizations and Society, 36*(1), 10–30.

Lambert, C., & Pezet, E. (2011). The making of the management accountant – Becoming the producer of truthful knowledge. *Accounting, Organizations and Society, 36*(1), 10–30.

Lambert, C., & Sponem, S. (2012). Roles, authority and involvement of the management accounting function: A multiple case-study perspective. *The European Accounting Review, 21*(3), 565–589.

Latour, B. (1996). On actor-network theory. A few clarifications plus more than a few complications. *Soziale Welt, 47*, 369–381.

Loft, A. (1986). Towards a critical understanding of accounting: The case of cost accounting in U.K., 1914–1925. *Accounting, Organizations and Society, 11*(2), 137–170.

Macintosh, N. B., Shearer, T., & Riccaboni, A. (2009). A Levinasian ethics critique of the role of management and control systems by large global corporations: The General Electric/NuovoPignone example. *Critical Perspectives on Accounting, 20*, 751–761.

Miller, P., & O'Leary, T. (1987). Accounting and the construction of the governable person. *Accounting, Organizations and Society, 12*(3), 235–265.

Morales, J., & Lambert, C. (2013). Dirty work and the construction of identity. An ethnographic study of management accounting practices. *Accounting, Organizations and Society, 38*, 228–244.

Mouritsen, J. (1996). Five aspects of accounting departments' work. *Management Accounting Research, 7*, 283–303.

Moustakas, C. (1994). *Phenomenological research methods*. Thousand Oaks, CA: Sage.

Nama, Y., & Lowe, A. (2014). The 'situated functionality' of accounting in private equity practices: A social 'site' analysis. *Management Accounting Research, 25*, 284–303.

Nor-Aziah, A. K., & Scapens, R. W. (2007). Corporatisation and accounting change: The role of accounting and accountants in a Malaysian public utility. *Management Accounting Research, 18*(2), 209–247.

Preston, A. M. (1992). The birth of clinical accounting: A study of the emergence and transformation of discourses on costs and practices of accounting in U.S. hospitals. *Accounting, Organizations and Society, 17*(1), 63–101.

Roth, J. A. (1963). *Timetables: Structuring the passage of time in hospital treatment and other careers.* Indianapolis: Bobbs-Merrill.

Sandberg, J., & Tsoukas, H. (2011). Grasping the logic of practice: Theorizing through practical rationality. *Academy of Management Review, 36*(2), 338–360.

Scapens, R. W. (2006). Understanding management accounting practices: A personal journey. *The British Accounting Review, 38*(1), 1–30.

Schatzki, T. R. (1997). Practices and actions: A Wittgensteinian critique of Bourdieu and Giddens. *Philosophy of the Social Sciences, 27*(3), 283–308.

Schatzki, T. R. (2001). Practice theory: An introduction. In T. R. Schatzki, K. Knorr Cetina, & E. von Savigny (Eds.), *The practice turn in contemporary theory* (pp. 1–14). London: Routledge.

Schatzki, T. R. (2002). *The site of the social: A philosophical account of the constitution of social life and change.* University Park: Pennsylvania State University Press.

Schatzki, T. R. (2005a). The sites of organizations. *Organization Studies, 26*(3), 465–484.

Schatzki, T. R. (2005b). Where times meet. *Cosmos and History: The Journal of Natural and Social Philosophy, 1*(2), 1–14.

Schatzki, T. R. (2006). On organizations as they happen. *Organization Studies, 27*(12), 1863–1873.

Schatzki, T. R. (2010). *The timespace of human activity: On performance, society, and history as indeterminate teleological events.* Lanham, MD: Lexington Books.

Schatzki, T. R. (2012). A primer on practices. Theory and research. In J. Higgs, C. Sturt, R. Barnett, S. Billett, M. Hutchings, & F. Trede (Eds.), *Practice-based education perspectives and strategies* (pp. 13–26). Rotterdam: Sense Publishers.

Schön, D. A. (1983). *The reflective practitioner: How professionals think in action.* New York: Basic Books, Inc.

Seo, M. G., & Creed, W. E. D. (2002). Institutional contradictions, praxis, and institutional change: A dialectical perspective. *Academy of Management Review, 27*(2), 222–247.

Siegel, G., & Sorensen, J. E. (1999). *Counting more, counting less, the 1999 practice analysis of management accounting.* Montvale, NJ: Institute of Management Accountants.

Simon, H. A., Guetzkow, H., Kozmetsky, G., & Tyndall, G. (1954). *Centralization vs. decentralization in organizing the controller's department.* New York: The Controllership Foundation.

Smith, J. A., & Osborn, M. (2007). Interpretative phenomenological analysis. In J. A. Smith (Ed.), *Qualitative psychology a practical guide to research methods* (2nd ed.). Los Angeles, CA: Sage.

Strauss, A. L., & Corbin, J. M. (1998). *Basics of qualitative research: Techniques and procedures for developing grounded theory.* Thousand Oaks, CA: Sage.

Suddaby, R., & Greenwood, R. (2005). Rhetorical strategies of legitimacy. *Administrative Science Quarterly, 50,* 35–67.

Taylor, C. (1995). *Philosophical arguments.* Cambridge: Harvard University Press.

Thornborrow, T., & Brown, A. (2009). 'Being regimented': Aspiration, discipline and identity work in the British parachute regiment. *Organization Studies, 30*(4), 355–376.

Vaivio, J. (1999). Examining "the quantified customer". *Accounting, Organizations and Society, 24,* 689–715.

Vaivio, J. (2006). The business controller, non-financial measurement and tacit knowledge. *The Finnish Journal of Business Economics, 2,* 194–212.

Vaivio, J., & Kokko, T. (2006). Counting big: Re-examining the concept of the bean counter controller. *The Finnish Journal of Business Economics, 1,* 49–74.

Weber, J. (2011). The development of controller tasks: Explaining the nature of controllership and its changes. *Journal of Management Control, 22,* 25–46.

Wertz, F. (2010). The method of eidetic analysis for psychology. *Les Collectifs du Cirp, 1*(special edition), 281–300.

Whittington, R. (2006). Completing the practice turn in strategy research. *Organization Studies, 27*(5), 613–634.

Whittington, R. (2011). The practice turn in organization research: Towards a disciplined transdisciplinary. *Accounting, Organizations and Society, 36,* 183–186.

Windeck, D., Weber, J., & Strauss, E. (2015). Enrolling managers to accept the business partner: The role of boundary objects. *Journal of Management & Governance, 19*(3), 617–653. https://doi.org/10.1007/s10997-013-9277-2.

Index[1]

[1]Note: Page numbers followed by 'n' refer to notes.

P. Chotiyanon, V. Joannidès de Lautour,
The Changing Role of the Management Accountants,
https://doi.org/10.1007/978-3-319-90300-2

The manufacturer's authorised representative in the EU is Springer Nature Customer Service Centre GmbH, Europaplatz 3, 69115 Heidelberg, Germany. If you have any concerns regarding our products, please contact ProductSafety@springernature.com

Printed and bound by CPI Group (UK) Ltd, Croydon, CR0 4YY

30/09/2026

02225660-0006